Trinity Tales

Trinity College Dublin in the Nineties

Trinity Tales

Trinity College Dublin in the Nineties

edited by CATHERINE HEANEY

THE LILLIPUT PRESS
DUBLIN

First published 2016 by
THE LILLIPUT PRESS
62–63 Sitric Road, Arbour Hill
Dublin 7, Ireland
www.lilliputpress.ie

ISBN 978 1 84351 679 8

1 3 5 7 9 10 8 6 4 2

A CIP record for this title is available
from The British Library.

Set in Minion with Akzidenz Grotesk display titling by Marsha Swan
Printed in Spain by GraphyCems

CONTENTS

FOREWORD

louise richardson

I ENTERED TRINITY an ardent nationalist with a one-dimensional view of Irish history. I left five years later, including a year out on a scholarship to the University of California, robbed of my certitudes and determined to get as far away as I could from what I then felt to be the suffocating constraints of Irish nationalism, and with a scholarship for graduate work on international relations in America. In short, I'd been educated.

Studying Irish history with James Lydon, Theodore Moody and R.B. McDowell caused me to question everything I thought I knew. I learned never to accept an assertion, however palatable, and no matter the stature of the authority making it, without creatively seeking evidence to support it. I learned the pleasure and excitement of trolling through original documents, trying to understand the thinking of eighteenth-century Irish radicals, and the government officials trying to suppress them.

I remember being told by K.C. Davis, who succeeded Moody as Head of History, that my handwriting was like wallpaper: beautiful to look at but devoid of function, as he could not decipher it – so I would go to his rooms in the Rubrics and read my essays aloud to him while he sipped sherry and appeared to listen intently.

Plutarch claimed that the mind is not like a bottle that needs filling, rather, like wood, it needs kindling. That kindling was everywhere in the Trinity I attended in the late seventies. It was in the lectures on the Scandals of the Medieval Papacy by Ian Robinson, in the tutorials with the late, great, and always eccentric R.B. McDowell, and in the *Kaffee und Kuchen* gatherings graciously hosted by Helga Hammerstein. It was in the mass democracies in Front Square, the debates at the Hist and the Phil, the earnest discussions about bringing an end to apartheid and blood sports, and planning the next demonstration against fees, library opening hours and the cost of food in the Buttery. Above all, it was in meeting people with different social backgrounds, different nationalities and with different world views than my own.

At the time we thought that having exams in the autumn was a terrible tyranny, requiring us to return early from our summer jobs to study around the clock in preparation. We were aware, however, even then, that having exams in the autumn freed us up to engage fully in all the distractions of student life, to read widely and throw our energies into all kinds of good causes while working to pay our way.

FOR MUCH of its history, Trinity appeared to the Ireland I came from as a place apart, a British outpost in Dublin. We were all aware of its international reputation and the quality of those who worked and studied there, but they were different. This was a place of privilege removed from our Ireland; it was part of a larger, wider world. My father cycled past Trinity every day throughout his school years, but he never went inside. He never walked under its arch until he came to see me there. It was, after all, a Protestant place.

Coming from rural Ireland, I didn't have any English or foreign friends before arriving at Trinity. As a student I had many. The English students were all on grants and even those not from wealthy families had plenty of disposable income. On Friday nights they would drink pint after pint while we tried to make our glass of Guinness last until it was time to head to the Magnet and dance our hearts out to the music of Hurricane Johnny and the Jets. It never occurred to us to think this was unfair – they were just lucky.

By the 1990s, the era remembered in these essays, Trinity had changed, as had its place in Irish life. While in the 1960s over half the student body were from outside Ireland, it became college policy in the 1970s to bring down the non-Irish student population to 15 per cent. And as the student body became more Irish, the profile of the academics became more cosmopolitan.

The student population also grew, as more and more people sought a university education. In the mid 1960s the cap on student numbers was lifted by a third to raise the number to 4000 (today it stands at around 17,000). In an environment in which many students continued to live at home, practical considerations like location greatly influenced student choice. Dubliners flocked to Trinity, and many of those on the northside opted for Trinity over UCD due to the shorter commute. The social exclusivity that had for so long been a hallmark of Trinity was eroded. This coincided with the Catholic Church finally lifting the ban on Catholics attending Trinity in 1970. The college also deliberately sought to attract smart students who would not previously have attended university – and certainly not Trinity – through the Trinity Access Programme (TAP). The first TAP student was admitted in 1993 and the programme continues today.

This opening up of the university to the city had its most dramatic physical manifestation in the inauguration of the new Arts Block on Nassau Street in 1978. Once begun there was no going back, and the trend has continued, most recently with the opening on Pearse Street of the Biomedical Sciences Block. Gone are the days when the door under Front Arch could be closed and the city kept out – Trinity is now part of the thriving, bustling life of Dublin with students, staff and visitors streaming across the many permeable boundaries. Both the university and the city are richer as a result.

It's odd, really, that a university situated smack in the heart of a city could ever have been so removed. For a long time, of course, it was part of the British ascendancy in Ireland and very much integrated with the civic buildings around it. But with the advent of Irish independence, Trinity retained its elite, British and outward-looking inclinations while the rest of the country turned inward. Both suffered as a consequence. For far too long, to borrow a line from Seamus Heaney's 'Villanelle for an Anniversary', Trinity's books did not lay open nor the gates unbarred. By the 1990s, emphatically, they did.

Trinity was a different, somewhat exotic place when I came to apply to university. I knew it was the best and that, quite simply, is why I wanted to go there. I didn't much care about the rest. While Robert Emmet and Wolfe Tone had studied there, as well as Thomas Davis and Henry Grattan, most of the names that stilled my childish play did not. Those who did – men like Swift, Burke and Goldsmith – were indeed 'of a different kind' ('September 1913', W.B. Yeats).

There were other attractions too. I remember being up in Dublin as a schoolgirl from County Waterford, and my desire to look as though I belonged was overwhelmed by the excitement of being in the front seat of a double-decker bus. As we passed through College Green, we were stopped in traffic in front of Trinity (some things never change), and looking out the window I saw a tall, blond and strikingly handsome twenty-something leaning on the railings near Front Arch. I assumed he must be a student and imagined that glamorous Trinity must be filled with such hunks. After four years there, and never encountering anyone remotely like him, I concluded he must have been a Scandinavian tourist waiting to see the Book of Kells.

Even if not in all other areas, when it came to its treatment of women, Trinity reflected the social mores of Irish society. I lived in Trinity Hall for a year and in rooms for two more. Trinity admitted women in 1904 and Trinity Hall, in Rathmines, was built to accommodate them a few years later. It was only in 1968 that female students were allowed to live in rooms in College – up until the 1950s, women had to leave campus by 6 pm. We use to wonder how the formidable Professor A.J. Otway-Ruthven, who used to drive an ancient Morris Minor magisterially through Front Square, must have managed. She was a lecturer in the history department from 1938–51 when she was named Lecky Professor of History, yet she had to be off campus by evening. We always wanted to ask her what it was like, but found her too terrifying to approach. As it was, we used to bridle at the injustice of the fact that there were guards at the bottom of the stairs of all the girls' wings in Trinity Hall, whose job it was to ensure that we did not entertain guests of the opposite sex – yet there were no guards in the boys' wings. The girls whose boyfriends lived in Trinity Hall were envied.

I HAVE STUDIED and worked on both sides of the Atlantic, on both coasts of the US, and both sides of the Irish Sea. Had it not been for Trinity I might never have left Ireland. Students arrive at university at seventeen or eighteen years of age and the next four years often set the trajectory of their lives, even if, like me, they don't realize it at the time. Universities are some of the most important institutions in our societies. As John Stewart Mill told us long ago, the purpose of universities was not so much to produce skilled professionals as thinking human beings. They serve a great many functions, none more important than pushing at the frontiers of knowledge and passing on what is learned to the next generation. Universities also serve as drivers of our economy, as engines of social mobility and indeed as the very foundations of our democracies.

Trinity today serves all these purposes. Historically, the beneficiaries used to be very few in number; by my day, the student body had begun to grow and to include more students from Catholic Ireland. In the 1990s, the decade captured in these pages, the process accelerated, and Trinity influenced a larger section of Irish life. Today, the idea of Trinity as a place apart no longer has any resonance.

Louise Richardson is Vice-Chancellor of the University of Oxford. She had served previously for seven years as Principal and Vice-Chancellor of the University of St Andrews, Scotland. She received a BA in History from Trinity College Dublin, an MA in Political Science from UCLA and an MA and Ph.D. in Government from Harvard. She was Assistant and Associate Professor in the Harvard Government Department 1989–2001, and served as Executive Dean of the Radcliffe Institute for Advanced Study at Harvard 2001–2008 where she was instrumental in its transformation into an interdisciplinary centre promoting scholarship across academic fields and the creative arts.

A political scientist by training, Professor Richardson has specialized in international security with an emphasis on terrorist movements. She has written widely on international terrorism, British foreign and defence policy, security institutions and international relations. Her work has won numerous awards including the Sumner Prize for work towards the prevention of war and the establishment of universal peace.

Professor Richardson received the Trinity College Dublin Alumni Award in 2009, the Harvard Centennial Medal in 2013, and in 2015 she was awarded honorary doctorates from the University of Aberdeen and Queen's University Belfast and became an Honorary Member of the Royal Irish Academy. She was elected to the American Academy of Arts and Sciences in 2016 and serves on the boards of a number of non-profit groups including the Carnegie Corporation and the Booker Prize Foundation.

INTRODUCTION

catherine heaney

LIKE ITS THREE PREDECESSORS, this fourth instalment of *Trinity Tales* gathers together recollections of a decade at Trinity College Dublin. This time, the story is taken up by 1990s graduates, those of us who passed through its gates as the twentieth century drew to a close, and through the forty individual voices assembled here, describing forty very different college experiences, a vivid portrait emerges of student life during those transformative years. As with previous volumes, royalties from the book go to the Long Room Library fund.

LOOKING BACK NOW, I see Trinity in the 1990s as a time and a place in between, a stepping-off point between one age and another. On the surface, College was the immutable place it had always been – all cobbled squares and sunlit playing fields, academic endeavour and *outré* characters. And as some of the contributors to this book attest, it was those timeless attributes that attracted many of us in the first place. In retrospect, however, it seems to me as if we were suspended between two different worlds. Our generation came of age in an Ireland caught between the grim, recession-ridden 1980s and the brash, moneyed 2000s, an almost unfathomable transition eclipsed only by that between the analogue and digital eras. An undergraduate entering Trinity in 1991, like me, still hand-wrote essays, researched using actual books and communicated with friends via notes left on library desks. Those arriving at the decade's end had email, mobile phones and the vast resources of the internet at their disposal. In addition, they were relatively debt-free (under-graduate tuition fees having been abolished in 1996) and every bit as likely to stay and find work in Ireland rather than getting on the first flight to London or New York. Reflecting this sense of rapid growth in the country at large, new buildings started springing up around campus, most notably the Samuel Beckett Centre and Goldsmith Hall (where I would later study for a master's in the then-pioneering 'multimedia') and as the millennium approached, College was expanding in all directions.

Historically too, the 1990s felt like a time of shifts and upheavals, as across Europe old barriers fell away and, in Ireland, the grip of the Catholic Church on society loosened further. As Luke McManus and Orlaith McBride recall, the debates around abortion and the availability of information raged on, coming to crisis point with the X Case in 1992. In November 1995 the divorce referendum only barely passed (almost inconceivable to Miranda Kennedy, recently transplanted to Dublin from the US). Over the course of the decade, a peace agreement for Northern Ireland went from blind hope to reality and, throughout it all, the digital revolution unfolded, changing the world in ways we could never have dreamed.

And yet for all that, there are features of Trinity life that seem impervious to change, and crop up again and again at both ends of this collection. The Ball, of course (and the 1992 quatercentenary extravaganza in particular); debates in the GMB, a training ground for future politicians like Paschal Donohoe; the machinations of the SU and the publications office, as recalled by Nick Webb, Aengus Collins and Declan Lawn; the complex social ecosystems of the Berkeley and Lecky libraries, described by Antonia Hart and Anna Carey; and the dramas played out (both onstage and off) in Players, where the likes of Dominic West, Mario Rosenstock and Hugh O'Conor cut their acting teeth. Somewhere between all of this, people actually managed to study, or even – in the cases of Philip Lane, Margaret Doyle, Barry McCrea and Heather Jones – become Foundation Scholars. For some, as John Boyne writes, there was acute loneliness amidst all the surrounding gaiety; for others, like Mark Pollock, both challenges and triumphs lay ahead.

But what is most touching in this volume, perhaps, is a collective sense of fondness for those naive, striving, occasionally daft younger selves reflected back at us in the following pages. And how, for so many, those formative years would provide an education that went far beyond our chosen courses, giving us precious time and space in which to take the first tentative steps into adulthood.

I HAD FOLLOWED my older brother Chris to Trinity in 1991, settling on a degree in history of art and English. And in spite of the fact that I continued to live at home in the city where I grew up, and had walked through Trinity many times, I had the slightly uncanny feeling of having entered a parallel universe on my first day. Of course it was the sheer physical grandeur of the place that underpinned this sense – that and being liberated from the deadening drill of the Leaving Cert – but meeting new friends was the real awakening. People like Ellen Rowley, who breezed into the history of art department on that first day like a freshening gust of spring air, and a group of funny, whip-smart girls from Belfast, who reminded us that there was a world beyond our middle-class Dublin upbringings, and in whose flat off the South Circular Road we sealed those early friendships over mix tapes and cheap cider.

Every day for the next four years we would spend endless hours in each other's company, in lecture halls and coffee shops, forensically analyzing love lives, fretting over essays and exams and experimenting with our new, grown-up personas. Eventually our group would widen to include people in the years above and below ours, and even – glamorously – a few from across the water. In second year I surprised myself by managing to acquire a sweet, handsome English boyfriend who seemed as worldly as I was green. To this day my closest friends (including that boy from Cambridgeshire) are those I met at university, and while I thrived in my studies – history of art in particular – that, for me, is its most lasting legacy.

One of Trinity's own in-between places was, and is, the Douglas Hyde Gallery, which I always think of as a sort of border crossing between the campus and the world outside. At that time, history of art students had the chance to work shifts on its reception desk and in my second, third and fourth years, this was how I earned my pin (or perhaps more accurately, pint) money.

In terms of student jobs, it was a peach: all you had to do was sit at the desk, ask visitors if they wanted to take a leaflet, and sell the occasional catalogue or copy of *Artforum*. What it lacked in excitement, it made up for by the fact that you were basically being paid to do what you would be doing anyway. Friends would stop by for long *sotto voce* chats, and there were quiet hours in which to catch up on reading or study or, as I seemed mostly to do, stare into space. (In my defence, there was always superb people-watching through the tall strips of window, as the constant flow of students, tourists and shortcutting commuters poured through Nassau Street Gate.)

The exhibitions at the DHG garnered mixed responses, to say the least. To his credit, the director John Hutchinson brought many international contemporary artists to Dublin for the first time (including a few from the then fledgling White Cube Gallery in London) as well as exciting younger Irish artists like Dorothy Cross and Kathy Prendergast, on whom I would write my fourth-year thesis under Dr Catherine Marshall. But some of the more minimalist exhibitions left viewers underwhelmed. I seem to recall a show of stark monochrome canvases drawing particularly blank gazes and dark mutterings, and I was once asked to explain an installation involving a bucket and a steady drip of water. It was, in fact, a leak.

However, there was one exhibition that in February 1994 transformed the usually pin-drop-quiet gallery into the one of the most buzzing spaces in the city. The Kalachakra Sand Mandala was created by four visiting Tibetan Buddhist monks, who crouched on their knees for three weeks and painstakingly funnelled coloured sand to make this large geometric artefact. Their task captured the public imagination: almost overnight, the modest number of daily visitors leapt into the hundreds as students and passers-by alike came back again and again to see the work progress. And progress it did, a jewel-coloured, intricate design slowly taking shape, like an exquisite rug unfurling on the gallery floor. At the end of it all, the monks swept up the sand and marched down to the quays to pour it into the Liffey. The transience of the mandala was part of its magic, and a photo of the riverside ceremony made the next day's *Irish Times*.

What I remember most, though, is not that final fanfare, but the opening day of the exhibition. I happened to be working on the desk that morning and, like everyone else, was utterly fascinated by the monks. They seemed so exotic in their saffron robes, and yet part of me felt protective towards them – how would these gentle holy men fare as they set out to get lunch on that first day, I wondered. Did they speak English? Would they be intimidated by the jostling crowds on Grafton Street? I needn't have worried: they returned to the gallery half an hour later, all four beaming, clutching large McDonald's bags.

THERE WAS A NICE final postscript to those many hours I whiled away at the Douglas Hyde in my undergraduate years. In October 1995 I had just started my first full-time, post-college job working as curatorial assistant in the gallery (so much for getting away from Trinity). The Dublin Theatre Festival was in full swing and I had gone with my friend Louise East – then a rookie journalist – to see a lunchtime play she was reviewing. Arriving back at the office, I was calmly informed by a colleague that there had just been a phone call to say that my father, Seamus Heaney, had won the Nobel Prize, and did I know where he was.

I didn't, and what happened next is still a blur. I remember increasingly frantic calls from newspapers and broadcasters enquiring about Dad's whereabouts (he and my mother were on holiday in Greece, and would remain obliviously so for the next twenty-four hours) – instead they had to make do with dazed interviews with my brothers and me. There was also a visit to the gallery, and a very nice bouquet of flowers, from the Swedish ambassador. I didn't get much work done.

A month later at my graduation in the Exam Hall, a Swedish television crew would record the entire ceremony for a documentary they were making about Dad. As I went up to receive my scroll, their camera captured a momentary look of pride on my parents' faces that I would never otherwise have seen, and that I will always hold dear. Afterwards, my classmates and I emerged on to Front Square, jubilant and relieved and awkward in our mortarboards. College was over; we were ready to say our goodbyes. Trinity had prised open my schoolgirl's mind, given me friendships to treasure and a space in which to start imagining a future – but now it was time to strike out. Beyond its walls, the rest of our lives waited.

Catherine Heaney with her parents, Marie and Seamus Heaney.

Catherine Heaney (TCD 1991–95, History of Art and English; 1996–97, MSc Multimedia) is a freelance writer and editor. She worked for many years in magazines in Dublin and London, including **Image**, **Red** and **The Gloss**, and was a regular reviewer for the Books pages of **The Irish Times**. In more recent years, she has worked in publishing, at Fourth Estate and later at Faber and Faber, where she ran the creative-writing school Faber Academy. She lives in London – for the time being.

Trinity Tales

Trinity College Dublin in the Nineties

THE PERFECT POLITY

margaret doyle

PIRANHA, College's aptly named satirical magazine, once dubbed me 'the woman least likely to be sexually harassed'. There are two ways of interpreting this dubious honour. I freely admit that fashion and appearance troubled me little at college, but I prefer to believe that I was seen as a woman not to be messed with. A certain reputation for toughness has followed me since and, while I consider myself to be kind and consensual, it's true that the worlds of finance, journalism and politics, where I have spent the intervening years, are not for shrinking violets. Trinity was a cornucopia of opportunities for anyone with the drive to take advantage of them, and I did my best to do so.

There was no question, in my bookish, bourgeois family, of my not going to university – and for me, there was no question about which one. I chose Trinity, knowing that it would offer new experiences to this Wexford girl. My eldest sister, Helen, had studied botany there, and brought home groups of – to my mind – exotic friends: a man who wore a skirt (not a kilt); Madeleine Reid, who took fennel on a trip to Schull, fearing it be unattainable there – somewhat ironically given that West Cork has become a foodie paradise; and Damian Collins, an opera lover who spent his career as a competition lawyer.

The discovery that Trinity had a scholarship exam ('Schol'), which appealed both to my swottishness and my ambition, confirmed my aspiration. While

UCD's commerce faculty had a great reputation, my choice pleased my mother. She had been prevented from attending Trinity thanks to the ban, imposed by the episcopal hierarchy, on Catholics attending what was still seen as a Protestant enclave.

I had never heard of Entrance Exhibitions, but was granted one nonetheless. College made these awards purely on the basis of Leaving Cert results and, while largely honorary, it did entitle me to rent sought-after rooms on campus long before final year. I was already enrolled in Trinity Hall for my first year, where I shared a room with a Loreto school friend. However, the Exhibition allowed me to secure Front Square rooms in second year, which proved handy for intense Schol preparation.

I studied economics within ESS (Economics and Social Studies). Lectures were supplemented by tutorials given by older students. I was tutored by Martin Coulter, a lanky and urbane oarsman, who enrolled in a MBA programme at the Harvard Business School the year after me, and then embarked on an entrepreneurial career in the US. John Fingleton, who became and remains a friend, tutored me in first year economics. He is even better connected now than in his days as a 'college personality', or CP. *Piranha* dubbed him John 'Tammany Hall' Fingleton after he ran Paul Caron's successful campaign to be elected Students' Union president in 1986.

Beyond study, there were other challenges. My father, who had been a heavy smoker, was, by the time I got to college, fatally ill with lung cancer. He was treated at St Luke's Hospital, near Trinity Hall, which meant that I could visit him easily. His obvious suffering during radium therapy contrasted with the frivolities of student life.

I stayed in Ireland that summer as it was clear his time was short, working as a brand assistant on Harp Lager under Jean Callanan, at Guinness' St James' Street headquarters. This position led to a gig as Guinness rep on campus the following academic year. In theory, this should have made me the most popular person on campus, as I was responsible for doling out kegs to clubs and societies. However, I failed to anticipate that for every club I gave a keg to, there would be others that I would disappoint.

Moreover, in second year, my focus lay on Schol. Fortunately, Professor John O'Hagan ('Johno'), then head of the economics department, took a great interest in his students in general, and Schol candidates in particular. He arranged the syllabus to suit the compressed timetable of the Schol exam. I wrote no fewer than ten Economy of Ireland essays in Hilary term, if memory serves, all of which Johno faithfully marked.

I made regular trips to the late-night newsagent on Grafton Street to buy chocolate-covered oat biscuits to sustain my essay-writing all-nighters. This unhealthy diet and a lack of exercise, compounded by grief, took its toll. By the time Trinity Week came around, I was plumpish and spotty. But I was also a scholar, and a Foundation Scholar at that – which was rare in social sciences – so it was a good trade.

(Six years later, in Boston, my mother and I were seated at the HBS Dean's table for the celebratory dinner for the forty Baker scholars, including me. The Dean's wife said to my mother, 'Isn't it wonderful that someone from a little country far away can come to a place like Harvard and do so well?' As this was kindly meant, my mother refrained from retorting that her daughter was a scholar of Trinity College Dublin, which had nearly half a century on Harvard.)

As it happened, any Schol-induced self-importance was punctured soon after that heady Trinity Monday, 1988. At the end of my Senior Freshman year, I took off for Paris with my friend Rosemary Ward, who was the year ahead of me in ESS, for the summer. We shared a small *chambre de bonne* at the top of a tall house (no lift) on the Boulevard Saint-Germain, in exchange for taking care of our landlady's disabled adult son. At that time, it was very difficult to get even the most menial of jobs: applying for a job as a chambermaid, I was asked about my training and experience, of which I had none.

While Rosemary and I did manage to visit museums, read writers' biographies and explore Rive Gauche literary haunts, the difficulty in finding decent paid work prompted us to do a flit, taking off for Amsterdam instead. The youth hostel we landed in was in the city's famous red light district. We spent a month in Amsterdam, working at Centraal station where we marketed a hotel to tourists. We lived on a barge hotel for a few weeks, and worked as chambermaids (Dutch hiring standards were clearly lower than French ones) in return for our accommodation.

At the end of our time in Amsterdam, we paid for a lift in a VW Beetle to Yugoslavia, a little over a year before the collapse of the Berlin wall. It was a historic moment at which to see that part of the world, although I have yet to fulfil my promise to myself to do a proper tour of the former Eastern Bloc, 'before it changes too much'. From Pirot in Serbia we made our way by train to Istanbul, where hawkers greeted the foreigners disembarking from the train, 'Hello, beautiful tourist people!' After our long train journey, that was far from how we felt.

When we got to our youth hostel, I phoned my mother. I managed to let her know that I was no longer in Amsterdam, but in Istanbul, before – in those pre-mobile phone days – the line went dead. She responded with more equanimity than I would in similar circumstances.

Back in Trinity, I lived in New Square in my sophister years, and had a bit more time to enjoy college life. I got more involved in the Hist, becoming treasurer in my final year. Some of the strongest recollections of my entire college career are of the endless elections and the associated machinations and politicking. Indeed, once I learned – in the politics course in ESS – what a 'polity' was, I opined that 'Trinity is the perfect polity'.

Niall Lenihan, son of the popular Fianna Fáil politician who served as Minister for Foreign Affairs during our college years, invited me to his inaugural address at the Phil. On the back of the invitation card, he had written, 'Hope you can make it – Niall'. I was touched at this personal gesture, until I realized that Rosemary, who was my New Street Square neighbour, had received the same message. Niall, who remains a friend, laughed sheepishly when I reminded him recently of his youthful ploy.

I was a reasonable public speaker – I was told by Malachy McAllister that I would have won the Hist's Freshers' competition had my speech not been too short (not a complaint I get very often). However, I had a lot to learn from a generation of superb debaters in the parliamentary tradition – Aidan Kane, Paul Gavin (now Pol O Gaibhin), Anthony Whelan (who won the *Observer* Mace with Malachy in 1989) and those in the years immediately after me who went on to take silk at the Irish Bar – my cousin, Marguerite Bolger, Bernard Dunleavy and Kerida Naidoo.

Trinity debaters held their own in a remarkable generation of debaters. These included Michael Gove, former President of the Oxford Union and now a Conservative MP, and Kevin Sneader, then at Glasgow, another debating powerhouse, who overlapped with me at McKinsey and Harvard, and who now chairs McKinsey's operations in Asia.

Kim Humphreys was not the Hist's finest debater, but was perhaps its – and College's – best-known personality. Everyone in College 'knew' Kim. The closest parallel in contemporary politics is Boris Johnson, the ex-London mayor. An Old Etonian whose mother is Thai, Kim was good-looking in a distinctly un-Irish way. He piled up votes in a Students' Union election in his final year, despite having already withdrawn his candidacy because his future City employers did not want him to defer entry.

I encountered Kim again in Conservative Party circles in the 1990s. He was hoping to be elected to parliament and, in an attempt to reach out to the common man, boasted in a speech that he had always lived in inner cities. This may have been technically true – Trinity is nothing if not central, and Southwark Council, where Kim led the tiny Conservative group, is an inner London borough. But Dulwich, where he owned a house, is a leafy upper-middle-class oasis in south London. I gave him the ribbing he deserved in a diary column in *The Daily Telegraph*, for which I then wrote. Kim, being Kim, was pleased at the publicity.

In final year I applied only for London jobs, in management consultancy or investment banking, and joined McKinsey. Like many emigrants, I vaguely intended to return to Ireland in a few (unspecified) years. But life, as is its wont, got in the way while I was making other plans. I returned to McKinsey in London after graduating from Harvard, but soon jumped to journalism.

My day job in journalism was always in print (*The Economist*, Reuters Breakingviews, *Global Agenda*, the Davos magazine, as well as the *Telegraph*), but I did a lot of broadcasting on the side – both TV and radio commentary for outlets in the UK, US, Ireland, Japan and beyond, and lots of presenting for BBC radio. I also discovered a facility for chairing conferences, which I continue to do to this day as part of my job as a partner in a big City professional services firm.

However, I have kept in touch with Trinity in the intervening years. At Johno's invitation, I launched the *Student Economic Review* (where I had served on an early editorial board) in 2002. I joined the advisory board of the Trinity-based Institute of International Integration Studies, alongside Peter Sutherland, a former EU Commissioner and College benefactor, and David O'Sullivan, now the EU's ambassador to the US. And, on the invitation of Gerard Lacey, a fellow Trinity Hall resident who became College bursar, I moderated the finance working groups at the Trinity Global Graduate Forum in 2013. I also participated in a panel on Ireland's banking sector at a joint EU/College conference in 2014, to mark Ireland's exit from its three-year bailout programme, at the invitation of Professor Philip Lane, a 1989 ESS Scholar, and now governor of the Central Bank of Ireland.

London's dominance as the world's international financial centre has only grown in the quarter-century since I graduated, and as long as finance is my *métier*, my work is likely to be here.

My Trinity education – and especially Schol – gave me the confidence to study and work at elite institutions. And the culture shock of going from being the proud Head Girl of Loreto College, Wexford, to a student in the bastion of liberal education in Ireland sparked an interest in Liberal and Radical ideas that continues to this day. But the most lasting legacy of my time in Trinity has been my fond memories and the warm friendships that I forged there.

Margaret Doyle (TCD 1986–90; ESS) is a partner in Deloitte in London. She began her career in McKinsey & Company before becoming a journalist. She has written for **The Economist**, **The Daily Telegraph** and Reuters Breakingviews and edited **Global Agenda**, the official Davos magazine. She has presented many flagship BBC radio programmes including **Today**, **Analysis** and **The World Tonight** (BBC Radio 4); **The World Today** (BBC World Service) and **Wake Up to Money** (BBC Radio 5 Live). As well as a BA from Trinity, she holds an MBA from the Harvard Business School.

A REHEARSAL FOR LIFE

ed brophy

WHEN I ENTERED TRINITY, Ireland was still mired in the grim despair of the unlamented 1980s. Any green shoots withered on fallow ground. Like today the political situation was unstable – this time with a minority Fianna Fáil government being supported from opposition by Fine Gael in the so-called Tallaght Strategy. The country had been in recession for what seemed like forever. Unlike today, however, the corner had not been turned and there seemed to be little hope of a decisive shift in our economic fortunes. Mass unemployment and emigration, culture wars and the IRA's misguided war in the North formed the public backdrop to my private misgivings about the law degree I was about to embark on. When I graduated in the early 1990s all had changed utterly; the first stirrings of the coming economic boom were plain to see. Suddenly emigration was not inevitable, divorce would soon be legal and the IRA had started the long journey to peace.

I fell into studying law as many swotty kids do. Then – as now – the points system dictated the career choices of too many people who didn't know any better. So armed with a sackful of Leaving Cert As and having been a somewhat sheltered teenager, I entered the Law School for want of something better to do. With a grand total of eight class hours a week, studying law in Trinity left you with a lot of time on your hands. Of course reading time was supposed to take up a lot of this slack. However, I soon discovered that I was far more interested in reading novels, history and philosophy than law. And with all that spare time there was plenty of space for any number of extra-curricular activities. My journey as an unremarkable law student and committed party animal had begun.

Trinity teemed with tribes. Marinated in the narcissism of small differences, disparate groups carved out *lebensraum* for themselves and their kinfolk. The Arts Block was all BESS students from fee-paying schools in South Dublin and Sloane Rangers studying history of art. No lefties dallied long there. Our spiritual home was the Junior Common Room – universally known as the JCR – where political activism and Nicaraguan coffee blended with beatnik existentialists and mavericks of all hues. Irrespective of what tribe you belonged to, most of us realized what a privilege it was to have this place of great beauty and grandeur as the canvas against which we developed and grew.

Politics in Trinity was dominated by the culture wars, particularly abortion – although the usual obsessions of student politics, like fees, grants and accommodation, also featured. The favoured response to any issue was either a demo or an occupation. Or even better a demo followed by an occupation. My friend Senator Ivana Bacik became president of the Students' Union in my first year and soon felt the full force of the law when the Society for the Protection of the Unborn Child brought her and the other union officers to court for having the temerity to continue to provide information to women facing crisis pregnancies, including abortion. Eventually the students prevailed and the right to information was enshrined in law following a constitutional referendum. Ivana's political courage and reluctance to be intimidated were qualities that made her the politician she is today. As chief of staff to the Tánaiste, it has been a privilege to work closely with her on reforming legislation, including recognition of transgender people and particularly marriage equality. However the big struggle we undertook over twenty-five years ago to secure a woman's right to choose remains unresolved.

The best gig in the Students' Union was entertainments – or 'Ents' – officer, where you were effectively one of the main concert promoters in the city for your year in office. Remember, this was a time when very few international acts visited Ireland and the range of festivals and venues we take for granted today was unthinkable. As a result the political battle for this gilded prize was intense. Edwina Forkin – now one of Ireland's leading film producers and one of the warmest human beings you will ever meet – was Ents officer the year I arrived in Trinity. She was always keen to have new faces on her team, so before long I was helping out in the running of gigs and events all over College. However, it soon became clear that I just didn't have what it took for the rock 'n' roll business, preferring the fun to the more prosaic work involved. Edwina, on the other hand, went from strength to strength, ending her year in charge on an incredible high note by putting on Public Enemy – probably the hottest band on the planet at that time – as the headline act in that year's Trinity Ball.

After Ents, my main focus was media. At the time, the satirical magazine *Piranha* was the leading publication on campus. *Piranha* had a proud history and was a rite of passage for many talented people who went on to become real journalists, but to most it was a gossip rag and there was often a collective sense of unease around the Arts Block the day before publication, fond as the magazine was of exposing the previous week's tittle tattle. My ears certainly burned more than once! The paper I wrote for was *Trinity News*. Liberal in its outlook, it was essentially a campus version of the *Irish Times* and those who wrote for it were often auditioning for the Old Lady of D'Olier Street. I was a regular writer for the paper under the editorship of Conor Sweeney, now a communications guru for Amazon.com.

Movies were another passion. Before the era of streaming, the College Film Society was at the height of its popularity, showing a mixture of classic and foreign movies that were unavailable elsewhere before the advent of the Lighthouse Cinema and Irish Film Institute. I worked for the society for most of my time in Trinity and eventually headed it up in third year. Being Trinity, we were able to attract really big names to come along and talk at events we laid on. One of my most surreal experiences was looking after Richard Harris when he came for a public interview. Harris the hell-raiser had long been sober, and was reluctant to accompany me to the Buttery for a pre-interview drink. He eventually compromised on being served a pot of tea, but the somewhat awkward half-hour we spent together in the bar as I sank a Guinness while he wrestled with his demons counts as one of the strangest encounters of my Trinity career.

While my extra-curricular activities blossomed, I became disillusioned with academic work. Trinity can sometimes feels insular and I was restless to get out into the world and make things happen – I felt I was languishing. Rather than quit, I decided at the end of my Senior Freshman year to take a year's sabbatical, during which time I would see some of the world beyond Front Square. It was the best decision I made, travelling through Europe and eventually to Germany where I worked and studied the language. That year turned into two, so that when I arrived back for my Junior Sophister year, there was a palpable change in the air. Trinity's quatercentenary in 1992 was the catalyst for renewal and a new direction.

I knuckled down and now enjoyed the academic work. No longer did law feel suffocating – in fact it was liberating. Some of this was down to the quality of the lecturers we were blessed with. Gerard Hogan, who wrote the leading book on constitutional law and is now a Supreme Court judge, was hugely dedicated to his students. And the late Brian Lenihan lectured us in the law of evidence in final year, before he became a Fianna Fáil TD. As the public was later to learn, Brian was a singularly charming man. He was also prone to the unpunctuality characteristic of many politicians – in part because he was juggling lecturing with a very busy practice at the bar. Keeping a lecture theatre full of students waiting for over half an hour late on a Monday afternoon would have been the death knell for anyone else, but Brian was able to win us over, breezing in as if nothing had happened and wearing an appearance of *faux* offence that we would even dare to grumble about his lateness. His subsequent political rise and willingness to do what was right for the country in its hour of need was no surprise to those of us who witnessed first-hand his unique combination of erudition and *sang-froid*.

Looking back on my time in Trinity, it feels like a rehearsal for life. My various acts since then have all drawn on the experiences and enthusiasms that first took root on those hallowed cobblestones. And in many ways I never really left. I returned for a master's in economic policy a decade ago and continue to maintain relationships and connections to the college. There is rarely a day I don't walk through Front Square on my way to Leinster House. But more than this, it is the emotional connection to Trinity that will endure for a lifetime. More than anything what Trinity gave was a sense of intellectual curiosity and respect for ideas – and the confidence to stand over them. It was and remains a beacon of open inquiry and tolerance that reflects the best of Ireland's past, present and future and I feel privileged to be associated with it.

Ed Brophy (TCD 1988–94; Law) is Chief of Staff to former An Tánaiste, Joan Burton TD. He has worked as a lawyer and public policy advisor in Dublin, London and Brussels. He lives in Dublin with his wife and four children. One day he plans to leave it all behind to go and live the good life in Italy.

TRINITY THEN AND NOW

philip lane

I ENTERED TCD in October 1987 as part of the intake for the then Economics and Social Studies (ESS) programme (subsequently relabelled as Business, Economics and Social Studies). I was following in the footsteps of my older brother Mark, who studied English and history a year ahead of me, while my sister Cloda also studied economics in TCD from 1991 to 1995. (Our younger brother Colum departed from this pattern by studying commerce at UCD.)

As was typical in the era before large-scale open days and marketing campaigns, I selected Trinity on the basis of remarkably little hard information. While I was sure I wished to specialize in economics, the multi-disciplinary and structured ESS curriculum was attractive to me, compared to alternatives such as commerce or arts in UCD. I also recall that the four-year nature of the TCD undergraduate programme seemed to offer the prospect of a deeper and broader education compared to the three-year alternatives at the other universities.

The years between 1987 and 1991 were an incredible period to be studying economics. At a European level, the decline of the communist bloc, the reunification of Germany and the deepening of the economic dimensions of the European Union through the 1992 Single Market project stimulated a wide range of fundamental economic policy debates. In Ireland, the fiscal stabilization that was initiated in 1987 after years of economic stagnation ulti-mately proved successful, even if that was not immediately obvious at the time. Ireland seemed destined to remain an underdeveloped part of Europe – the remarkable subsequent growth boom was not on the horizon at that time. A high proportion of the class of 1991 was destined for long-term emigration, facilitated at that time by the windfall of the US Donnelly visa programme.

As with all students, my memories of the Junior Freshman year are domi-nated by personal and social experiences. The transition from the all-male and fairly homogenous environment of Blackrock College to the diversity of TCD was exhilarating, while the presence of various school contemporaries (and an older brother) provided a basic initial social network.

Most importantly I met my wife Orla, a fellow economics student, in Freshers' Week and the development of our relationship during that first term really defined college for me at a personal level. We were soon part of a wider group of classmates that bonded over daily breaks for coffee and biscuit cake in the Arts Block. In the evenings, the diverse offerings of the city centre provided a daily reminder of the superiority of TCD relative to UCD's Belfield location, even if Belfield has been transformed in the last twenty years.

The economics-related courses (economics, mathematics, statistics) in the Junior Freshman year of the ESS programme were relatively straightforward and already familiar to me. Still, even if the content was not too surprising, lecturers such as Doug McLernon and Andrew Somerville made quite an impression in terms of presentational styles. I still retain quite a bit from the introductory courses in sociology, political science and law. Among the lecturers in these disciplines, I was especially impressed by Michael Marsh, Ron Hill, James Wickham and Alex Schuster. Ron Hill's module on the Soviet Union was especially fascinating: in 1988, we had little clue as to the speed of the disintegration of the Communist bloc.

A broad-based first year has many merits in allowing students to learn more about different fields before committing to a specialization. It also has an important social value in bringing together a more diverse group of students, even if students from other parts of College might unfairly classify ESS students into a single and defamatory 'type' that might correspond to a more studious version of Ross O'Carroll Kelly!

The large size of the ESS cohort meant that many first-year lectures were held in the Ed Burke and effective lecturing required a deft combination of showmanship, storytelling and the occasional imposition of disciplinary measures on giddy or inattentive students. The 1980s method of taking hand-written notes in real time during lectures (and deciphering the scrawl months later during the revision period) is at a far remove from the contemporary norm whereby lecture materials are uploaded online in advance and many students take notes on laptops during lectures (while simultaneously main-taining social media accounts and trawling the web).

The tutorial system provided excellent supplemental support, while the small-group format also made it much easier to get to know fellow students. At that time, tutorials were typically delivered by final-year undergraduates: the confidence, expertise and friendliness of these older students was quite reassuring. One of my economics tutors was Kieran McLoughlin, now the CEO of the Ireland Funds. TCD continues to support small-group tutorials, which have been dropped by many other universities due to the high costs.

I occasionally attended the debates put on by the Phil and the Hist. While the debate format could be entertaining, it seemed to me that the adversarial format contributed little in advancing common understanding of the topics, even if it served to highlight the weaknesses of the arguments advanced by either side. I was much more impressed by various evening lectures by external speakers. I mostly attended events that related to the economic events of the day: the prox-imity of TCD to the Dáil meant that there were plenty of speeches by govern-ment ministers and opposition politicians. In addition, as an avid reader, I also enjoyed public readings by various authors. I plucked up the courage to speak to the American novelist Richard Ford after one such event, who was very gracious and kind. I still treasure my signed copy of *The Sportswriter* from that evening.

For me, the Senior Freshman year was pivotal. My strong academic ambi-tions and deep interest in economics meant that the Foundation Scholarship (Schol) exams were the primary focus and I undertook an intense study schedule in preparation. This was made easier by the fact that many of my friends were also preparing for these exams – there was a shared focus (albeit with different degrees of intensity) and a common *esprit de corps* among our group. The support provided for the scholarship group by the economics department was extraordinary, through the provision of extra tutorials and specific preparation for the unique format of the Schol exams. The encouragement and enthusiasm of staff members such as John O'Hagan and Dermot McAleese left a lasting impression. I was very pleased to be announced as a Scholar in Economics on Trinity Monday along with my friends Ciaran (C.J.) O'Neill, Tony Annett and Mary Kelly (a dual scholar in economics and German), even if it was difficult to witness the disappointment of other friends who did not make it.

Being a scholar was a defining experience for me. Living on campus vastly enriched the final two years of college – I shared rooms with Ciaran O'Neill in House Two in Front Square as a Junior Sophister, and House Twelve in Botany Bay as a Senior Sophister. Our rooms were a social hub for our group of friends, while the Botany Bay courts were an added bonus for the occasional game of tennis in my final year. These college friendships have largely been maintained over the years: as well as the aforementioned Ciaran, Tony and Mary, I am glad to remain in touch with fellow students such as Joe Smyth, Alan Cox, Dan McSwiney, Joe O'Brien, Sophie Bury, Elaine Whelan and Stephen Walsh. The daily Commons dinner provided an opportunity to get to know other scholars from across the college: while we studied a diverse range of disciplines, our academic orientation provided a genuine common bond.

The scholar status offered affirmation that my hopes for an academic career were realistic. It also provided an important benchmark: since previous scholars had subsequently succeeded in top US doctoral programmes, it gave me confidence that I could follow the same path. An internship with John O'Hagan in the summer after my Junior Sophister year provided further exposure to the academic life and a strong foundation for postgraduate research. The economics department hired several interns that year, so that it was enjoyable to spend the summer as a group rather than working away in pure isolation – and Ireland's unexpected success in the Italia 90 World Cup also meant that the summer of 1990 was a great time to be in Dublin. The tradition of hiring summer research interns continues in the TCD economics department, benefiting both the students and the staff, who receive valuable research assistance from eager and clever interns.

During the sophister years, my interest in economics was further deepened by a group of dedicated lecturers who were highly committed to nurturing the cohort of single-honours economics students. In keeping with the multifaceted nature of economics, I learned strong analytical skills from Andrew Somerville and Daniel Seidman (now at Nottingham University), the value of a policy-orientated approach to understanding economic problems from Alan Matthews and Frank Barry (a guest lecturer from UCD at the time, now a member of the TCD Business School) and the foundations of monetary economics and international economics (these would be my specialist areas in my subsequent career) from Antoin Murphy and Dermot McAleese. The high degree of personal interaction between students and the academic staff and the smallish class sizes created a true 'community of engagement' that was ahead of its time in terms of modern understanding of best practice in university education.

The Junior Sophister year was also marked by interaction with the group of visiting Erasmus students, including one Marius Brülhart from Frieburg in Switzerland, who was to become a lifelong friend. Marius is now an economics professor at the University of Lausanne, after having returned to TCD for his doctoral studies. At a time when the undergraduate student population (and the general Irish population) was considerably less diverse than today, the Erasmus programme played an important contributory role in building a greater understanding of wider European culture. The limited commitment of one-year visiting students to their landlords also meant that they hosted more raucous house parties – one such night in a Rialto terrace is burned in the memory of all who attended.

Supported by the department, TCD economics students had launched the *Student Economic Review (SER)* in 1987 as an annual journal of student essays. Since many courses required essays for assessment purposes, there was plenty of excellent material available for inclusion. Each year, a committee drawn from the Junior Sophister group was tasked with editing and producing the *SER*, with high expectations that each year would surpass the previous one in terms of content and production values. I was selected as the managing editor for the 1990 edition, with my room-mate Ciaran O'Neill taking the role of general manager. While I had the comparatively easy task of leading the selection of essays for inclusion, Ciaran suffered through a series of late nights in the Arches computer rooms, grappling with the rudimentary IT equipment of that era (some early generation Apples and a single printer) to convert the essays into a nicely produced physical format.

In parallel to the production of the journal, the SER committee also organized a series of student debates on grand topics such as the survival of capitalism, the implications of German reunification, the implications of the 1990 budget and the measurement of poverty. In more recent years, this series has been extended to include highly competitive debates against rival universities such as Cambridge and Harvard. The thirtieth edition of the SER was launched in March 2016, with many past members of the committee returning to TCD for a celebration to mark this milestone. An array of alumni speakers credited the SER as an important influence in their subsequent career trajectories in many fields (publishing, project management, economics, finance). In recent years, other parts of College have been inspired to launch similar student-led publications in other fields, but none can match the history and track record of the SER.

This year also sees the retirement of John O'Hagan, who has been so central to the success of the SER and, more generally, has been the standard-bearer in developing and maintaining the commitment of the economics department in fostering a vibrant community spirit among its undergraduate population. A major challenge for the future is to ensure that this undergraduate-focused culture continues to thrive, despite the increasing time pressures on the academic staff due to the growth of postgraduate education and the greater emphasis on high research productivity.

I am eternally grateful to Trinity (especially the economics department) for providing me with strong foundations for my career. After doctoral training at Harvard University and an initial spell as an assistant professor of economics and international affairs at Columbia University, I returned to TCD as an academic staff member in 1997. A career highlight was to be appointed as Whately Professor of Political Economy in 2012, one of the oldest chairs in economics (originally founded in 1832). Although I have taken on a new career challenge as governor of the Central Bank of Ireland, I am proud to remain part of Trinity's academic community during my period of leave.

Philip Lane (TCD 1987–91; ESS) is Governor of the Central Bank of Ireland and Whately Professor of Political Economy (on leave) at TCD. Having studied economics at TCD, he returned to the academic staff in 1997.

BOHEMIA HIBERNIAE

dominic west

EDUCATING RITA was in some part responsible for my going to Trinity. In the play by Willy Russell, Rita attends a redbrick university in the north of England and I was struck that the film had transposed her to a beautiful campus of classical stone facades and cobbled squares, filled with bright, questing, long-haired students. I later discovered this was Trinity College and that it was bang in the middle of Dublin, a town I had long mythologized from reading Leon Uris, as the spiritual home of my courageous forebears.

My mother read law at Trinity in the 1950s, but hadn't lasted very long because of strictures imposed on her by Archbishop McQuaid. As a Catholic, she was forbidden to attend but since she had grown up in England, and so was probably damned anyway, he granted her dispensation to go, provided she only went to lectures and didn't socialize. She had to be off campus every day at six and regrettably, after only a year, she left in search of wider confines. Nevertheless, she cherished a romantic yearning for Ireland, not least because her parents were Irish, and she passed that on to me.

My grandfather had gone to the Royal College of Surgeons and my sister was in her final year there when I arrived. She lived in Galloping Green, Stillorgan, with two friends. I went to live with them, cycling up and down the dual carriageway every day to and from our box housing estate, which

Brendan Kennelly later referred to as the sort of doll's house Ibsen was writing about.

It wasn't quite the romantic Dublin I'd had in mind. That came later in the person of Juliette Gruber, a wonderful actress and the niece of Walter Matthau. She was in her final year studying philosophy and lived with Vanessa Soudine, a Trinidadian/Irish beauty. Vanessa's spray of curly dark hair perfectly complemented Juliette's spray of blonde curls as they studied together in the Berkeley Library or at the Winding Stair Café or sauntered picturesquely up the Liffey to their flat in Arbour Hill. I was entranced and learned poems to woo her.

Together we explored the romantic corners of old Dublin: Boland's Mill and the Grand Canal Basin; Beggar's Bush Barracks; Smithfield; the Dockers Pub; St James' Gate; Mountjoy Square; Poolbeg Street; North Great George's Street – all untouched for decades and incredibly atmospheric in their decay. Juliette brought me to the house in Henrietta Street where she had lived for two years with the Casey family: two artists and their six children, living frugally but magnificently among the bare floorboards and crumbling walls of a dilapidated Georgian palace. I was transported. This was it. *Bohemia Hiberniae*. I'd come home.

I studied English and drama. The drama department was still in its infancy, founded and run by John McCormack in rooms on Westland Row. I only just missed the boom time, when Ireland took off and the spectacular Samuel Beckett Centre was opened. In 1991 it was all pretty rudimentary: creaky floorboards and sash windows like guillotines, that Steve Wilmer, the department number two, would crash down to rouse us from slumbers induced by the history of Kabuki theatre.

John McCormack was a gentle soul completely obsessed with puppets. He directed us in several shows, most memorably his own translation of de Musset's *Lorenzaccio*, which ended with a puppet show that was unquestionably John's favourite part. He had been a star of the French department, like Sam Beckett, to whom he wrote to ask if he could name his new drama department after him. Beckett's reply was pinned to the wall: a postcard with two words: *Yes. Sam.*

I soon joined Players, which was run by Gemma Bodinetz, a sassy, raven-haired dynamo, who now runs the Liverpool Everyman Theatre. I remember her rolling around a rehearsal room floor shouting, 'I am Woman!' She had me do something similar in a play called *Fando & Lis*, which I did with Juliette and my great friend Dominic Geraghty. It was intensely serious with lots of bondage and whipping and the first of many shows, which my embarrassed sister would find 'a bit rude'.

Gemma was a volunteer drama teacher at Arbour Hill prison along with another sexy Trinity student, Caitríona Duffy. Their classes were heavily over-subscribed but eventually had to be cancelled when one of the resident sex offenders got out of hand. I had directed a stage version of Dylan Thomas' *A Child's Christmas in Wales* and Gemma arranged for us to perform it there, as it was the least inflammatory material then in Players' repertoire. I remember waiting nervously behind an improvised set as the prison hall filled with noisy inmates. Hoping for silence, we dimmed the lights and the whole place went bananas. An angry screw swatted me aside, slapped the lights back on and we proceeded to shout our way through the play in record time, the delighted audience baying throughout.

We did a lot of devised story theatre, principally influenced by Annie Ryan, who had come to Trinity for a year from Chicago. Over there, she had acted with John Cusack and Jeremy Piven in their company New Crime. They developed a style based on updated forms from Commedia dell'arte: grotesque make-up, expressionist delivery and stock characters. Annie still uses it with her company, The Corn Exchange, to great acclaim; I have always loved it. We did several shows together at Trinity and in the years since, after Annie married Michael West.

Michael had played the lead in *Lorenzaccio* and then focused his considerable talents on writing plays. He looks a lot like Beckett, whose influence was clear on *A Play on Two Chairs*, which Michael wrote and directed and I performed with Amanda Hogan. It was a great success both in Players and at the ISDA festival, where I think we won a prize. Someone took it to Utrecht, where Michael, Amanda and I spent a lively few days watching it being performed in Dutch.

Michael shared rooms with fellow scholar Lenny Abrahamson. Lenny had switched from physics to philosophy, for which he won a gold medal, but his real interest was in film. I went with Lenny, Mikel Murfi and Gary Cooke to

Galway for a week to develop Lenny's first film, *Three Joes*, which we shot in moody Jim Jarmusch-style in Lenny's kitchen in Harold's Cross. Ed Guiney produced and Stephen Rennicks wrote the score – the same team that made Lenny's latest film *Room*, nominated for four Oscars in 2015.

NEAR THE END of my second year, John McCormack interrupted one of Steve's interesting lectures on the Ontological Hysteric Theatre of Cruelty to ask: 'Does anyone want to study in Paris for a year?' No one replied. Silence. I looked around, incredulous, then put my hand up: 'OF COURSE!' And so for my third year, I studied drama and English in Paris, at the Sorbonne Nouvelle, free of charge as an Erasmus student. Oh the glories of the prelapsarian European Union and of the days before student fees and email.

I lived initially with three Trinity girls in two rooms near Montparnasse. As we were the first Erasmus students to go from TCD to l'Université Paris III, the lines of communication between the two institutions were a little patchy and all correspondence seemed to come through us. It was the final year of my drama degree, for which I had to attend excruciating two-hour lectures in French on Meyerhold and Grotowski and the operas of Handel. I was at sea. But no matter, for I was twenty-one and Paris is a moveable feast, and I confess I took advantage of the patchy lines of communication and marked myself. I had a friend, now a distinguished QC, who had perfected the idiosyncratic handwriting of the French academic. Almost all have the same careful, curling script and with this we contrived a glowing report in dubious French, ultimately awarding myself a modest low First.

DURING THE SUMMERS I did a lot of travelling. I hitchhiked across Eastern Europe with Juliette in 1991 just after the fall of the Berlin Wall. The following year we walked to Santiago de Compostela with Vanessa and some depressed Parisians. After Juliette had graduated and moved away, I hitchhiked in Ireland, to Connemara where I had been as a child with my grandmother, and to Borrisokane, where my grandfather was raised. I walked all around the north coast, from Belfast to Aran Mór island. I remember being rescued at 2 am from a mountainside near Larne: a colossal rainstorm had washed my tent away and I'd made it to a road where a woman was searching for her lost bantams. She picked me up and took me to a cottage where her husband was playing a bouzouki and drinking whiskey in front of a blazing fire.

I returned to Dublin for my final year and rented a flat on the corner of Mountjoy Square in a huge Georgian townhouse with delicate fanlight. It was freezing but wonderful, with views in three directions and a turf fire in the bedroom. I was on the top floor and below me was a sparky American, Aileen Corkery, and her boyfriend Maurice Culligan, who played piano with The Big Geraniums. Below them was Mannix Flynn, who was talked about in hushed tones but mysteriously never appeared.

The walk home from Trinity up O'Connell Street through Parnell Square was a journey into the exotic: turf-scented twilights; rough pubs like the Hill 16; Tops in Pops the greengrocer; lovers' fights outside the chip shop: 'Of course I love yer! Sure don't I buy yer chips and ride yer?' Kids were always playing on the street, one of whom, a three-year-old, wise beyond her years, I once found crying. She had fallen over. 'Are you ok?' I asked and she fixed me with a furious glare: 'Ask me arse!'

My last show with Players was a seventies disco version of Dante's *Divine Comedy*, which I staged in the Atrium, using all its levels to delineate Hell, Purgatory and Paradise, and featuring big dance numbers like 'Disco Inferno'. For the climax, when Dante sees God, we blasted The Jackson 5's 'Can You Feel It' and everyone got up and danced. We had rehearsed in the freezing cold of Castletown House in Celbridge because one of the writers, Ben Flynn, had use of an entire floor there. I remember we hired a double decker and bussed everyone out there for a party after the final show. It was so cold you either had to dance or jump into bed with someone.

The Dante show consumed most of my final year, at the end of which I was hopelessly unprepared for exams. My degree was in English literature since Shakespeare, but the only book I really knew well was fourteenth-century Italian. Fortuitously, my first exam was on English literature in general and I remember one suggested essay title was 'Exile'. It was my only chance. I waxed lyrical on Dante's expulsion from Florence; his yearning for Beatrice … for Virgil … for the Jackson 5 … the 1970s … I couldn't entirely remember which quotes from the show were Dante's and which were Boney M. Surprisingly, it worked. I think the examiner actually commended me for the breadth of my reading.

I fear too little of my time was spent reading the great novels and too much trying to work out how to sound like I had. Once I had to give a paper on *Middlemarch* and the tutor Anne Clune asked me, after twenty minutes of guff, if it was George Eliot's *Middlemarch* I was referring to, or somebody else's. But I did – amazingly – read *Ulysses*.

I loved David Norris's brilliant lectures on Joyce and enjoyed a whole year of his seminars on *Ulysses* without ever actually reading it. David lived near me on North Great George's Street and I called around to him the day before the final Joyce exam, desperate and panicking. He was as kind and generous as ever and eventually said 'Well, we're not trying to catch people out here, so I might as well give you a hint as to what might come up.' I returned home feeling considerably calmer and sufficiently inspired to open up *Ulysses* and read the whole book straight through. I stayed up all night in my flat, looking out over Mountjoy Square and Fitzgibbon Street, which both feature in the book, and as dawn came up over Dublin and the city bustled back to life, I read those great final words, 'and yes I said yes I will Yes'. I closed the book and sauntered down Gardiner Street to the exam. It was magical.

THERE'S A GREAT exchange in Tom Stoppard's play *Travesties*, when someone asks Joyce, 'So what did you do in the war?' and Joyce quips 'I wrote *Ulysses*.' Well, in terms of academic work, that's what I did in four years at Trinity: I read *Ulysses*. In other terms, it set the course for the rest of my life. It gave me a lifelong love of Ireland; it made me decide to become an actor and it made me friends I still see and love. One in particular.

When I returned from Paris, Dominic Geraghty kept telling me about a second-year student called Catherine FitzGerald who was causing quite a stir. Beautiful, intelligent and spectacularly disdainful, she had won a scholarship and so had rooms in Rubrics, which of course made her even more attractive. A mutual friend – appropriately called Charity – introduced us in Marks Bros café on South Great George's Street. Catherine thought very little of me and I thought everything of her, and little changed for seventeen years, when I finally persuaded her to marry me.

Her room in Rubrics was just along from Michael West's. Annie Ryan had returned from Chicago to be with Michael and I remember her collaring me in the corridor one morning after Catherine had sashayed past, and murmuring in her Chicago drawl, 'What's up with Lolita?' We were together for my last four months at Trinity, travelling to her family home, Glin on the Shannon, and sunbathing on the roof in Mountjoy Square with all of Dublin spread out beneath us.

Brendan Kennelly said he had given my patchy course work the benefit of considerable doubt because I had fallen in love with Catherine, whose mother he knew from Kerry. He understood my obsession and thought it should count as extenuating circumstances. Only a poet would think like that and probably only an Irish poet. Such depth of humanity: it's what university education is all about.

Dominic West with Catherine FitzGerald.

Dominic West (TCD 1989–93; English and Drama Studies) studied at the Guildhall School of Music and Drama after graduating from Trinity, and has since acted in plays at The Almeida, The National Theatre, The Donmar Warehouse, The Crucible Theatre in Sheffield, and in the West End and Broadway. He has starred in films including **Richard III, Chicago, Awakening, Pride** and **Money Monster**; and on television in **The Wire, The Hour, The Affair** and **Appropriate Adult**, for which he won a BAFTA for Leading Actor in 2012.

PUBLISH AND BE DAMNED

nick webb

TRINITY AT THE END of the 1980s and start of the 1990s was an insane amount of fun if you didn't mind getting into trouble. I didn't. I read history of art and history, and got chucked out of college in the quatercentenary year. (There were limits, it seems.)

I arrived at Trinity in the autumn of 1989, a wannabe cartoonist in a denim jacket. Early in my first term, I'd heard that *Piranha* – the college's satirical magazine – was looking for a new illustrator. Its previous one had graduated. I met the editor, Vincent Piat Kelly, and we instantly hit it off. He wanted to stick his finger in the eye of some of the more pompous and self-important people and bodies on the campus. It's a hard habit to kick.

Piranha had been around for about ten years and was run out of the publications committee offices, on the third floor of House Six on Front Square, looking out over College Green. It was a double-sized room with a dilapidated sofa and a bunch of mismatched tables and chairs. The walls might have been yellow and fluorescent tube lighting cast a glare over it all. There was also a broken window blocked up with cardboard. Across the corridor was the Ents office, with the Happy Mondays playing on a loop and the vague whiff of hash.

I became editor of *Piranha* at the end of 1990 when Vincent graduated – it became a crash course in how not to manage or edit a magazine. The first print technology revolution was unfolding at the time, and Trinity was ahead of the curve by giving us beige, box-like Macintosh computers loaded up with Adobe PageMaker design software. It's not a million miles from how newspaper pages are designed today. Copy would be dragged into columns and made to fit into spaces. Then we'd print the pages out and glue on photos or illustrations. These were then laid out on the floor in order and carefully put together in a folder to hand to the printer – a guy a called Terry on Pearse Street. Having no computer skills (not unusual in those days), I persuaded a friend of a friend to help me design my first edition. As the deadline approached for the issue to go to the printer, I had a blazing row with him – things may have been thrown. He walked. There was no way of completing his half-finished work on the Mac and I ended up handwriting headlines directly on to the proofs. It looked terrible. Even so, I managed to edit seven more issues over the following two years.

The magazine was about twenty-eight pages of whimsy, vitriol and fart humour. It ranged from cut-out condoms to photo stories copying the style of teen-girl magazines like *Jackie*, to salacious and probably inaccurate gossip. Nothing too serious. After a while I started doing photo-bubble covers like those of *Private Eye* and *The Phoenix*. These were in particularly poor taste. I think the first one featured a photo of serial killer and cannibal Jeffrey Dahmer, who'd just been collared by the Feds. The caption just read 'Burp'. And it probably wasn't the worst.

The magazine was partly funded by advertising, and we would sell ads to the shops around Trinity. There were big plans to ramp up revenues – I even remember talking to a proper grown-up ad sales man to see if he'd do it on commission. He wouldn't. The men's clothes shop Kennedy & McSharry was our core advertiser. The Stag's Head used to give us a keg. Most of the income came from selling the magazine from a table in the Arts Block and a couple of roving sales people. We managed to whack up circulation a fair bit but we never broke the thousand mark.

Piranha, and the publications office in general, was a lot of fun. There were other magazines and publications being run out of the offices at the same time: *Trinity News* was the big one. It was staffed by very serious reporters, guys like RTÉ's David Murphy, Bloomberg's Dara Doyle and former *Irish Times* writers Liam Reid and Conor Sweeney. And lots of people who wore sensible shoes.

We were definitely seen as messers by them, but we always had gorgeous girls hanging out when we were in production. *Trinity Miscellany* was a bit more fun – intellectual in tone and well written but largely produced by men with beards. *Icarus* was the college literary magazine, and it was full-on bonkers.

As well as the day-to-day shenanigans of House Six, there was always terrific intrigue as the publications committee had a large presence in the Central Society Committee that oversaw all of the College societies. There were shaftings and coups in smoke-filled rooms. I was appointed to be the publications representative for the Trinity Week quatercentenary year, in 1992. The attraction was that it came with free tickets to the Trinity Ball and a champagne reception. All I had to do was produce a commemorative magazine that people received when they arrived at the ball (and then chucked in the bin). The CSC gave me an early grounding in why you should never, ever go to meetings and I suspect I went to very few. The magazine came out on time. Just. Also, I met my beautiful wife at the ball.

Academically, I was a glorious failure. I read history of art and history and had a total of around four hours a week of lectures and seminars, though I probably only made it to four hours over the first two and a half years. Mind you, I do know enough to spoof my way through a conversation about seventeenth-century Spanish painting – thanks to Dr Peter Cherry, I can sound vaguely credible about the composition of Velázquez's 'Las Meninas' or the Rokeby Venus.

Midway through my third year, things went pear-shaped. It was hardly a surprise: there was a lot of partying and very little academic application. I racked up a bundle of N/S or 'Not satisfactory' reports at the end of each term, to add to the ones I'd got in second year. And first year. I moved from tutor to tutor. I'm pretty sure that I didn't actually meet them all, and any of the ones I did go and see looked at me sternly as I promised to pull up my socks.

It didn't happen. My days were pretty much dominated by *Piranha*, or at least hanging out in the publications office, or loafing in pubs with writers. Long before Buzzfeed, we had cornered the market in trashy listicles. It was a great way to shift copies – put the names of 300 people in the magazine and write something bitchy about them alongside. Dumb, perhaps – but boy, did it sell.

In February 1992 as the deadline loomed for the Valentine's Day edition, an envelope was pushed under the door of our office. Inside was an anonymous article called 'The Hit List' – four pages of typeset copy, perfectly laid out and ready to go. It was a list of about 150 prominent names in Trinity, largely the most noted or most beautiful people on the campus social scene. And it trashed them. It was puerile, offensive and spectacularly nasty … but bloody funny in places. In other words, exactly the kind of piece *Piranha* always published. And more importantly it was printer-ready.

There may have been libel training offered by the publications committee in 1991, but either I didn't bother going or simply missed it. In any event, my understanding of libel laws was close to zero – I thought that the general gist was that certain words relating to the, um, female undercarriage couldn't appear in print. And that was pretty much it. Truth? Accuracy? Meh. So I cut out replacement words and glued them over the one or two examples of profanity and let it go to the printer.

Whoah! Big mistake. Within minutes of *Piranha* going on sale, the sky caved in. My sales people were told to stop selling it in the Arts Block. There had been a flood of complaints. My recollection is that there were about sixty-plus objections – probably half of all those featured. There was also talk that two people had made complaints of sedition. I honestly can't remember much of what happened next. I do remember being hauled in front of officialdom and carpeted, and I'm pretty sure that I was made to resign as editor. Then I think I probably drank some beers.

At the same time as *Piranha* met its end (it was subsequently resurrected), I was informed that I wouldn't be sitting my exams that year. Given that I'd never failed an exam in my life, it probably kept my record intact. I would have to repeat the year. Several months later, over the summer holidays, Trinity sent me a letter telling me not to come back the following year. I kept the letter for years and always meant to frame it.

Eventually, in 1994, I would go back to Trinity to finish my degree, while working for a magazine on Liffey Street. All of my friends had graduated, and I don't remember those final two years as being much fun (which might have been for the best). Even when I did complete my finals, I still didn't graduate because I had racked up a huge library fine. The following year my mother paid the fine and I got my piece of paper – just.

Nick Webb (TCD 1989–95; History of Art and History) is a journalist and former Business Editor of the **Sunday Independent**. In 2009 he was named National and Business Journalist of the Year and is author of the bestselling books **Wasters** and **The Untouchables**.

THE MAKING OF A MEDIC

larkin feeney

BEING RATHER INDECISIVE, I had the pleasure of spending eight years as a TCD undergraduate: 1989 to 1997. I had gigantic glasses and floppy hair but thankfully Trinity was a more stylistically forgiving place in the 1990s – grunge was very convenient for cash-strapped students. My friend Rory Egan and I embarked on a very in-vogue European studies degree but quickly jumped ship to English literature and history when we realized that the French and German components were more gruelling than we had reckoned upon. Two fun-filled years in and around the Arts Block followed before some subconscious urge drove me to the science end of campus, and medicine.

Walking into the *mêlée* of Freshers' Week with societies baying for my interest is a strangely happy memory. Somehow this clichéd and parochial demonstration gave me a sense of worldly possibilities beyond the narrow confines of a south Dublin secondary school. Like most, I joined many societies that first week but stuck with almost none. Tales of my parents' student-protesting exploits led me to the very radical-sounding Socialist Workers' Party. There followed a year or so of delusional meetings above Conway's pub and weekends outside the GPO trying to sell tabloid newsletters announcing the impending revolution. The efforts it took to escape their clutches when I finally got fed up of it all put me off organized politics for life.

Players was another early enthusiasm. My Fresher's year play was *Lysistrata* by Aristophanes. I fondly remember prancing around that tiny stage in the corner of Front Square with a balloon for a sword/penis. I was a dreadful actor but Players was inclusive enough to allow me to occupy some minor roles alongside the bright talents of Dominic West, Cathy Belton, Gavin Kostick, Mario Rosenstock and others. My denouement was a horrific effort to bring Raymond Carver's marvellous poetry collection, *A New Path to the Waterfall*, to the stage. Back then, *The Irish Times* prominently reviewed all Players productions and its formidable critic Victoria White wrote that the play killed both poetry and theatre and had the feminist bristles rising on her neck. I would like to take this opportunity to belatedly apologize for that humiliation to my fellow director, Una Bradley, and to actors Jo Mangan, Jack O'Driscoll and Emma McIvor.

Socially, life in the Arts Block was wonderful. There were all these seriously intellectual Northerners and glamorous American exchange students to chat to in the Junior Common Room by day, the Buttery by evening, and on into the small hours at countless overpopulated flat parties. Joseph O'Gorman was often there and I still cannot walk in the front gates of Trinity now without instantly recalling his booming declarations of Trinity's delights while conducting tours for international tourists. Another unforgettable feature of Trinity at the time was Matteo Mattubara, aka 'Matt the Jap', a shuffling, hard-of-hearing Asian man, who seemed to be everywhere and about whom all sorts of magnificent rumours circulated.

Although Brendan Kennelly's passionate renditions of Yeats and stories of life were genuinely inspiring, academically I never quite felt at home in the arts. The professor of medieval English had the most apt name of any academic I've encountered since: Scattergood. I dabbled in poetry, short stories, journalism and tried to write amusingly for Nick Webb's wonderfully anarchic *Piranha* magazine. In the end I figured out that my talents lay elsewhere and decided to take the plunge into pre-med.

MEDICINE WAS an altogether different venture. Suddenly I jumped from eight to thirty-five hours of lectures and practicals a week, with plenty of study to boot. I found it academically liberating. Although physics, chemistry and biology dominated that first year, it seemed as if every scientific department had a little bite at us: anthropology, archaeology, psychology, sociology, computer science, even botany. The nineteenth-century science buildings we inhabited fittingly conveyed a sense of deep tradition rather than cutting-edge science. The highlight of that first year was my chemistry professor, Dr Roy Brown, and the pipe cleaners he commanded us to mould into 3D representations of all sorts of molecules. Anatomy and the unforgettable Professor Máire O'Brien loomed large in second and third years. The steeply tiered, circular anatomy lecture theatre felt like something out of Rembrandt painting, a stark contrast to the ultra-modern Hamilton building, which became our new home shortly afterwards. In the anatomy dissection lab there were eight students to each body and together we excavated until every nook and cranny had been explored. In the way these things tend to happen, my wife Jennifer Donnelly and many of my best friends to this day, Susan Hopkins, Cartan Costello and Anna Beug to name just a few, worked on that same anonymous woman or her immediate neighbours. To them I am eternally grateful.

After my switch to medicine, the self-conscious intellectuals of the JCR were replaced by a much more eclectic group. International students abounded, with Malaysians and Singaporeans most prevalent, and the exposure to their cultures and cuisines was hugely enriching. Medical student life didn't leave much time for serious extra-curricular pursuits but there were plenty of parties, the most memorable of these being the quatercentenary Trinity Ball of 1992. The whole campus was opened up, with ten stages and over 10,000 in attendance. Chumbawamba; Toasted Heretic; pre-*Grace* Jeff Buckley on a tiny stage; Kirsty MacColl (I think) in front of the Moyne Institute in the small hours: what more could you want? I was supposed to be working security but this in no way restricted the freedom or fun of that night.

Having done some teaching on research methodology since, I often bore students with a story of my participation in a randomized controlled trial in the Trinity Dental School in the early 1990s. My friend Paul Balfe and I answered an advertisement as we were attracted by the offer of a small amount of money and a wristwatch. Shortly afterwards we reported to the dental school and had our gums unpleasantly prodded as a researcher recorded how much we bled. We were then each given a box containing numerous bottles of mouthwash and told to rinse thoroughly, morning and evening, and to come back in a month to be prodded again. Our bottles looked the same but of course we decided to open them up and taste each other's. His tasted pleasant; mine was caustic and nasty. We assumed his was placebo and mine was the real deal. Somehow we separately contrived not to bother with the mouthwash. However, I assiduously brushed my teeth for the next few weeks while Paul did the opposite and we duly presented, slightly shamefacedly, to collect our loot. It only dawned on me years later that we may have contributed to a useless mouthwash making it to the shelves.

Perhaps the best thing of all about my time in Trinity was the four-month-long summer breaks. There was no pressure to do anything career-related, so like droves of other Irish students we headed off in small groups to German biscuit factories and North American cities. I enjoyed more of these sojourns than most: London, San Francisco, Montpellier, Montreal, Vancouver. In fourth year, medical students had a tradition of raising money to fund summer trips so that they could gain experience in the developing world. One of our enterprises was the insensitively named Club Foot, which we hosted in the nightclub of Blooms Hotel. I got to go to Trinidad, which felt like cheating, but those few months in Port of Spain General Hospital were exhilarating, humbling and edifying.

Fourth year brought us properly into the hospitals. The Trinity Centre for Medical Sciences had recently opened in St James' Hospital and our lectures increasingly took place there. I did my clinical placements in the dilapidated Meath and Adelaide hospitals. The Adelaide had nurses with quaint polka-dot uniforms and starched caps and a ward called Featherstonehaugh, which nobody could pronounce. The consultant teachers were a memorable bunch, as were the patients; I particularly remember one very grand, and not very ill, older lady who was in for months, feeling poorly as a result, she said, of eating an ornamental gourd.

At the time we used to host 'Res parties' on Fridays in the Doctors' Residence – a distinguished-sounding name for a poky collection of sitting rooms and bedrooms in the hospital basement, harking back to the days when junior doctors lived in. I remember the fire brigade evacuating us during one of these, probably when the night sister could no longer tolerate the racket;

such a thing seems unthinkable now. It was during my intern year that the Adelaide, Meath and National Children's hospitals finally closed their doors and were amalgamated in a shiny new facility in Tallaght. Somehow, this break with nineteenth-century traditions – the real end of an era – seemed a fitting way to bring my own Trinity undergraduate days to a close.

Larkin Feeney (far right) *with, from left, Jerry Chan, Anna Beug, Ti Wei Foo, Susan Hopkins and Jennifer Donnelly.*

Larkin Feeney (TCD 1989, European Studies; 1989–91, English Literature and History; 1991–97, Medicine; 2004–06, MSc Health Informatics) embarked on a career in neurology but soon realized that he was drawn to Oliver Sacks more for the human stories than the fascinating conditions, so he became a psychiatrist. He works as a community general adult psychiatrist in south Dublin. Among his interests is the interface of the arts and medicine. He is married with three children.

FAST TIMES ON FRONT SQUARE

mario rosenstock

THERE WAS only ever one reason I was going to Trinity: Players. That was it. The BESS degree I took to get there was really just a means to an end. From my mid teens I knew without a shadow of a doubt that performing was something I really wanted to do and I had been told by people who had gone to Trinity in the 1970s – in the glory days of Michael Colgan, Susan Fitzgerald et al. – that if I wanted to act seriously, then Players was where I wanted to be. And so Trinity was the only choice.

By that point, acting had already become something of an obsession. After a couple of years at Newpark Comprehensive in Dublin where I discovered girls, Van Halen and pierced ears – all in a frenetic attempt to shake off the culchie in me (I had been brought up in Waterford) – I simultaneously began to fail all my classes. So my parents decided to send me to Rochelle House, a boarding school in Cork. It was on a trip there the year before that I saw my brother René perform in a male musical version of *Cinderella*, called *Mr Cinders*. He stole the show and I was mesmerized. By then I had metamorphosed from teen rocker into an even more objectionable Don Johnson clone, circa *Miami Vice*, 1985. White blazer: check. Sleeves rolled up to the elbow: check. Pastel blue t-shirt: check. Studied stare into the middle distance: check. Sonny Crockett had arrived in Cork. Watching René on stage, listening to him sing 'Spread a Little Happiness', seeing the reaction of the girls in the audience, I had what I could only believe was an epiphany. This was it. This is what I wanted to do. And I thought, 'I want to be in that space.' Fast.

The next year I had the lead in the school production of *Death of a Salesman*. For a sixteen-year-old playing 63-year-old Willy Loman, it was heavy going, inhabiting all his turmoil and pain – but I loved it. I loved the *esprit de corps* that you get working so closely with others, the deepening of friendship and trust, which is by necessity fast-tracked on our exhilarating journey together. On the fourth and final night, I remember going out to the steps behind the theatre after the play had ended, and starting to cry uncontrollably. About an hour later I figured out that it was because I wasn't going to be able to revisit Willy's life the following night; I was leaving him behind. It was an utterly transformative experience. I had a brilliant drama teacher – in the Robin Williams *Dead Poets Society* mould – and I remember having conversations with him about taking acting more seriously. His encouragement, I would say, spurred me on.

OF COURSE the next step wasn't that straightforward. I had been told that if I studied drama, I wouldn't be able to join Players – that was the rule back in those days – so instead I opted for law. I missed it by a point but, undeterred, repeated my Leaving and missed it again, and ended up doing BESS. It was probably just as well – I think law would have been too dry for me, and the politics and economics of BESS offered some colour. Eddie Hyland's suitably bearded figure pouring forth on Socratic thought while simultaneously rolling a cigarette in the Edmund Burke Hall; Plato through a plume of smoke. It couldn't happen now!

It was a fascinating time to be studying politics. Ron Hill was probably the most charismatic of the lecturers, and taught a module in Soviet society and studies. He would regularly appear on radio and TV too, which lent him an added glamour. But in October 1991, just as we were about to begin the course, the Soviet Union collapsed. So Ron walked into class on the first day and, with his usual brisk delivery, announced, 'I have news for you all – there will be no course this term, because there is no Soviet Union.' And so it became more of a journalistic course – we read newspapers and magazines and analysed the events as they unfolded. Wonderful stuff. In the early 1990s there were also a lot of professors, like Basil Chubb, who had been at Trinity for time immemorial. My uncles would ask me, 'Is so-and-so still there?' – enquiring after some lecturer from their day – and, inevitably, they still were.

BECAUSE I HAD repeated my Leaving, my brother René and I entered College the same year, and I suppose we stood out a bit – both in Players, both with unusual names. It didn't go unnoticed. During first term, I remember a friend saying to me, 'Mario, someone's got it in for you,' and thrusting a copy of *Piranha* into my hand. There, in the notorious Sybarite column at the back of the magazine, was written something along the lines of: *Rumour has it that our hallowed institution is being infiltrated by complete [insert unrepeatable word here] – people with names like 'Mario' and 'René', who describe themselves as 'thespians'. The Mario creature wears an Aran jumper and a silk scarf. He is a charlatan and should be avoided at all costs.* Probably sound advice. Yet it led to my first encounter with Nick Webb, *Piranha*'s editor, who would go on to become one of my best friends. Handsome and raffish, Nick had a line in humour so dry it made Angus Deayton look like a panto dame.

I occasionally dipped into the Hist and the Phil but I always found that there was a bit of antipathy towards the fact that I was a performer. The truth is that I was a snob. To my mind, the people in those societies were wannabe actors who weren't quite good enough. I used to debate at school so I liked the idea of tackling subjects and using my performance skills to win the day by injecting humour and bringing some individuality to the performance. But in the Phil and the Hist, you'd see these guys who you knew were all destined to become barristers and they all seemed to have that same sense of humour, and that same condescending legalese banter. To me they were robots parroting the same hackneyed old phrases back and forth at each other: 'Well I'm afraid that would be a matter for yourself entirely – haw haw haw ...' Bollocks. So in the end, I stuck to Players.

I DID sixteen plays in my four years at Trinity – around one a term – and played the lead in eight of them. Out of sheer good luck, I struck gold with my contemporaries. Annie Ryan, who founded the now-famous Corn Exchange theatre company was one of the first people I worked with. She had already been in big movies like *Ferris Bueller's Day Off* as a teenager and was passionate about performance. She introduced me and many others to the magic of Commedia dell'arte. Dominic West was there at the same time, and he and I acted in plays together. He was a charismatic stage presence and there was a sense, even then, that he was one to watch. My first time seeing him was in *A Play on Two Chairs*, a charming two-hander written by another budding genius, the playwright Michael West. Dominic was also a genuinely lovely guy with a generous booming laugh and a zest for life. He also had a real curiosity about people, which I think was one of the reasons for his talent. Gemma Bodinetz was another powerhouse. She and Cathy Belton – now one of Ireland's most accomplished actresses – cast me in my first role, in the Freshers' Co-op production of Aristophanes' *Lysistrata*. I remember auditioning for these two nineteen-year-old girls, who were utterly serious about what they were doing, and getting the part of the magistrate. From then on, I thought, 'I'm in here.'

Meeting those people who had theatre flowing through their veins was completely formative. They weren't just in it for a bit of craic or sophomoric exhibitionism – they were there because they too had an inkling that this was what they might do for the rest of their lives. There was a fairly high degree of professionalism – in terms of ideas, and detail and commitment. We might go out drinking all night on Saturday, but we would be there at 8 am on Sunday morning to put in a day's rehearsal. And it would be focused. Being around these people made you want to up your game. We were also competitive with each other but good-naturedly so. Back in those days, Players' productions were reviewed by *The Irish Times* – by Derek West and David Knowlan. The legendary Con Houlihan would even come in from *The Evening Press*. They reviewed in a way that did not cut much slack: they expected something decent from us, and we would be determined to deliver.

Gemma directed Dominic and me and another actor called Rod Chichignoud in a beautiful absurdist play called *Fando et Lis* by Fernando Arrabal. I remember being incredibly proud of the fact that the play was her thesis and that she was trusting us to execute her vision. Very few people would even see it, yet I remember the depth of thought she and then we put into it. Cathy and I were in *Translations* together – she as Máire, me as Yolland – and we did a brilliant spoof musical called *West Brit Story*, written by Paul Gavan.

In 1992 as part of the College's quatercentenary celebrations there was a production of William Congreve's *The Way of the World*. Congreve was a graduate of Trinity and along with the now-legendary ball, our play was the centrepiece of Trinity Week. I played the lead, Mirabell, and it was directed by Judy Boland and produced by Frank Mannion, who has gone on to be a successful film producer and even then was something of a legend. College had given Frank a budget of £400, but with his spectacular gift for making things happen, he had managed to raise £10,000. The play was a huge success – we had period furniture brought over from London for the set, the costumes were practically made from gold, and it went on to win all the awards at that year's ISDA student drama festival in Belfast.

Fool for Love by Sam Shepard was another highlight, as was Edward Albee's *Zoo Story*, a two-man play starring Rory Egan and me. At the end of it, I got stabbed and we thought it would be more authentic to use an actual knife – the old theatre in House Four was so tiny that the audience would be able to see it was real. So I'd strap foam bricks around me under my coat, with a balloon filled with fake blood, and Rory would plunge the knife in. But towards the end of the week, the foam became a bit tired and the tip of the knife ended up going into my belly. That, perhaps, was a little too method.

Still, we always strove for a high degree of authenticity. For *The Hanged Man*, written by a visiting American student playwright, we hired a stuntman to rig me up with a harness in which I was hanged every night. It was on the morning after one of those shows that I had the kind of moment that young actors dream about. I was walking past the Players' noticeboard under Front Arch, as I did every day, and on it was pinned a thick white envelope with my name on it. I reached in and grabbed it. It was from a brand-new company called the Lisa Richards Agency, and inside was a letter that read: *Dear Mr Rosenstock, my name is Richard Cook – I came to see you last night in* The Hanged Man *and I think you could be a wonderful professional actor. Would you like to give me a call?* I was walking around on a cloud for the rest of the day, smiling and clutching the letter. A few days later I met Lisa and Richard at their office on Merrion Row – where there was one table and one chair – and chatted to them for half an hour. At the end of it I asked when the interview would be, and they said 'That was the interview. And you're in.' I was their third client. Receiving that kind of validation was life-changing – soon afterwards, I got a part in *Glenroe*, and things took off from there. Twenty-five years later, I'm still with them.

EVEN AT THE TIME I remember being cognizant of the privilege of going to Trinity, and being very proud of the fact. There we were in a wonderful, historic city university in the centre of a European capital; in a bubble, totally protected, and free to do pretty much whatever we wanted. The idea of an eighteen-year-old being able to walk into a campus wearing ripped trousers, a cravat and eyeliner (don't ask) and going up to a barman at 11 am on a Monday morning and ordering a pint of Guinness; and being served? You'd have been kicked out if you tried that anywhere else – imagine doing that in Longford.

There was much more of a drinking culture back then and I saw some young men and women turn into alcoholics before my eyes, in the space of a few months. We were childish and fairly reckless, and part of the reason was that you were more or less guaranteed that no one would find out – or kick you out. No phones, no Facebook, no Snapchat; if you went out and misbehaved in broad daylight (and we did), the only people who'd know about it were the ones you were with. It was madness.

We bunked into the Quatercentenary Ball in 1992 by hiding out in the underground space beneath the old Players theatre. We had meticulously prepared it for weeks – cleaned it out, brought in a couch and bunks so that we could hide out down there for around eight hours before the ball began. Nick Webb brought ten packs of Camel with him. We heard the sniffer dogs barking above us, but got away with it.

In third year, Johnny O'Reilly and I set up the Aeronautics Society. This was basically a scam to make us some cash and – for £1 each – we offered trusting Freshers the chance to go up in a hot-air balloon or a light aircraft, knowing we'd never deliver it. A lot of unhappy punters. For the rest of that year, angry young men would come up to us in the Buttery, jabbing fingers in chests, asking about their plane ride or parachute jump, and we'd tell them we hadn't the slightest idea what they were talking about. Well weren't we just right tickets altogether!

The Classical Society would hold 'toga parties' – yes, you read right. A society that threw parties offering free wine and the chance to 'discuss

Bacchanalian excesses' with fellow students dressed only in togas. Needless to say the waiting list for membership was lengthy.

Sometimes we took our antics off-campus. A memorable trip to Cork – supposedly for the ISDAs – ended up with us throwing lifebuoys into the Lee, getting arrested and thrown into the Bridewell for the night, being charged by a judge and fined £250, meeting a naked madman in a pub, nearly being arrested again, hitchhiking as far as Tipperary, sleeping in a barn and being chased by a shotgun-wielding farmer. All in the space of thirty-six hours. I really think we had watched *Withnail and I* once too often.

THE COMBINED DEMANDS of Players and partying meant that I failed my exams every year (except for my finals) and had to repeat them in September. I'd be home all summer studying and watching cricket on TV, while Rory and Johnny and Nick were in France, stealing chickens and getting off with women and sending me the postcards to prove it.

We coasted and we took a lot for granted, but I will always be grateful to Trinity for giving me time and space. Time and space to exercise an obsession, to immerse myself in it and to start learning who I was. I couldn't have done that at UCD – I'd have been kicked out after first year, I reckon.

There's one memory I have that seems to me to capture the harmless ambition and aspiration to the high life and, perhaps, our youthful arrogance: it is of me and Frank Mannion in his rooms, drinking £9 champagne from Dunnes, and Frank taking a call from Alan Dershowitz. (Ever the big thinker, Frank was trying to produce a retrial of Oscar Wilde, with Dershowitz defending, though sadly it never happened.) At moments like that, you realized just how ridiculously lucky you were to be living in this giddy little playground where you were treated like an adult yet were little more than a child.

Many years later I got married in Trinity's wonderful chapel to my wife Blathnaid, who also studied there. And every few years, someone from the Hist or the Phil contacts me to be a guest. I'll ask them, 'Didn't you call me about this three years ago?' and they'll say, 'Nah, not me. I'm nineteen – three years ago I was doing my Junior Cert.'

I forget that, like us, they're all just passing through on their way somewhere else.

Mario Rosenstock (TCD 1989–93; BESS) is an actor and writer, and the creator of **Gift Grub** on Today FM. Having first come to public attention in the 1990s in **Glenroe**, Mario went on to develop comedy and satirical sketches for **The Ian Dempsey Breakfast Show** on Today FM, where **Gift Grub** premiered in May 1999. He has won numerous prizes for his writing and performing, including **Magill** magazine's Political Humourist of the Year 2005 and the PPI Outstanding Achievement Award in 2011. While broadcasting, he continues to act in plays and films, and in 2012 he brought his many characters to TV in **The Mario Rosenstock Show** on RTÉ2, now in its fourth season. In recent years, Mario has performed eight sell-out nationwide stage tours of his one-man show, and has sold over half a million CDs and DVDs. He lives in Dublin with his wife Blathnaid and two children.

A PLACE APART

orlaith mcbride

THE TRINITY CAMPUS is like a cowl in the middle of the city; a protected space, an urban snug. It contains imposing public stages within, settings for occasion and grandeur. Arriving there, my schoolgirl self saw only difference and vast scale compared to what I was familiar with, and sophistication all around; in hindsight I see a great schoolyard for the still growing-up. Every tiny detail of independent living was a rite of passage. Negotiating strangeness and aloneness were part of the growing up. So too was the freedom to talk almost any talk with little of the burden of responsibility – that made for freedom unprecedented at home or at school, and enjoyed only seldom afterwards in a world of small but never-ending obligations.

To the seventeen-year-old decanted off the Lifford bus in September 1989 onto the streets of a grimy old town full of faded charms, Trinity College was a world away from home and an end to childhood. From knowing everybody to knowing nobody, from being senior at school to being a 'Fresher', it wasn't just alien, it was a whole new and exciting world. Stepping into Front Square was transforming, life-changing. Then, there was wide-eyed wonder, vocalized in a Donegal accent that didn't fit. The most valuable thing I took away from Trinity was the slowly acquired self-confidence not to fit in. My accent was as wide and my *blás* as big on the day I left as the day I arrived. That's what

Trinity did for me – it allowed me to be proud of just being myself.

I wish I could claim that I was inspired by a convent education or *The Nun's Story* to become a doctor. Whatever it was, the motivation can't have been very deep because when I filled in my college application form, medicine – which had loomed large up until this point – was peremptorily abandoned for English and philosophy. The MacGill Summer School near my home in Donegal was an open university in a small village. My contemporaries went to Trinity for the learning and the company of people like Brendan Kennelly and David Norris, but those luminaries had already come to Glenties to talk in a hall much smaller than most of the lecture theatres in Trinity. Brian Friel and Seamus Heaney were frequent guests on the main street, which became an open-air parlour during the week-long event. It would be an exaggeration to say I took it all in, but I had enjoyed passing familiarity with great names.

The exhilarating talk of those writers led me to seek their written words and in the end, that was what brought me to Trinity. I wanted to learn more about Anglo-Irish literature, and philosophy seemed necessary for any enquiring mind. So with enthusiasm for what I hoped to learn, and curious notions that did not survive impact with reality, off I went. Flat-hunting was the first imperative education, and Ranelagh was student central. The daily purchase of the *Evening Herald* and the race to be top of the queue for the grim viewings of damp bedsits and freezing flats is unconscionable now in our digital era. The Celtic Tiger was then an economic embryo, but to us the gentrification of Ranelagh remained unimaginable. The nascent peace and prosperity of the 1990s began to dawn only as my class graduated in 1993. Nineteen-eighty-nine and the four years that followed, in economic terms, had more in common with the long, unhopeful decade of the 1980s.

The glamour of living away from home with friends came up against the reality of a freezing cold flat. Reverse-charge phone calls recreated the umbilical cord with telephone wire. Mammy and Daddy, tolerated by my teenage self, were a lifeline again. But things settled – I was quickly in love, in love with Dublin, in love with Trinity and in love with my first college boyfriend. The shift came subtly as my confidence grew. There wasn't one other person from Donegal in my class, but I made friends with the large number who came from Northern Ireland. Our accents were similar. Many of them came to Donegal during the marching season every July, and they weren't from Alex or Gonzaga. We gravitated towards each other – strong Ulster friendships developed, which continue today. Familiar echoes were recreated on new territory.

Studying English was exhilarating. If beans on toast made up the daily diet, the life of ideas and literature was rich. We had exceptional teachers: David Norris and his exuberant Joyce tutorials, Professor Scattergood's gentle introduction to medieval literature, the intensity of a Chaucer lecture from Dr Gerald Morgan, and lecturers like Terence Brown, Antoinette Quinn, Gerald Dawe and Nicholas Grene had a profound effect on me. They opened up new ways of seeing the world and it was invigorating.

Beyond the lecture halls, the election of a new Ents officer and the hustings on the Dining Hall steps were as critical in our world as the New Hampshire primary in a US presidential campaign. I recall weeks of campaigning for a classmate and fellow resident in House Nineteen in 1992. Campaign teams were deployed. This was our first brush with democracy. It tested us, tested our convictions and allowed us speak unedited in a protected, privileged world.

The wider world did impinge, though, and 1992 was the year when abortion, the right to travel for one, the right to have information about one, and the attempt to rule out suicide as basis for accessing legal abortion under the eighth amendment to the constitution were pulverizing issues. For me those campaigns were an awakening. We marched for the right to information, for the right to travel and to insist that the tiny chink of constitutional light, where a suicidal woman could avail of abortion, be allowed through. Nearly a quarter of a century later, the central issue, unbelievably, remains undecided. For me, that campaign then was the moment when the long decade of the 1980s was finally over: nothing would ever be the same. The unspeakable was shouted. Out of tragic, unprepossessing circumstances cultural, a revolution began.

Outside Trinity's walls, Marks Bros café and Bewley's Café Museum were regular haunts, and my friends and I would sit for hours over a single coffee. But mostly our social life was lived around the Arts Block – the brutalist building was our window onto the world. On the eve of an as yet unforeseen electronic revolution, old-fashioned notes on scraps of paper were left on library desks identifying where coffee was being consumed, and with whom. If the Lecky was for browsing and socializing (given our lectures averaged about nine hours a week), then the Berkeley was for serious study when essays were due or in the final weeks of the Trinity Term when thoughts of returning in September were thrown into sharp focus and exams needed to be passed. A biting north wind caught your breath upon exiting its unwelcoming entrance hall. This austere building offered no guarantees, only the promise of hope if we were willing to take it. And take it we did – we committed the month of May to its silent walls of study.

There was little in the way of Dublin nightlife, and The Stag's Head, Grogan's and, most of all, the Buttery were where we were to be found, in animated discussion and a constant cloud of smoke. We tackled the big issues in our lives, gender politics in the contemporary American novel, existentialism in the plays of Samuel Beckett or Edward Said's theories of post-colonial literature. With each glass of Guinness the conversation became more abstract, more esoteric and more pretentious, but such was the privilege of being an undergraduate.

It says something of that undergraduate life, and more for life generally, that entering Trinity seemed like a great adventure but leaving was a natural progression. At the end of four years, I emerged wiser, calmer and more prepared to deal with the uncertainty of what lies ahead after an arts degree. Above all else, those four years rooted me in myself and laid the foundations for what would come next with confidence and self-belief. It was more than a university, it was an endowment for life. Trinity College, like County Donegal, is extra-territorial, a place apart. Therein lies another life, a dual citizenship, a charmed world for its denizens.

Orlaith McBride (TCD 1989–93; English and Philosophy) graduated from Trinity and then completed post-graduate studies at the University of Ulster and University College Dublin. She is Director of the Arts Council/An Chomhairle Ealaíon. Prior to this, she worked in the arts across a broad range of arts organizations. She served as a member of the Arts Council from 2003–11, was a member of Dublin City Council Strategic Policy Committee (Arts and Youth) from 2004–09 and of the Special Committee on the Arts and Education. She was President of the National Youth Council of Ireland, 2010–11 and is a member of the Governing Authority of Dublin City University.

ALONE IN THE CROWD

john boyne

BETWEEN AUTUMN 1989 and summer 1993, a young man attended Trinity College where he studied English literature. He shared the same name as me, looked exactly like me and had the same parents as me. He took the same bus into College as I did, shared my aspirations to be a novelist and was coming to terms with being gay, just like I was. But he wasn't me. He was someone who, more than twenty years later, I barely recognize. A loner. An introvert. A complete mess. A total disaster.

There's a condition known as Avoidant Personality Disorder, which marks the sufferer out with social inhibition, feelings of inferiority and a compulsive need to avoid any form of public interaction, despite a desperate longing to be part of a group. It's an ailment that I suffered from during my days at Trinity and which effectively caused me to waste four years of my youth that should have been overflowing with adventures and excitement. Afterwards, knowing how much I had missed out on, I had to work hard to overcome it. Had I not succeeded, I simply would never have been able to live the life that I live today.

My APD displayed itself in the following ways: hovering in the hallway before lectures, I would wait until the professor had entered the theatre and the room had gone silent before slipping in and taking my seat at the very back. By doing so, I would not be forced into conversation with anyone before the lecture began. And once it was over, of course, I would gather my papers and flee. Tutorials were more difficult. For these, I preferred to arrive first, in order to ensure a safe seat, one where there was less possibility of me being called upon to engage in the discussion. While my classmates chatted amongst themselves as they arrived, I would be furiously scribbling in a notebook, giving off every sign that I didn't want to be disturbed. Strangely enough, one-on-ones with my advisors were fine. I seemed to have no problem interacting with adults; it was people my own age who I feared.

I was living at home during those early years and, more often than not, I would retreat there at the end of the day to the safety of my room, my books and my records, like a reclusive teenager who emerges only to eat and growl at his family. I longed to join the other students in the Buttery or the city-centre bars but having failed so terribly during my first term even to engage in conversation with others, I knew that this was a lost cause. By Christmas 1989 I was sure that the possibility of a social life was lost to me and, in persuading myself of this, the problem became self-fulfilling. I was terribly lonely. And I felt like a complete failure.

I lost myself in two things. The first was writing. When I was not at lectures or tutorials I could usually be found in a quiet corner of the Lecky Library, working on short stories. I knew that I wanted to be a writer and must have completed close to a hundred stories over the course of my degree, most of which are lost to me now, but some of which got published and gave me a much-needed boost of confidence. I liked the solitude that came with writing, the fact that I could express all my thoughts and feelings on paper and never have to explain them aloud. I liked creating characters that weren't me but were the types of 'me' that I wished I could be. I still like that feeling. I'm at my happiest alone at my desk, working on a novel. The public aspect of it, the interviews, the book launches and the endless tours are a source of increasing misery to me. Other than reading aloud to an audience – which I love – I could quite happily walk away from the rest of it forever. But that's impossible to do, of course, for publishing doesn't work that way. Particularly if you're actually interested in selling a few books.

My second outlet was the cinema. I had a weekend job in a bookie's and used most of my money to watch afternoon films in the many cinemas scattered around Dublin: the Carlton, Adelphi and Screen, all of which are gone now, the old Lighthouse on Abbey Street, which has since re-opened in Smithfield, and the Savoy on O'Connell Street, where in 2008 I would host the world premiere of the film adaptation of *The Boy in the Striped Pyjamas*. I saw everything. Blockbusters, art-house films, trashy comedies, award-winning dramas. Being alone in the dark for a few hours made me feel safe. Once those lights went down, I felt an overwhelming sense of calm.

When I would observe students socializing together around campus, apparently completely at ease in each other's company, I could never understand how they did it. I envied them, tried to figure out what their secret was, and on the rare occasions when I found myself trapped in conversation with them, I was sure that every sentence that came out of my mouth was even more idiotic than the one before, that I was a complete bore and they were silently judging me as they looked around for some way to escape. None of these things may have been true, of course, but it was how I felt.

It didn't help that I was struggling to come to terms with my sexuality. I'd known since I was about ten years old that I was gay and, ironically, the one area of my life in which I had no difficulty pursuing social opportunities was my sex life. But of course this was the early nineties, a very different time to today, and everything I did, everything that we all did back then, was covert and felt both sordid and dangerous. I knew nothing of romance or love, nor did I give any thought to it. All I was interested in was fucking, as often as possible with as many different people as possible and, the deed over, making my way home as quickly as I could. In those days, young gay people didn't date. Even the concept would have been fairly ridiculous to us. You got together with someone for one reason and one reason only and, for both parties, it was an entirely successful arrangement. Again, I seemed to be at my best in the dark, where people could barely see me and absolutely no one was interested in talking.

None of this, it needs to be said, was the fault of Trinity College. It was simply the person that I was at the time. I was inadequately prepared by my school for life outside its rotten walls and perhaps there is a part of every writer that is naturally introverted and prefers solitude anyway. In the end, when I left Trinity I took a year off and travelled before undertaking the Creative Writing

MA at the University of East Anglia. On my first day there I determined not to allow the same thing to happen to me during my post-graduate year as had taken place during my undergraduate ones and made a determined effort not only to be part of a social group but to throw myself into the very heart of it. I succeeded, quite quickly in fact, and somehow the disorder that had marred four years of my life began to fade and eventually disappear entirely.

Most memoirs of university life are happy ones, filled with a love of learning and the dramas that go hand in hand with youthful partying. And that's as it should be. But my story is a different one. It's hard for me to look back at those years without feeling an unhappy and embarrassing combination of pain and regret. I don't dwell on it – it's more than twenty years ago, after all, and my life has moved on – but I can't forget it either. Perhaps it's one of the reasons why I am so disciplined and ambitious as a writer. It's important for me not to be on the outskirts anymore, not to hover around while others capture an audience. I need to be in there. I need to be part of the conversation. I need to have a voice.

John Boyne (TCD 1989–93; English) is the author of nine novels for adults, five for younger readers and a collection of short stories, including the international bestsellers **The Boy in the Striped Pyjamas**, **The Absolutist** and **A History of Loneliness**. His novels are published in over forty-five languages.

THE LATE BLOOMER

trevor white

I SORT OF went to Trinity College for a couple of years in the early 1990s. Here is what I learned: don't write the first thing that comes into your head. That's what idiots do. Don't write the second thing. That's what clever people do. Write the third thing.

'Words are just a conclusion.' Antonin Artaud. It's a theory.

I can't remember the third thing.

LOOKING BACK, Trinity is a blur. It feels incidental, because it happened to someone I hardly know – a stranger, even – and because I was there on the edge, just for a while, looking for a party in a flat near town. This tall kid from Raglan Road with floppy hair and a boarding-school accent. (A woman once stopped me on the street to compliment my performance in *Four Weddings and a Funeral*. It wasn't the compliment that made me feel like a fraud. It was when I heard myself say 'Thank you.')

Admission to the diploma course in theatre studies was by audition alone. As my older brother put it, 'You can be a gobshite and still get into Trinity.' For my audition I chose to perform a speech from the end of *Philadelphia, Here I Come!*. In a classic Irish love letter, Gar tries to get through to his father one last time: 'And you know why I'm going, Screwballs, don't you? Because I'm twenty-five and you treat me as if I were five.'

It did the trick. On the first day, at the beginning of October 1990, my classmates and I learned that several hundred applicants had been turned away. The syllabus included acting, dance, movement, voice coaching, drama theory and acting for film. As the Soviet Union spluttered to a halt, I was busy learning that words are only a conclusion. Artaud discovered this just before he went mad.

The goal of drama school is to shed one's inhibitions, explore character, become a 'thespian' and say that word without blushing. Painfully self-conscious, I never got over the fact that we had to wear a black leotard all the time. In week one I wanted to join the French Foreign Legion. In week two I skipped class to pick magic mushrooms.

At that time, the Samuel Beckett Centre for Theatre Studies was housed in Westland Row at the arse end of college. It felt miles from the campus, a distancing effect that Bertolt Brecht would appreciate. Stanislavski, Artaud and some other people – who knows – were also on the curriculum. You would race past our building to catch a train in time to get home to watch the first Gulf War unfold on the evening news.

We were discouraged from engaging in College life – I'm still not sure why we weren't allowed to act in Players – and the course was tough. Long hours. Emotionally exhausting. I remember that most of the boys came out, and that one of our teachers, Nigel Warrington, saw himself in the *auteur* mould. I saw myself as the token bourgeois dilettante. For one project we had to become an animal in the zoo for forty-eight hours. As you may know, polar bears sleep a lot.

There were sixteen students in the class. By the end of the first week everyone knew that one of us would become a star. Derbhle Crotty had already done a law degree in UCD, which is bomb-proof. She remains my favourite woman on the stage. Then there was Gerry Stembridge, ebullient teacher and future collaborator. On Saturdays Dominic West and Catherine FitzGerald were the best-looking couple on Grafton Street. (I belonged to a small group of *amadáns* who thought we could woo Catherine away from Dominic. Miracles belong to the young.)

At the 1992 quatercentenary Trinity Ball, I remember feeling part of something larger than myself. That solemn invocation at dawn: 'This is the greatest night of my life.' In the early house that morning, the best talkers were not students but stragglers. The yoghurt to Beckett's 'cream of Ireland'. Earlier, 14,000 people watched bands play on ten stages across campus. The names might be googled. All I remember is the White Horse Inn at 8 am: the decrepit charm of men who drink before work, the churning jaws and the puke-stained dickie bows, the girls who held onto their makeup, and the girls who didn't. The most amusing characters in that pub were not destined for success of any sort.

A few weeks later, steeped in early house drivel, I got my diploma, left for Bermuda, became a journalist and never went back to study for a degree. Shame. Yet that was not the end of this ill-starred relationship. For we continue to see each other on a regular basis, and the whole matter has taken on a new complexion, like a friendship that begins from a distance, and is now all the closer for it.

Trinity's position in the heart of the city requires it to be hospitable, a role it is happy to play until someone smashes a car through Front Gate. Once or twice a month, I walk through College Park, and as a cyclist I have occasion to flout its hallowed by-laws. Then there's the odd game of cricket, the occasional lecture, launch or topical debate, the historical conferences and the late summer sunshine.

As a student, I played no part in the life of the College. In recent years it has become a sweet, fragile part of my own life, like a bunch of lilies that refuses to die. Last summer I went to a party in the Pavilion Bar to celebrate a handsome new edition of J.P. Donleavy's *The Ginger Man*. In the Long Room Hub I met Malcolm MacArthur at a lecture on Hubert Butler by John Banville. And a few months ago, at a wedding in the College chapel, the groom, Professor Patrick Geoghegan, told me that Daniel O'Connell sent two of his sons to Trinity. It has taken me twenty years to understand why anyone would bother.

I remember the third thing. 'You should have studied history.'

Trevor White (TCD 1990–92; Theatre Studies) was born in Dublin in 1972. After College he worked as a journalist for many years and in 2001 launched **The Dubliner** magazine and **The Dubliner 100 Best Restaurants**. The author of two books, **Kitchen Con: Writing on the Restaurant Racket** and **The Dubliner Diaries**, Trevor is director of The Little Museum of Dublin.

MORRISSEY ATE MY HOMEWORK

tom farrell

TRINITY IN THE NINETIES: Spiritualized in the Ed Burke; Cornershop in the Buttery on Friday night (ask your grandfather); the yard of ale; the Iron Stomach; Matt the Jap; QuarkXPress; Kevin McAleer competing with Snoop Doggy Dogg on the ghetto blaster; incompetent tennis in Botany Bay; snooker in the GMB; the collective Chicken Bovril from a thousand student welcome packs; Panic – Thursday night at McGonagles; evening football outside the Pav; chess in the Theological Society; the Arts Block ramp; 'neither Washington nor Moscow but international socialism' – but while I'm here I'll have a cup of tea and a scone; a midnight bollocking from Brendan Kennelly during a nocturnal football match outside the Sam Beckett … and I'm sure I managed to fit in a couple of lectures as well.

I walked through the soot-stained, darkened walls of Front Arch in 1990 and emerged from the pristine, sunlit Portland stone of same in 1994. Sand-blasting time. Any half-decent writer would extract some inspiring analogy of personal growth from the fact that my time in Trinity coincided with the great quatercentenary clean-up. But I am not that man, and I don't remember it that way.

In a similar vein, it might be a stretch to argue that my long and frankly undistinguished career in the Irish tech space owes much, if anything, to my

College days. I'm not going to lie: my tech experience added up to sitting down in front of an Apple Mac in the Arches in order to type up an essay, failing to figure out how to turn the thing on, and leaving after an acceptable amount of time and in a manner that was intended to suggest I knew what I was doing. Well, that and overnight sessions on Sid Meier's *Civilization* in the publications room. In fact, inside or outside college, playing computer games remains pretty much the only thing I've ever managed to do 'all night long'. While others were presumably dancing and making love (I am basing these assumptions on pop music – those people seem to know what they're talking about) I spent too many college nights negotiating complex peace agreements with Shaka, leader of the Zulus. Never let it be said I don't know how to parley.

But let's rewind (something else we did in the 1990s). I tumbled headlong into Dublin. Fresh off the boat from England in September, by January I was so immersed in College life that my parents suspected I was somewhere at the bottom of a canal. However, not quite so immersed in College life that I was around to hear the enquiries as to my whereabouts delivered at the start of lectures.

As the proud possessor of a UK grant I was able to fund a place to stay independent of adult supervision. My father travelled with me to help select suitable digs; he seemed particularly concerned about the existence or other-wise of a desk. I couldn't fathom why that could possibly be of any importance. Perhaps we had different priorities.

In the end, I escaped from 'our' chosen quarters within about four weeks and via a series of fortunate events ended up living with three girls from Omagh in a single-storey house in St Mary's Place – an interesting experience for a green-as-grass boy from Cheshire, but one that I took to like a duck to water. That house has since been demolished and if truth were told it was already part way there. Fortunately they didn't take the memories with it.

Dublin was all new to me. Not just the hallowed halls of Trinity but the city around it. On those rare occasions when I passed up the discounted beer of the Buttery (£1.48 old money for a pint of Guinness – when I die they will find that written on my heart, like 'Calais' and Queen Mary, but with booze), I had a whole city to explore for the first time. A city with neighbourhoods – something that for whatever reason struck me as impossibly glamorous. In my first months of College I partied from Blacharostown to Blackrock, went to the movies in Harold's Cross and Rathmines – and stood on the corner of Dorset Street and Granby Place, looking down the road in the twilight to the lights of a distant Texaco filling station. Was this Phibsboro? It wasn't – and Phibsboro turned out to be something of a disappointment.

The shops opened late. They were full of exotic foodstuffs that a simple boy from the English provinces had never seen or tasted before (Waffles, Chipstix, Rancheros, Silvermints). When, early on, I enquired where I might find a second-hand coat, I was directed down a laneway under something called the 'Central Bank' to a small enclave of shops in an embryonic part of town called Temple Bar. Don't bother looking for it – it's not there anymore. So although a large part of my Trinity career – but certainly no more than 95 per cent – was spent smoking and playing chess in the rooms of the Theological Society (an organization slightly, but only slightly, more fun than the name suggests) it was still a thrill to know that the city was out there somewhere.

I studied BESS. Somebody had to. For an idealistic eighteen-year-old raised on a diet of English, maths, history and geography, the social sciences hold an almost fatal attraction, but I soon figured that the sociology and business side of things were not to be. So when Morrissey lifted my newly purchased sociology textbooks aloft as he exited stage left at the climax of his comeback gig in the National Stadium in 1991, he kind of made my decision for me. I'd only popped them on the stage for safe-keeping, but presumably he assumed they were some form of poetic offering.

Anyway, politics had plenty of advantages. Some of the department's more Marxist elements had a wonderful habit of letting you know what questions you'd be asked in your final exams. If that was Stalinism, then I am all for it, but at the time it felt crazy (a bit like Stalinism in that respect too, I suppose). It felt as if somebody somewhere was cheating. But if you were given the opportunity to pass – with flying colours – a course in political philosophy without having to read a word of Hegel, you'd stay quiet and keep your head down too. Anyway, from a vantage point in the world of work, it now feels like a sensible way to go about things. It is over twenty years since I left College and this much I've learned: it's not often something comes up that you haven't revised. And anyway, you're allowed to use books.

My exposure to politics wasn't limited to the theoretical either. I am still not quite clear who or what persuaded me that a run for Student's Union President was a good idea, but in my final year in 1994 I decided to give it a go. My profile was zero but with key contacts in *Trinity News* I was assured that a favourable write-up would see me cruise to victory. It didn't quite pan out like that, but as a crash course in parish-pump politics it couldn't have been bettered. Despite promising coffee machines, bar extensions, textbooks, computers and the rest I finished in a disappointing third place. On the flip-side I won the official Trinity College Air Guitar Championship two years in succession. Swings and roundabouts …

So what did I take away from those four years? There's an easy answer to that. One marriage – that took place years later in the College chapel – and a whole heap of friends for life. The former is a long story that we don't have time for, but it does involve rolling tobacco, compromise rules, Crunchy Nut Cornflakes and my first visit to the Phoenix Park.

As for the friends? Well, they say you make a lot of them in your first term in college – and spend the next year slowly getting rid of them. Twenty-five years into that process I am making little progress, and not for want of trying. I've made every effort, even going so far as to make a new friend (in 2010) who went to a different college entirely. But it appears I am stuck with them. Thanks Trinners.

Tom Farrell (TCD 1990–94; Economics and Politics) left Trinity for a short stint on social welfare before going on to work at Irish software company IONA Technologies. For six years he was Digital Brand Manager for Paddy Power and is presently VP of Marketing at Swrve. He has three children and is currently in a complicated love triangle with a wife and a one-eyed sausage dog named Gussie. He has reached Island Nine in Tiny Wings and is the longest-serving member of Sheridan's Cheese Club.

A RAMP FOR ALL SEASONS

evelyn o'rourke

IT'S ABOUT fifty feet long.

Nowadays, they would probably measure it in metres, but back in 1990 we thought about things in feet, so I am sticking to that. The Arts Block ramp, I'm talking about – it's about fity feet long. It's not much to look at it compared to the rest of campus – it merely links the Nassau Street entrance to the Arts Block and then leads you out to the side of the 1937 Reading Room. To a passer-by it is just an anonymous, grey, sloping bit of concrete, but for four years it was a kind of home for us.

A stage.

A catwalk.

A runway.

Hanging out on the ramp. Meeting friends and swapping stories on the ramp, or 'gories' as we used to call them. 'She did whaaaaat to him?' Hands rubbing with glee.

We needed the ramp because we had no Facebook. News shared on the ramp could go viral. Some days we spent hours there just talking. Swapping ideas. Big and small.

'With the text of *Tristam Shandy* filled with allusions and references to the leading thinkers and writers of the seventeenth and eighteenth centuries, to what extent can we see influence of Pope and Swift on Sterne's groundbreaking work? Discuss.' 'Eh, anyone got notes on that?'

'Are you going to the Phil debate tonight about the advantages of Europe?'

'No, they're a crowd of pillocks.'

There was always company. Just as one of you would move off, another would come along and slip into their spot and the chat would rumble on seamlessly. From Parkey to Emma to Ems to Mar to Cregan to Murinn to Una to Colman to Judy to Callso to Ann, and on and on. The conversational baton thrown lightly but endlessly between us all.

Some days you would have a real reason to be there, cemented to the spot in the hopes of 'running into' someone special. 'Funny meeting you here!' you would hope to be able to say, four hours into the vigil. On other days – even more perhaps – you would be desperate to avoid the scrutiny. Depending on how Thursday night at the Buttery had gone, the next morning could see you owning the ramp or disowning it. Scuttling out of the Lecky and taking a swift left out on to Nassau Street to run away for fear of your own blushes.

I was an irritating Players-head, which meant that along with my friends I spent hours decorating the ramp with posters of our latest production. Please come to my incredibly innovative and groundbreaking reimagining of Chekhov's *The Three Sisters* in Esperanto. It is a seven-hour production and honestly, it will change your life (free sandwiches thrown in).

And it wasn't just us Players types who claimed it as a base – there were the BESS girls, flicking their hair, like they were the queens of the catwalk. Ambitious leaders of the future would plaster the noticeboards in election posters. Vote for me. I'm powerful. Strong. Going places. And I have a ridiculous sub-Morrissey haircut to prove it. The postering could get viciously competitive: my poster is bigger than yours and I will show you no mercy. I WILL cover you up for the greater good, because these students aren't going to entertain themselves without me as an Ents officer to guide them.

A few lecturers got in on the act: Gerald Morgan was often there on a personal mission, putting up posters reminding us about Irish soldiers who fought in the First World War. And all posters would be fighting for space with the societies, trying to tempt you to come to their latest events: Come play Tiddlywinks through French! Meet at the ramp, 4 pm Tuesdays.

The professionals knew that you needed thumb tacks too. Sellotape was for amateurs.

Another ramp regular was Professor Brendan Kennelly, who would wander up and down, happy to talk to any eager undergraduate about the reasons he gave his students the exam questions beforehand. And it was on the ramp that we discussed the irony of his first lecture to us, where he warned of the dangers of being too impressed with anyone. We were so impressed by this that we broke into spontaneous applause. Scarlet now.

It was also there that we spotted our first celebrity academic – Senator David Norris. We'd nudge each other and point him out because he mattered. He was important and he was here and maybe if we saw enough of him, a shred of his charisma, intellect and honesty could rub off on us. God knows he had plenty to spare.

It was probably on the ramp that I described my disappointment after my first tutorial with him when he looked – not unkindly – at us all and said: 'I have far too much information to store in my brain, so I'm not even going to pretend to ask for your names as I just won't remember them. Sorry. Anyway – let's begin. Heaney, *Death of a Naturalist* …' And on he went to discuss the great poet with a passion, love and insight that illuminated the poems so wonderfully that, even though he had just told me that he would never know my name, I fell under his spell immediately.

It was on the ramp that I met my parents when they came in to see the first play I ever directed in Players theatre. (They had parked on Merrion Square and walked over. Fierce handy.) They could see how happy I was and were so proud of my little lunchtime production, *After the Picnic*. We walked across Front Square together, weaving our way through the crowds of students and tourists milling around, making our way to House Four, the original home of the Players' theatre. Three years later I would win Best Director at the Irish Student Drama Awards, which was a golden moment. 'You see,' I'd tell them, 'it's not all idle chatter on the ramp. Sometimes we are creating things.' Swapping ideas. Big and small. It's a bittersweet memory now as my dad died just some short years after that.

Talk of the ramp wasn't new to them, mind you. At the time, my parents were very friendly with the Trinity theologian Professor Seán Freyne. Seán sadly passed away in 2013, but back when I started college in 1990, my mother asked him to keep an eye out for me – to, you know, 'make sure Evelyn was alright'. A few months into term, she rang him to check up on me and he said, 'Every time I see her, she is on the ramp surrounded by friends, chatting … I think she's fine'. Ramp surveillance.

Life on our sloping outpost could offer up some great entertainment. If you stood there long enough you might pick up a dodgy invitation to some random-er's party. You would pretend that you weren't sure if you could go, while discreetly checking your wallet to see if you could rise to grabbing some cans from the Pav, where you could get Carling Black Label, six for £4. Expensive I know, but sometimes you had to push the boat out.

And the porters, of course, loved us. They sat in their glass box and looked out fondly as we horsed around, loving nothing more than finding a missing student card or taking details of your favourite scarf that had gone MIA. Or maybe not. In truth, they would stare gimlet-eyed at us, as if we were an alien species – and to be fair, all these years later, I can't say I blame them. We must have been a complete nightmare with all that yackety-yack.

The ramp was a place for all seasons too. It was a safe haven in winter because part of it was covered over – come rain or hail you could still squat there for hours and keep an eye on all the action. In summertime though, things changed. The tourists hit town, and boy did they love stalking Trinity. The coaches lined up on Nassau Street and their human cargo came pouring in, busload after busload after busload after busload. They arrived into College and acted like they owned the place. Bleedin' tourists. Annoying.

'No, I don't know where the bathrooms are.' 'Nope, no clue where the Book of Kells is, but if you LOOK OVER THERE AT THE LARGE QUEUE OF TOURISTS CLUTCHING CAMERAS, THAT MIGHT GIVE YOU A HINT.'

And as the college year drew to a close, on the night of the Trinity Ball the ramp would have its own gig going on. There would be Portaloos lined up outside the Lecky Library and wherever there is a Portaloo, there is action. I remember tottering my way across Front Square in heels, and then seeing the old familiar Arts Block and knowing that if I could just limp my way over to the ramp, I could kick off my towering shoes and sit down and relax. It was a useful spot on a night like that because it was good and dark. It had quiet corners, ideal for sneaky fags, and covert kisses. But enough of that kind of detail – that is between the ramp and me.

TO HELP research this piece, I decided to bring my young two sons to visit the ramp, to see what they made of it. They didn't seem to find it one bit weird that I was quizzing them about a sloping stretch of concrete. They instantly saw the opportunities it offered as they ran up and down ten times and counted out the footsteps. Twenty-three steps for Oisín aged six. Twenty-five steps for Ross aged five.

'So, what do you think of it, boys?' I asked.

'It's good,' said Oisín.

'Yes,' nodded his younger brother.

'Yes, it's a proper, good ramp,' Oisín added. And then Ross nudged him and they ran off laughing towards Front Square leaving the ramp behind. I stood rooted to the spot, staring at their retreating backs and then I looked around, and I have to say I agree with them.

The Arts Block ramp. Revisit it sometime.

After all, it's a proper, good ramp. Even a six-year-old can see that.

Evelyn O'Rourke (TCD 1990–94; English and Drama Studies) is married to John and they live in Dundrum in Dublin with their two boys. She is a broadcaster with RTÉ where she presents and reports on a wide range of radio and television programmes. From co-presenting **The Irish Book Awards** for RTÉ One to reporting on **Today** with Sean O'Rourke on Radio One, Evelyn spends her life talking for a living. Happily, it seems that all those years chatting on the ramp paid off in the end.

DIFFERENT TIMES, DIFFERENT SPACES

antonia hart

I **PASS THROUGH** Front Gate, and the racket of College Green diminishes. It is October 2015 and I cannot get enough of looking at these gold and orange trees. There are four years to come. I have been granted four burning college autumns, four floating springs of pink-tinged, tissue-light blossoms. I have been allocated a desk in the Berkeley Library. Through the low, oblong window beside it I watch the students below, stooping over smartphones as they round the southeast corner of Fellows' Square on the hour.

I turned seventeen just before taking the Leaving Cert in 1989, and for reasons that even I can barely knit together now, spent the following academic year studying for A Levels at Dr Barcroft's Dublin Tutorial Centre in Mount Street, and attending Greek language lectures at Trinity. I wasn't registered as a Trinity student, but nonetheless I bought my copies of *Reading Greek* (one text, one grammar and vocab) and pitched up to the fifth floor of the Arts Block, a high point over Nassau Street, where I immediately failed to translate 'the ship sails to Byzantium'. But that pair of textbooks – their closely-packed Greek characters in three columns of vocabulary or chunks of text for translation, illustrated only occasionally by a map of a naval battle, or a bit of pottery, their casual references to rhapsodes and *dicasts* and the aorist – made me see my schoolbooks as children's books. The only thing I could say for sure about the aorist was that it was something verb-related, but I knew I wanted to align myself with what these adult textbooks represented.

At seventeen, eighteen, nineteen, underexposed to everything, your outlook changes from Friday night to Saturday morning. By the following October *Reading Greek* was shelved and I was registered to study law, on the third floor. The Law School quickly evacuated the Arts Block and resettled in New Square, peaceful home to the croquet lawn, the Museum Building and the rose garden. It was harder (though still pretty easy) to escape notice in the more domestic proportions of the House Thirty-Nine rooms than it had been in the rippling acreage of the Arts Block lecture theatres. Niall Osborough taught all the most interesting subjects, like constitutional law, legal and constitutional history, and jurisprudence, and I stalked his teaching timetable through my subject choices. He danced ahead of us for an entire term teaching rights of ferry. I longed for him to throw me a bone, and fortunately he took a multidisciplinary approach to his teaching.

'Who was it,' he asked the ferry rights class, 'who went to sea in a sieve?'

Fifteen Bics paused over foolscap, ruled feint. I leaned forward over my half-desk with the smug confidence of a *University Challenge* captain who has not conferred.

'The Jumblies,' I supplied. It's not for me to describe it as the establishment of a relationship of intellectual equals, but it is God's truth that Professor Osborough nodded in my direction.

When you weren't astounding revered members of the teaching staff with the quality of your legal brain, there was always drink. My locker, between the fire hose and the Arts Block A stairs, was crammed with gin and tonic for the quatercentenary Trinity Ball. The ball was fabulously glamorous for about forty-five minutes. When by day you were as carelessly dressed as we were, in unravelling cardigans, oxblood Docs and one pair of jeans for the week, evening dress and make-up meant a significant transformation. I still have my Trinity Ball dresses: a wiggly John Selby number with huge orange and turquoise flowers, which had belonged to an old aunt; a black silk fifties full-skirter with a buttoned bodice, a precious purchase from Jenny Vander's vintage rails; a full-length deep blue taffeta, boned and petticoated, which I made myself on my mother's sewing machine. But after a few stiffeners from the locker bar, the ball was less about elegance and more about doing the kind of dancing that jolted every hairpin from your up-do, and holding your vintage silk skirt away from whoever you were minding while they vomited in the bushes.

Senior Sophister year was my first living in, and my sister and I shared the biggest and best set of rooms I've ever seen in College. 40.0.04 was on the ground floor next door to the Law School, and leaving aside my bedroom window overlooking the rose garden, our giant kitchen, the rare luxury of a sitting room, and being able to receive notes on our bell, the best thing about that year was setting my Digicube alarm clock for 9:58 and being on time for a ten o'clock lecture. A trapdoor, irresistibly, dropped from our kitchen into a cellar beneath, and one evening I followed Edward Wingfield through it into the underworld. In the pitch-dark space beneath the houses we felt through rooms, and half-dived, half-squeezed through openings in the walls between them. When we found another trapdoor, Edward shouldered it open, and we hauled ourselves out into the empty kitchen of Pamela McEvoy's rooms, and, grimy and triumphant, ran back to 40.0.04. The whole of College perched on an underground world, though other spaces were more easily accessed than our filthy cellar maze: the half-submerged Lecky, the airless bunker of Periodicals beneath the Berkeley, the subterranean tunnel ending in the turret stairs to Early Printed Books, the passage from the Long Room to the Reading Room. There were permanent residents, too. When builders began to dig out the foundations of the new Ussher Library, they turned up the bones of twenty or so dismembered eighteenth-century children, and at least one camel, all supposed to have been disposed of by medical students; and you had to pass a tiny graveyard on the way in to the Buttery, under the Dining Hall steps.

Friday night meant pints down there in the black-barred Buttery, the vaulted cellar, where, if you were unlucky, a forming band might be playing. The floor was still sticky, the night's choreography still evident in the positioning of stools, when we reassembled for thick white mugs of coffee on Monday morning. In the Buttery, over that muddy coffee and Crosaire, I met a fellow law student, tall and intelligent, barely eighteen and infinitely gentle. He didn't propose then, but did tell me that he wanted to marry me. We went on to other lives, but twenty-one years later we did get married, in the College chapel, yards from where we first met.

I typed my vaguely legal essays on a manual typewriter, but I knew rich technology pickings when I found them in the science end skips. I sourced a large, wood-effect television for 40.0.04, which showed RTÉ One in green and grey through the traditional sorcery of a metal coat hanger, and a sweet Mac Classic complete with HyperCard, which ran off a floppy disk. It seems impossible that less than two years later I was back at Trinity, legitimately in the science end myself. In June 1994 I didn't have an email address and in October 1996 I was one of the first crop of multimedia master's students, the only inhabitants of the newly opened Goldsmith Hall on Pearse Street. We were dizzy with breathing space and spacious offices, showered with EU funding, overwhelmed by the kit in our fully equipped computer lab. In that space and for that year I felt for the first time as if I were involved in a process of discovery rather than the assimilation of facts. Technologies were evolving, being abandoned, replaced. Computer science was blending with the humanities. Everything was interesting, everything was worth trying, everything was a blast. When we were fed up with being pioneers of the digital era we crossed into Mahaffy's for pints and toasties, or pierced the still air of the lab with the smell of vinegary chips from the Sea Shell Fish Bar in Townsend Street. We scanned its menu, and marketed the Sea Shell from a College server as the world's first online chipper, because it might have been.

I graduated, and got a job, but once a week through the winter of 1997 I sat on the floor in the Writer Fellow's rooms in Front Square. It was Anne Enright's year and I would have sat on the icy cobbles outside if it meant being part of her writing workshop. I carried my second-hand copy of *The Portable Virgin* in my bag for eight weeks but was never brave enough to ask for her signature. The same winter I threw pots and made sculptures at the Trinity Arts Workshop, guided by Kathy, a talented Australian, whose tiny, dry-backed hands drew slim-necked vases up from the wheel as if she were a snake charmer. My friend Lynn and I drank pints of Carlsberg and ate crisps in O'Neill's across the road afterwards. Flakes of dried clay from our fingernails mixed with the crisp crumbs.

'I'm pregnant,' I told her.

'You'd better put down that beer, then,' she said.

My baby came the following summer. I was working for a campus company and statutory maternity leave was a heartbreakingly short fourteen weeks. I interrupted my working day at lunchtime to creep along the upper floors of the Arts Block to find a quiet corner to unwrap the baby from the sling on his father's chest. I sat cross-legged on an orange wire-haired box – a chocolate box, in College-speak – and fed my son, then hugged him until we both felt the satisfying rumble of his burps.

Other decades, other spaces, and in 2005, at thirty-three, I left a detested job in an advertising agency to settle into the luxury of a year at Trinity's Oscar Wilde Centre. Oscar Wilde was born at 21 Westland Row, now a School of English enclave in the science end and home to an M.Phil. in creative writing overseen by Gerald Dawe. I workshopped most of a novel there, and, as greedily as I'd gone to Greek, sat in on classes put on for students on our sister M.Phil. in Anglo-Irish literature.

Ten more years have passed. I have given up trying to decide what to do in favour of doing everything I can. I start my Ph.D. in the School of Histories and Humanities, back on the third floor of the Arts Block. Space has been conjured. Classics is no longer on the top floor: a sixth has been built. From the lower ground floor, an unpromising fire exit sign leads to a pretty cobbled path and a fig tree. Here are the newly refurbished Provost's House stables, where history of art researchers work in the horse stalls, their reading room the hay loft, and I go to a weekly seminar in the carriage house. Back in the Berkeley, I kneel at my lidded window, twisting until I can see the foot of the Long Room Hub, the tall new neighbour of the 1937 Reading Room. Although the '37 has been given over to postgraduates, I don't work there. The books have been taken out, and the space is too restless, too resonant with the sucking of coffee beakers. For now, I relish the uncompromising concrete of the Berkeley, its stern silence. This is a library that means business. It is twenty-six years since I opened *Reading Greek* and wanted to be an adult, but there are still undiscovered spaces between these walls.

Antonia Hart (TCD 1990–94, Law; 1997, MSc Multimedia; 2006, M.Phil. Creative Writing) is a Ph.D. candidate in the Department of History at Trinity College. Her book **Ghost Signs of Dublin** was published in 2014. She is married to Rory Mulcahy and has three children.

THE TASTE OF POSSIBILITY

luke mcmanus

EVERY WINTER there was smog in Dublin. On icy evenings it lay heavy and acrid, over Cabra and Crumlin, Kimmage and Artane. The poky concrete houses and draughty terraces of the city needed coal like a body needs a heart, so the smoke crept from squat chimneys, hanging low and still in the night. The city stank with a cancerous smell: the smog killed thirty-three people in its deadliest year. London had banished it in the 1950s, but it took forlorn, sluggish Dublin thirty years to get the message. The bituminous coal that caused the murk was eventually banned. The fires were laid with smokeless fuel and the air smelled fresher and tasted cleaner.

This was September 1990, the same month that I entered Trinity, where the rank-tasting brain-fog of school was about to be blown away. I'd spent the previous three years in a priest-ridden south Dublin boys' school, plodding through my preparation for the Leaving Cert. The place was an efficient production line of bankers and flankers, with a culture of elitism, religion and conformity that, to my eyes, was both monotonous and absurd. For a nerd like me, the transition from there to Trinity was like shedding a skin.

AT COLLEGE GREEN, buses and taxis roar through the streets' tangled curves. This is Dublin's true centre, the point where the raffish axis of O'Connell Street and Westmoreland Street collides with genteel Grafton Street. To cross the road and enter Trinity, first you must dodge the traffic. Then the honking, brake-screeching din of College Green starts to roll away as you pass through the railings and walk towards Front Arch. It's a surprisingly small doorway, just wide enough for two or maybe three people to pass one another. As narrow as a birth canal. Your eyes struggle in the darkness of the arch and the sound of the street is quickly left behind. To your right, the mighty stairs that lead to the JCR, a hint of stale dope smoke lingering in the stairwell. Another five steps and you find yourself at a perfect vista: the most glorious square in Ireland.

The sober columns of the chapel and Exam Hall face each other, flanking the proud Campanile, a stone Saturn V waiting for lift-off. Beyond lies an uncharted world: Botany Bay, the Rubrics, the Buttery, the Pav, JCR, GMB, the 1937: places with names like codes, secret signs, a hidden language. I had occasionally wandered (and wondered) my way through Trinity as a schoolboy. Now I was here as a student, a few weeks after my eighteenth birthday, while the new decade was still an infant.

The euphoric afterglow of Italia 90 was palpable, its warmth lingering in our hearts. But the 1980s had been a hard time for Ireland and that gloom was hard to shake. When I walked into Trinity that day, I fully expected that in four years I'd be heading straight for the boat to England when I left.

Even so, I didn't feel despondent. Front Square usually has a sweeping majesty that makes a symphony swell in your mind, but on the first day of Freshers' Week it is quite different: a friendly gauntlet of enthusiasts bellowing at their stalls, signing you up for societies and clubs of every kind.

College life at Trinity was extraordinarily rich, crowded with unions, publications, sports clubs, societies, a myriad of ways to spend your time on pursuits more enjoyable than anything the libraries and lecture halls could possibly offer. It quickly became clear that the place was also bursting with characters and eccentrics of various kinds. After the meaty male scrum of school, Trinity was a human safari park, teeming with exotic species.

Though the southside of Dublin was undeniably well represented there was also a heady mixture of tribes I hadn't met before. The gruff, garrulous Nordies who freely drank their government grants in September – by May they would be poverty stricken and vaguely remorseful. Then there were the plummy, tweedy ones, both Anglo-Irish and English (very hard to distinguish to my untrained ears). The list of types was long: the actors, the aristocrats, the anarchists, the philosophers, the debaters, the geeks, the stoners, the gays and even the occasional genius.

In my class were faces, some familiar, most new. One skinny Chesterman: Tom Farrell had an indie rocker's mop of hair and a whimsical line in English humour. One night, early that term, he got lucky with one of those grant-bearing Nordies, a girl from Omagh who was studying English. One of her housemates had gone off with my tobacco, bought from a dodgy character on Moore Street. (Bargain basement smoking was a mainstay of student life back then.) So I had the perfect excuse to head round to see them the next day and I persuaded a dithering Tom to come along. I remember doing most of the talking that afternoon, while Colette and her friends Deirdre and Bronagh peered at us with frank curiosity.

Nine years later I handed Tom a ring to put on Colette's finger. It was in the most fitting of venues, Trinity's chapel on Front Square. That was how it was in College. That's how things are when you are falling into adulthood – one random encounter can change your ultimate trajectory. The passing influences and chance meetings of those few months last forever. I have never felt as comfortable, anywhere, as I felt in Trinity at that moment. I floated weightless in the amniotic fluid of college life. Warm, happy, home.

BUT THE SCREENWRITING manuals and story gurus all agree that a good tale must contain an adversary. For drama to occur there must be an antagonist, an enemy at the gates. Around this time, the great enemy of post-war Western Europe was withering away. I had watched the televised delirium as the Berlin Wall collapsed the previous year. Just twelve months earlier I'd passed through Checkpoint Charlie on a school tour. One of my politics lecturers was finding the rapid pace of change exhausting: Professor Ron Hill was a highly regarded expert on Soviet politics. It must have been a touch discombobulating to see the old Soviet regime disappear before his eyes.

He hid it well, and remained a lively, engaging presence at the lectern, though he took to opening his lectures with, 'Now all of the following was true until … (looks at watch) … about three weeks ago. Now it's all up in the air.'

(Rueful shrug.) But though the struggle between capitalism and communism seemed to be coming to an end, the battle for the soul of Ireland still raged bitterly. In this conflict, Trinity was firmly on one side, the Catholic Church and their friends in the pro-life movement lined up on the other.

The year before I had arrived at College, the Society for the Protection of the Unborn Child had taken the TCD Students' Union to court for distributing information on the availability of abortion in the UK. The shadow of prison had fallen on students who had simply printed pamphlets or distributed a phone number (679 4700 – I can remember it today without the slightest effort). Anger is an energy, as Johnny Lydon said, and a poster of the day that simply read 'SPUC OFF' summed up our response. In the autumn of my first year (or Michaelmas term of Junior Freshman in the pleasingly archaic language of Trinity) Mary Robinson was elected Uachtarán na hÉireann. Fianna Fáil's death grip on the presidency had been broken by a doughty opponent of SPUC – and a Trinity woman to boot. It felt like the tide was beginning to turn.

Then, fourteen months later, the X Case put the issue back onto the front pages. A fourteen-year-old who was pregnant as a result of abuse by a family member was prevented from travelling to England for an abortion by the Attorney General of the FF–PD government. The Students' Union of Trinity led the protests outside Leinster House, and these angry gatherings resounded across the land as the country began to realize what terrible damage the so-called Pro-Life Amendment of 1983 had done to the rights of Irish women. Twenty years later I found myself in precisely the same spot on Molesworth Street, protesting the death of Savita Halappanavar, who was refused treatment in a Galway hospital because of the same law. It felt horrible. It turns out that nostalgia has an evil twin: a nagging, angry déjà-vu, and an overwhelming sense of futility.

Politics might have been the serious business of extracurricular College life, but Trinity also provided a dizzying variety of hedonistic possibility, from sipping Pimm's on the croquet pitch to necking pills at the Trinity Ball. Alcohol was like fresh air to a student, and getting free booze was a breeze if you were a dedicated ligger, willing to consume wine of questionable quality.

We crashed one memorable Atrium reception for the writer J.P. Donleavy, downing grim Pedrotti wine noisily as the great man read. Donleavy's career was based on *The Ginger Man*, a novel that celebrated a carousing, dissolute

Trinity student. So we were perplexed to find that our antics were met with icy disapproval by the literary types at the party – it seemed that while it was fine to read about drunken College messers, rubbing unsteady shoulders with them was a different matter.

The Trinity Ball was the greatest all-night party in the country, even if over-indulgence occasionally claimed victims. The stories were legion, if somewhat incredible. Everyone seemed to know the chap who hid up a tree in Front Square for six hours only to be kicked out just before the event began. Or the one who gobbled too much acid, then thought it would be a wheeze to strip naked and run babbling in and out of traffic as it circled round onto Nassau Street (though that one was definitely true). It always seemed a rougher deal for women at the ball: hours of careful preparation could be easily undone by a half-dozen shots of vodka, smeared lipstick and tears. Ball gowns can rip, stain and disintegrate in a number of interesting, sometimes horrifying ways. Tottering on a broken high heel, a victim of the cobbles, or grimly barefoot, carrying shoes, shivering in the heatless sun of dawn … by comparison, the boys had it easy. There are few men who don't look their best in a black suit and a white shirt, and the spilled Guinness just blended in.

As the sun came up, we would emerge blinking into the city's bustling morning, finding our way to a greasy spoon caff for soakage (the Alpha, upstairs on Wicklow Street, RIP) or staggering to an early house to kick on with a few breakfast pints. Our bow ties were left dangling open, badges of rakish honour, so that the shoppers and tourists couldn't miss the fact that we had just come from the Trinity Ball. Back in those days, the ball was held right at the end of the academic year, so the release of tension was extremely welcome. Exams were only days away, and in fourth year not just any exams, but that chilling word: finals.

Thanks to some miraculous intervention, my finals went well. By the time I left Trinity in 1994, something had changed in Ireland. That expectation I'd had in first year, that I would emigrate after college, had shifted. The boat ticket to Holyhead remained un-bought. Friends and peers were picking up work in Dublin, some of them in ingenious computer companies that had been started in Trinity by our peers. The city was throbbing with a bassy cocktail of economic optimism, youthful energy and ecstasy. Temple Bar was having its brief interlude of cool. Ireland was in the World Cup again, and if we could beat Italy 1-0 in New York, surely getting a job wasn't entirely impossible?

Although life beyond Trinity's walls was a little more welcoming than I'd expected, cutting the cord was still painful. The real world, with all its unknowns, was a daunting prospect. Trinity had bewitched me, defined me and in a strange way, almost cheated me: I had expected that after four years in the best university in the land, I would be a fully fledged adult with a plan, and the wit and gumption to put it into action. This, unnervingly, was not the case. Two decades later I'm still waiting for that plan. And for the wit and gumption too.

In the end I went to Berlin. The wall was pretty much gone at this stage, but the twilight streets of Prenzlauer Berg and Friedrichshain retained their le Carré shadows. I came back months later to graduate – smiling on the surface, nervously unsure of my next move underneath.

The air tasted good in Dublin, fresh with the smell of saltwater on the easterly breeze. The delirious hot summer of 1995 was only months away. My friends were (mostly) still around, a few of them were even still at Trinity. The College remained the axis around which the city turned.

Though I'd have to make my unsure way in a cold, bright world, I'd always have Trinity around me. And inside me.

Luke McManus (right) *with Cormac Barry and Tom Farrell.*

Luke McManus (TCD 1990–94; Economics and Political Science) is a filmmaker and television director. He lives in Dublin with his wife and son.

REBELS WITHOUT A DESK

claire kilroy

TRINITY POSSESSED a romantic quality in my mind long before I attended it. It meant 'not here', as in, not the awful convent school I attended in Clontarf where everyone (it seemed to me) aspired to a job in PR and marketing, and art was the preserve of weirdos and losers. The weather, I used to think, got better when you emerged from that dark tunnel onto Front Square. My grandfather, Joseph Long, had done a postgrad there, having been granted a dispensation from John Charles McQuaid, whom he loathed. Joe was the formidable one, the one who read Joyce and was bolshie and anti-establishment and fun. Nicky Byrne went there too, and she was one of the most beautiful girls on the peninsula of Howth. Nelson Mandela told her that if he weren't already married, he'd propose. Trinity equalled freedom and, all through the bleakness of the eighties, it was the straw I clung to. I was off to read English, and that was the end of it, even if it was a fast track to unemployment. There was no Plan B.

The Trinity I entered and the Trinity I left struck me as very different places. When I arrived in the Arts Block in 1991, several professors still wore black academic cloaks. They stood at podiums to lecture into the middle distance about things of which I knew nothing. They seemed elderly, antique, stumping along as if on wooden legs, navy and maroon hardbacks stacked under their arms. Their canon stopped in the 1800s. This was the School of

English, Michaelmas Term. I was a Junior Freshman, just turned eighteen.

Their store of knowledge was vast and intimidating. They spoke with genuine passion about poetic language, poetic imagery, poetic truth, poetic beauty. This was the world they had dwelt in for decades, these were their marble halls, and they were intimate with every corner. They sat in offices lined with books, having devoted themselves like monks to lives of contemplation. The first-year booklist they set us ran to something like 400 titles. If it was designed to cow us, their strategy worked. A bunch of us sat there during Freshers' Week examining it, our stomachs sick. Our Leaving Cert As were no good to us here. Nobody knew what ontological meant – we'd only gotten as far as metaphysical. As for Old English, a whole different language? To open your mouth was to expose your ignorance. The safest approach was that of Stephen Dedalus: silence, exile, cunning. I took notes and kept my head down.

Then, during my sophister years, a critical theorist arrived, and with him, critical theory. It swept through the School of English like wildfire. We were given new words like deconstruction and ideology and post-Marxism, and we knocked them about like hammers. Anyone who disagreed with you was declared a fascist. That shut them up. The theorist was witty. He had charisma. Instead of a cloak, he wore a leather jacket. He didn't bother with the lectern, but instead wandered up and down the stage, discoursing with his hands in his pockets. Lectures became performances. He told us he never again wanted to read another sentence beginning with the words 'What Shakespeare is trying to say is …' as if Shakespeare were groping around for the right words but we could nail it. Literary texts stopped being about truth and beauty, and started being about revealing who had the power, and who they were oppressing with it. You had to deconstruct everything in order to reveal what it truly meant. Hamlet, it was explained, was *homme-lette*, which sounded like omelette but which meant little man. Wow, I thought, scribbling this down in the lecture hall, this is amazing. It almost made sense. Those people in the black cloaks banging on about lyricism and imagery? They were the liberal humanists, we were told. Liberal humanists were the old guard. They were the house we had to burn down. Yeah, what he said, went up the cry.

A spirit of rebellious excitement began to brew, though there was frankly little for us to rebel against. Fees were already in the process of being abolished by the government but we had to agitate about something, so we agitated about the, um, library. There were not enough seats to go around, and we were the children of the seventies baby boom – we had had to compete hard to get into college, and we continued to compete hard when we got there. So we read on window sills or steps or those poxy orange boxes or even on the floor. This was hardly the worst state of affairs: we were young – we did not yet suffer from backache, and it was collegial enough in its way. As a generation, we were used to being squashed in. The protest was a bit of diversion, a flexing of our new-found wings. One of the JCR heads strung a banner across Front Arch. *Paris 1968, Dublin 1993*, it proclaimed without irony to the traffic on College Green. A classmate carted a desk out to Front Square and sat there with a sign reading *This student is out here because there is no seat for him in the library*. There was an empty seat for him at his tutorials. (I googled him after I wrote this, the classmate who had lugged a desk out to Front Square. I discovered he lives in Melbourne now. Then I googled the girl he started seeing the summer after we graduated and were loitering about, not knowing know what to do with ourselves now that our studies in Going on the Dole were complete. She was in Melbourne too. Sweet.)

There was a march about the, um, library. We got up on our hind legs and strode down O'Connell Street on a sunny spring afternoon, disrupting the traffic, making noise. There we all were the following day in the paper, to our delight, quite a large photo, as I recall, which alas I couldn't find, prancing around in our element, revelling in our heyday. I think of yearlings bucking in meadows just because they can. The march wasn't really about the library at all. It was about being young in early spring and having had the tools of the intellect recently handed down to you, and seeing what you could do with them for the few years that you were protected by that lovely walled city, the moral high ground inalienably on your side. The liberal humanists were right, of course: it was beauty that mattered in the end. The beauty of the young, the fresh, the untrammelled, the hopeful and the hopelessly optimistic, setting off into the world.

Claire Kilroy (TCD 1991–94; English) is the author of four novels: **All Summer, Tenderwire, All Names Have Been Changed** and **The Devil I Know**, which was described by **The Guardian** as 'a satiric danse macabre of brio and linguistic virtuosity', and by the **New York Times** as 'savagely comic ... and great fun'. She has been shortlisted three times for the Kerry Group Irish Novel of the Year, and was awarded the Rooney Prize for Irish Literature in 2004. She lives in Dublin with her husband and child.

THANK YOU JOHN MAJOR, OR THE ARCHITECTONICS OF TRINITY IN THE EARLY 1990s

ellen rowley

IF I WROTE LETTERS home during my four years at Trinity, ostensibly spent reading English and history of art, those letters would have overflowed with happiness: slovenly, hungover, hot-eyed and empty-pocketed happiness, but happiness all the same. Instead, as a Dubliner, I was still under my saintly parents' roof and so, while no letters were written, my mother would have surely welcomed more information on my questionable comings and goings. Us suburban Dubliners, it would seem, took advantage of the large-ish population of 'out-of-towners' and stayed about four nights a week on their sofas and floors. Mostly hailing from Northern Ireland and living on relatively generous student grants, these attractive creatures with exotic accents and strange hobbies (like rowing and seventies disco), rented flats in redbrick basements in parts of the city to which I had never before ventured.

A new map was being made.

And as I, with increasing resentment, caught the 48A bus home – usually with one or two of these new friends in tow – to replenish stocks and maybe attend local weekly mass, my psycho-geography was altering forever. The suburban landscape and fairly privileged homogenous cohort with whom I'd grown up were being added to and ultimately replaced by central-city streets and late-night venues, by an eighteenth-century palette of granite and Portland stone and by a colourful bunch of like-minded peers. There was the flautist from Booterstown and the rosy-cheeked beauty from Santry; the famous poet's lovely daughter and the quick-witted wonder with the Benson & Hedges; not to mention the Northern crew, the soccer lads and a couple of kooky Quakers. Everyone appeared to love novels and second-hand clothes, and to have a shared propensity for doodling. 'Thank you, John Major,' said the particularly mischievous short-haired one from East Belfast, as she withdrew another twenty quid from the Banklink and we headed into the vaulted spaces of the Buttery.

THE MAP DEEPENS. Added to these new people – lifelong friends, I now know – and to the new streets, was a new way of learning. First, we had the lecture. Delivered in the raked subterranean theatres of the late-1970s Arts Block, it seemed to me that the lecture was not an altogether successful means of communicating to a gang of post-teens – especially ones with their eye firmly on the next black-tie event. From the outset though, with focused visuals and quite brilliant performances, it was clear that the art history lecturers understood their clientele better than did the English department. The latter, experiencing some kind of existential crisis brought on by the over-consumption of critical theory, expressed itself to itself. Only the dramatic overtures of a Joycean scholar and the cynical accusations of a soon-to-be-retired poet made an impact. The rest was self-referential, or so I thought. Comparatively, the lectured journeys in and out of canvases, up and down arcades, and through the – let's face it – archly traditional corridor of art history, were a wonder. While the subject matter lent itself more naturally to this mass force-feeding teaching method, the art historians were, to my naive mind, excellent teachers. Our learning seemed to matter to them.

Second, juxtaposed with the scribbly, sleepy lecture, was the excruciatingly silent and squirmy seminar. From passive anonymity we were plunged into its extreme opposite: active learning in a small group. Again, the architecture was windowless, a condition of the late-twentieth-century university experience across Europe, but now I was always red-faced and on high alert. Like the Arts Building itself, I was overwrought. Inheriting from my mother the need to fill silence (and to boost a teacher's confidence), I nodded incessantly, turned pages desperately so as to (mis)locate Shakespearean passages, and asked superfluous questions. And though for a while – certainly for the first two giddy years – it all seemed hopeless, the learning began to settle and to sink in.

THE MAP DELINEATES. Maybe it was the disappearance of half the gang to Poitiers, Strasbourg and London's Royal Holloway on Erasmus programmes, or the steadiness brought on by being in a first-love relationship with an soccer-playing engineer on a scholarship? Either way, in my third year, learning shifted and deepened. At about the same time, the campus opened up to reveal its many quadrangles. Previously locked in to the multipurpose, multi-storeyed Arts Building, with glimpses of sky and fresh air coming from the damp courtyards that punctuate its bulk, I now had to venture eastwards to the 'sciences' and the newly-completed Hamilton Building to meet the engineer. College had, up to that point, consisted of a well-trodden path from lecture halls and seminar rooms to the glazed carpet-tiled spaces of the Lecky Library, via an overly long smoking break on the ramp. Sometimes, in the first year, we would wander over to the beautifully scaled Botany Bay to where my older brother – a renowned fourth year and captain of College's soccer club – lived in ground-floor rooms. Other afternoon diversions brought us to the Buttery Bar but without awareness of or interest in the Palladian Dining Hall overhead or the postmodern Atrium to the side. And of course, the end of year saw us sweat under the Examination Hall's neoclassical elliptical groin-vaulting, surrounded by the barely noticed portraits and College's own secular *Pietà*, the Baldwin Monument. Trinity was then, for my first years, a limited place. It had to be.

However as things settled, the horizon widened. There was more to this walled city and my reintroduction to the place came through a superbly rigorous teacher, the Architectural Historian of the piece. It probably all began with fear. If we arrived in to his lectures late, he might snipe; if we whispered or distracted, he might bang his large stick, a pointer of sorts, on the podium floor. In near darkness, he could discern bodies slouching to share gossip, and his beard would bristle. As we progressed – akin to a new father's initial distrust of his newborn starting to fade – the architectural historian warmed, and by the third year, if effort was made during his trying seminars, all was well. I learned so much that my brain now hurts to think about it. Off our feet and out of the airless windowless seminar room we were marched, to stand in front of his hand-drawn plan of Borromini's Sant'Ivo church, pinned to notice-boards in the public areas. 'What is going on here?' He pushed and prodded until we responded and got it, until we understood something of the exigencies of baroque geometry. In these oft-calamitous situations, my colleagues became brothers in arms, and more friends were made. This time, mature students took centre stage, joined by a bespectacled boy who always wore a denim jacket regardless of the weather, an old school friend, reincarnated, and a diamond heiress who sounded like the Queen Mother. By our final year, some of us chose to take the bearded Architectural Historian's special subject: Dublin in the long eighteenth century.

At last I grasped the narrative of Trinity's outside spaces. I learned that Library Square was the oldest and most intact dimensionally, deriving as it did from the junction of the one remaining Rubrics range and the stoic Old Library of the early 1700s. It turned out that New Square, which looked just as old as anywhere else, was a late nineteenth-century space feeding the magnificent Museum Building of the 1850s and ignoring the beautiful (dinky) 1730s Printing House. Beyond that, we were entering swampy cadaver territory, rationalized through the nineteenth and twentieth centuries. Past the green fields of College Park, several small copies of the Museum Building, built from the 1880s, accommodated the medical and scientific arts, and by the 1970s, a new quadrangle was attempted in the form of Ronnie Tallon's Luce Hall. I did not know then that this was an Irish nod to Chicago and Ludwig Mies van der Rohe. Nor did anybody tell me that the Berkeley Library was an internationally important late-modernist building and an exemplar of poured-concrete technology. We were instead encouraged to look at the older stuff and to understand floor plans, relationships to the ground and fabric. This was possibly enough for us, and College's backlands with its late-twentieth-century endeavours were to be known only as places for dubious behaviour.

Really, the crowning discovery was that Front Square was a ruse. It was never supposed to be so big, and likely its symmetry was accidental, organic even. I learned of the distinct and rich intersection of social and political histories with architectural history. The Act of Union brought not only a deluge of books to Trinity, but the end of a building campaign that left nineteenth-century equivalents of derelict sites in its wake. So that, upon entering College through that tiny opening past Front Gate, the visitor was hit with a blank space and an unsatisfying lack of perspective. By the 1830s there was a call to fix the absence. A failed competition led to the decision to build a 'small but highly architectural object', out of which Trinity's beloved Campanile was made, in 1849. The Architectural Historian set our small class the task of unpacking the Campanile and for the first time (aged twenty-one), I undertook primary research.

My journey through College's spaces intensified as I excavated the library's treasures on a trek to the manuscripts department, and to early printed books, both housed in the pavilions of the Old Library but only accessible through the bowels of the Berkeley. As the Architectural Historian had promised, the manuscripts' collection contained Trinity's account books, commercial portraits of a place and an unrivalled resource. Poring over them, squinting at the barely faded ink in a florid hand, I fell in love with this process: such investigative rigour, brought to bear outside, in the reading of how buildings were made and who was paid for what.

MAPPING BEYOND COLLEGE. Twenty years have passed now. The friends remain, constant, stronger than ever even. Trinity has gained at least two important buildings since I graduated – little did I know that the mechanical engineers were capable of hatching such a marvellous lab building (Parson's Lab, begun in 1996) or that the Provost had such a fine structure for his horses (the stables having been converted in to a study centre in 2005). The research rigour and processes introduced during those precious four years have developed, and a fresh appraisal of Dublin's twentieth-century architecture is being written. The Architectural Historian should know his legacy. Writing to him, and to my saintly parents, I would thank them for the happiness and the privilege.

Ellen Rowley (left) *with, clockwise from left, Damien Bennett, Jez Paxman and Catherine Heaney.*

Ellen Rowley (TCD 1991–95; History of Art and English) is a cultural and architectural historian, educator and writer on twentieth-century Ireland. Her essays on modernism and Irish architecture focus on themes of Catholic patronage and suburban development, concrete technology in post-1916 Dublin and everyday architecture in Ireland, 1940–80. She recently co-edited **Architecture 1600–2000**, Volume IV of the landmark series, **Art and Architecture of Ireland**. Ellen has led and designed an innovative research project into the twentieth-century architecture of Dublin city since 2011, for Dublin City Council, published in three volumes from 2016 and entitled **More Than Concrete Blocks: Dublin's Twentieth-Century Buildings and their Stories**.

UP FROM THE COUNTRY

michael bowman

THAT PRETTY MUCH sums it up. That's exactly what I looked like, and that's exactly what I was – an eighteen-year-old from Mayo, just landed in Dublin. In October 1991 all young Irish men – and indeed the country – still had an extra spring in their step after the national football team's exploits in Italia 90 the previous year, and while the summer of 1991 brought with it the slight downer of the first Iraq war, that didn't intrude too much upon my preparations for life as a first-year Trinity law student. I spent those months working as a kitchen porter on a campsite in Jersey, living in a tent, saving up my pounds while living on a staple diet of potatoes. (Potatoes are Jersey's largest export outside of tax exiles, and my brother, who spent the summer picking them, brought home a stone-weight bag of Jersey Royals each Friday, which we would have literally for breakfast, dinner and tea.)

Such hard-earned cash afforded me the luxury of calling Hatch Hall, a Jesuit hall of residence on Lower Hatch Street, home for my first year in Dublin. I was in good company – 103 other rurally inclined young men, about to be let loose upon whatever third-level institution they were fortunate enough to get accepted into, were to be my study companions for the year. I buddied up with a great guy from Borrisokane called James Lyons and was as enthused as any young man could be about what I fully expected to be a colourful voyage into the unknown. I was fortunate in that two friends from school in Castlebar had come to Trinity the year before I did. Aodan Bourke and Cathal Hanley together with Billy O'Connell, my only friend from Dublin, had established a FOB (Forward Operating Base), which afforded me a springboard into campus, so at least I could pretend to know where I was going.

My introduction to the law course took me quite by surprise. My first lecture was criminal law, a subject I presumed would be engaging and challenging. I expected Alan Dershowitz or Johnnie Cochran to bestride the lecture theatre, grasp the lectern and put the fear of God into those who were late, ignorant, or both. I could conceal my tardiness by getting there on time but God forbid my ignorance would be exposed by even the most rudimentary of questions. Amidst a class of what looked to be ninety-odd people, about two-thirds girls (never a bad thing), I positioned myself mid theatre, new pen, new notepad and ready for action.

I think everybody was taken aback when a petite brunette entered the room and turned left to address the lectern as opposed to right to find a seat. This very pleasant and engaging, and very young woman announced herself to be Professor Úna Ní Raifeartaigh. She held a professorship in criminal law, and she was going to lecture us for the next year. There was a ripple of excitement amongst the girls as they realized anything was now possible in this brave new world, and a quizzical smile from not a few of the male members of the class.

Professor Ní Raifeartaigh did not disappoint, and held us all spellbound for the duration of criminal law during that first year. Not only that, but when the option later presented itself to study criminology under her, the class was vastly oversubscribed. The other lecturers in first year, whilst I'm sure they were hugely competent and highly recognized within their field, failed to capture the imagination to the same extent. She enthralled us with cases from the eighteenth century, such as Dudley and Stephens, a well-known case of cannibalism among shipwrecked sailors that featured an unfortunate and ill-fated cabin boy.

Perhaps everybody else was as deluded as I was, but I began to fancy myself thinking that maybe I too could be a young, engaging, debonair professor. Maybe I could hold a class of 2001 or 2011 spellbound with tales of *mens rea* and *actus reus*. However, every future legal luminary must first pass their exams and as the year wore on, my target fell from aspirant professor, to accomplished academic, to competent student, to ultimately 'maybe 40 per cent is about as much as I need for the moment …' And so it proved.

I would remind myself that this was a marathon, not a sprint, and to injure myself at this stage of such a journey could be deemed foolish. In any event, I thought my time was better spent familiarizing myself with every blade of grass, every dark corner, where something new, novel and inviting might be found. I was going to take this journey at walking pace, lest I miss anything of interest. By this stage, I had discovered a new (to me anyway) breed of individual, commonly referred to by those in the know as a 'West Brit'. With its distinctive accent, this was indeed a foreign and exotic creature, most definitely something to be observed from afar and approached with the utmost caution. Having been originally wary and suspicious of such parties, I quickly learned that they possessed an appetite for mischief, nightlife and success with the opposite sex to which I could only aspire.

Allied with this was another alien creature, the 'Northerner'; again, an item of particular curiosity. Rough around the edges, usually unkempt, showing a very healthy disregard for authority and convention and an unquenchable thirst for Buckfast. Those were just the girls! The guys were quite simply wild. They even had cooler names than us: Rusty, J.B., Magoo and Pedro.

Law had a disproportionate representation of both Northerners and the West Brits, keeping as it did approximately 40 per cent of its places open to A Level graduates. I would have to concede that they brought more colour and passion to any and every social gathering we were at than all the natives combined. I became fast friends with a crew of Northern guys and girls, whose social tentacles spread well beyond the law class and indeed Trinity.

Because most of them had cars (something else the natives did not possess), I found myself going on weekends away to locations as diverse as Sherkin Island in West Cork to Essex, home of an English gent called Nick Hayes. But for the name you would not have guessed that Nick's dad, now a bigwig in the City of London, was originally from the Liberties, having taken the boat across in the fifties. Same with Shane Ruddy – this Harrow-educated young man's father proudly wore the green and red of Mayo, hailing from Belmullet territory!

But it wasn't all sweetness and light. Oh no – long before Frank McCourt published his 1996 memoir *Angela's Ashes*, I had known all too well the sort of hunger and misery that he would later communicate to a worldwide audience. Fortunately, not for my friends and me the poorhouse or eating coal. No. We had the Mont Clare Hotel. The Mont Clare, for those of you not familiar with it, was a large hotel located near the Lincoln Gate end of Trinity, which routinely held, amongst other functions, twenty-first birthday parties. The beauty of the twenty-first was that if you arrived late enough in the evening, you were most probably assured of well-inebriated company, free booze and certainly the tail end of whatever rations had been laid on for the well-heeled debutante celebrating this auspicious milestone. The ballroom of the Mont Clare became a familiar stop-off point on the way home from a lengthy evening in the Pav. Those evenings generally began with my friends and I discussing, in gentle tones, the issues of the day, and concluded with us shouting at one another, or indeed anybody who was in earshot, the righteousness of our respective positions.

I distinctly recollect one such evening involving myself and a gentleman best described, to preserve his anonymity and current respectability, as Long John Kelly. Long John was so known because of his conspicuous size, which was matched only by his appetite. Having arrived at the Mont Clare, we realized much to our disappointment that there was no twenty-first that evening. Undeterred, we decided to go straight to the source and having behaved, we believed, in an utterly inconspicuous manner and presented as residents, we skulked through the ballroom and found our way into the kitchen. Long John proceeded to find the walk-in fridge and, therein, a six-pound smoked salmon. However, it soon became apparent we were not alone in the kitchen, as some diligent staff member had noted this odd couple stroll through the foyer, and we had to beat a hasty retreat, going in opposite directions to confuse the Securitate who were well on our heels.

Being thoroughly nondescript in physical appearance I simply put my head down and kept walking. However, Long John was easily identified – not only by virtue of his size but also the presence of a 6 lb side of smoked salmon under his arm – as he devoured the ground beneath him and, reminiscent of Cúchulainn, straddled the north side of Merrion Square in almost one mighty stride.

His liberty was to be short-lived. Famed for his quick thinking, Long John had decided he could outwit the police who had now arrived on the scene (always a bad idea to get involved with this sort of late-night antic so close to Government Buildings with its ever-present Garda sentry). He quickly took a right turn, then fell to one knee, feigned injury and when the Gardaí arrived within a matter of seconds, wasted no time in telling them that the culprit they were seeking had gone 'that way', having kicked our hero in the stomach for no apparent reason.

Unfortunately the police had not been socializing for the preceding seven hours, and observed it was unlikely that there was another gentleman measuring six foot seven in the vicinity, who by pure chance happened to have concealed about his person a side of smoked salmon. Ever the pragmatist, Long John realized the game was up, came clean and invoked the *Les Misérables* defence – no more than our hero Jean Valjean who stole a loaf of bread, Long John was driven to such an act of madness by desperate starvation. He was promptly marched back to the Mont Clare where he was identified by no fewer than three irate staff members, to whom he was made apologize and hand back the salmon. This he duly did. However, strong as an oak, he refused to bend the knee and give up his confederate.

DAY-TO-DAY undergraduate life in the early 1990s had some other distinctive features. It would not be unusual on any given morning to find a cohort of students congregated on the Arts Block ramp, possessed of a certain nervous or giddy energy. Their appearance was strikingly similar – all had a deathly pallor, large grins and eyes as wide as saucers, resembling two holes burnt in a sheet. This was, after all, the time of the emerging rave scene in Dublin, where a night out could extend to anything from ten to thirty-six hours. Trinity, like the rest of Dublin, pulsed to the beat of the KLF, Dee-Lite, The Prodigy and The Shamen's dance anthem, 'Ebenezer Goode'. Curious as to what all this was about, myself and some similarly uninitiated friends went to a cultural evening in the Tivoli Theatre off Francis Street to see a rising young act called 808 State. We arrived just in time to see three young men from Manchester dressed like lumberjacks introduce a guest star, who described himself as 'MC Tunes', and who immediately announced he was about to Split the Atom! There followed three hours of high-octane beat-driven music without a single word offered. When at one stage I needed some respite, I retreated to the bar and asked for three frosty pints of lager. 'You must be fucking joking!' replied the barman – the Tivoli didn't have a dance licence mid week but I could have as much water as I liked, he told me, or as many minerals as I could stomach.

So this, I thought to myself, is what all the fuss is about. The following year, Hugh Murray became the Ents officer and brought over some of the biggest dance acts from the UK, not just to the Trinity Ball, but throughout the year, and gave us all a deeper appreciation of what MC Tunes was trying to achieve.

I ALWAYS FELT that every student had an obligation to give something back and make a contribution to the glory of Trinity. To that end, I fell into the company of Gavin Lyons, a gentleman now the editor of a successful Dublin publication, and who at that time was instrumental in breathing life back into the Dublin University Boxing Club. A club with an illustrious and trophy-littered history, it had fallen on hard times in the 1980s, a decline that looked to be terminal until Gavin got involved and brought an infectious enthusiasm back to the club. I have no idea how it came up in conversation but it struck me that there could be no better way for a student to demonstrate his loyalty and affinity for his college than to put his body on the line and shed his blood, and so I volunteered to fight for my college. (I had no problem with the glory part but shedding of blood was a different matter altogether.)

Fred Tiedt was the then trainer and coach to the Trinity Boxing Club, a man singularly distinguished in Irish amateur boxing and who had won a silver medal in the 1956 Olympics in Melbourne – though it was a widely held opinion that he had been robbed of the gold. I was certainly fortunate to have him in my corner and I am sure he probably felt the same about me, although being a consummate professional he chose the motivational tool of hiding his respect well.

After hours of intensive training, fight night arrived. I remember Gavin appearing at the gym with the tournament gloves, which felt like taping cement blocks onto your hands and hurt just as much. Fortunately we were provided with headgear, which ensured you'd be able to stay on your feet long enough to provide a suitable spectacle for the baying horde. A ring had been assembled in the JCR – normally home to communists, the Workers' Party, student politicians and every manner of pinko leftie within the university – but, which for one night only yielded the floor to something more akin to a scene from *Gladiator*.

The place was packed, and due to the fact that I was fighting as featherweight, the lightest man on the card, I had the singular honour of opening and breathing life into the Trinity UCD Boxing Colours tradition, fighting for what was then the Harry Preston Trophy, but has since been renamed in honour of Fred Tiedt (Fred passed away from a long illness in June of 1999). I had intended being led into the ring by a lone piper, who required £20 for his three-minute introduction. He demanded money up front and because I had neither a good agent nor a manager, I foolishly handed over the money half an hour before my entrance, and to nobody's surprise but my own, Jock and his bagpipes were nowhere to be found, having last been sighted bellowing around Temple Bar outside The Foggy Dew.

At least I can say the fight lasted longer than the entrance: my opponent was a little-known but well-fancied UCD student by the name of Alan Moore. He poured the pain on me from the first bell to the last minute of our not-so-evenly-matched contest. It was a unanimous decision in favour of Moore from the blue corner, while I received a sympathetic and appreciative round of applause from the home crowd. I have yet to come to terms with the travesty, which was that decision. The night wore on and Trinity overcame its ignominious start to regain for the first time in seventeen years the Harry Preston Trophy. I thank Gavin for the pain and the memories every time I see him.

FROM THE ridiculous to the sublime: I recollect a party in a friend's house one summer's evening, and spotting a young lady of striking and unique beauty across the room. In truth, I had seen her around before, but lacked either the opportunity and/or the guile to make an approach. Now, good fortune came to my aid: she was seated on a couch talking to a friend of mine, and I immediately effected my introduction and perched on the corner of the seat. When my friend moved off through the crowd, I availed of the spare seat beside her. I engaged in such witty conversation and banter as I possibly could and lost no opportunity to acknowledge common ground and taste, whether real or imaginary.

This marked the beginning of a thoroughly unexpected but most fondly remembered chapter of my time in Trinity. At first I struggled to understand or articulate what was going on, and maybe even fought against it, but the truth was incontrovertible and undeniable: I had found my first true love.

MY LAST YEAR in College was spent in rooms in New Square, on the ground floor. I fell into a routine of walking over to the Kylemore Bakery on Nassau Street, where I would buy three fresh, full-butter croissants, then retreat to the sanctuary of my rooms, make a coffee, throw open the window and watch those less fortunate who had just commuted from God-knows-where pass my window. In the summer, the smell of freshly cut grass would drift into my room as the Croquet Club pitched up in New Square, its competitors possessed of a frightening and violent intensity, using words I would never have imagined hearing from croquet players. (It just goes to show if you eat nothing but cucumber sandwiches all day and pour bottle after bottle of Pimm's into any athlete, the result is inevitable.)

In many ways I look back on those four years and smile when I think how ill-equipped I was to commence a career in law – although ultimately that's what I did. The petite and inspirational criminal law professor who left such an indelible mark upon so many young, impressionable students, I am now fortunate enough to consider both a colleague and a friend. Indeed I have had the pleasure of being both prosecuted by and defending with the same professor, from whom I continue to learn on an almost daily basis.

What I took away from Trinity cannot be measured in terms of percentages, grades or even degrees. It introduced me to so many wonderful people, so many novel experiences, and so many bizarre circumstances, that what it really, indisputably gave me was an invaluable education for life.

I still love to stroll through College, entering either from College Green or Lincoln Place, and to walk the full length of the campus, ambling around New Square, Library Square, between the cricket crease and the rugby pitch, where on balmy summer's evenings the hordes still habitually gather on the playing fields to rest their weary bodies. It was and remains reminiscent of a biblical scene – the only thing missing being some class of a messianic figure to appear on the steps of the Pav and deliver a sermon to the multitudes. They all look impossibly young to me now, but the friendships and relationships that I forged in College remain as strong today as they were then, and I am fortunate to count amongst them some of the rarer breeds already identified: the West Brits, most of whom are now returned to the mainland; the Northerners, who have spread far and wide; and those creatures of rare beauty, the southside Dublin girls.

It's only when you cast your mind back with the benefit of twenty years of post-college life that you fully appreciate the expression 'youth is wasted on the young'. Maybe so, but it is probably also true that youth can only truly be enjoyed and experienced by the young. To prepare myself for writing this piece, I took my one-year-old son on a walking tour of my old Trinity haunts (in honour of the great Joseph O'Gorman, whose tours in the 1990s featured a sense of colour and pageantry not seen since). I told him of the exploits and past glories associated with the buildings on campus, although I'm not sure if he fully appreciated their significance – it's hard to explain to a one-year-old the passions that fuelled the SU sit-in of 1993. But I felt safe in the knowledge that I had begun to pass on to the next generation an appreciation of that most unique of academic and social environments, planted deep in the heart of Dublin, surrounded by its ancient walls, and cocooned in the memories of so many graduates.'

Michael Bowman (second from left) *with Andrew 'Rusty' Russell, Mark Cummings, Donal Flannagan and Peter 'Pedro' Haughey.*

After his time at Trinity, **Michael Bowman** (TCD 1991–95; Law) did a post-graduate business course at UCD just to see what the college life there was like (nothing much to report). He spent a year in London pursuing his academic studies in the company of some of the aforementioned characters and returned to Dublin with another degree. He entered the Honourable Society of King's Inns and ultimately settled for a career at the Bar, which had the distinct advantage of no interview process or requirement to send in a CV. Criminal law became his natural home and he has not strayed too far since.

OF BOOKS, BANDS AND THE BALL

aengus collins

MY FINAL YEAR in Trinity was spent in the ramshackle world apart of the Ents office, two floors up in House Six and blessed with an incongruously stately view of the Campanile. But over the four preceding years, most of my time on campus was spent facing a wall in the Lecky Library, at a desk which from early on I claimed as my own.

This desk was the closest thing to solitude that the Lecky offered. It was the left-hand bay in a brace of wall-facing desks tucked away in a corner of the lower ground floor. To my left, bookshelves. To my right, another desk, at which sat a parade of fellow students over the years; but with a partition of sorts between their desk and mine, they might as well not have existed. As desks go, it was powerfully immersive. I knew concentration sitting there that I had never known before and that I have never recaptured since. I would physically surround myself with books, piling them high on both sides (a working habit I have retained over the years, even as it has become less necessary).

Mornings started early, waiting outside the library, sipping bad black coffee from the café. Then the opening of the doors and fifteen minutes or so of preparatory activity before my day got going in earnest. It's hard to describe the perfect stillness of the library at that time of the morning. Each day would progress in crescendo, but during those first few minutes the Lecky was a thing of beauty, a place of hushed and ordered plenitude.

I would go downstairs to claim my desk for the day, before returning upstairs to collect from the librarians the multiple armfuls of books I always had on hold from stacks. I would bring these back downstairs, placing them in neat piles on my desk, before making a tour of the open-access shelves to retrieve whatever additional books I might need for the day ahead; another pile or two on my desk. I would arrange my several months' worth of notes in front of me. I would open a fresh page on a crisp block of A4 paper. I would begin.

With hindsight, all these preliminaries seem a bit over-engineered. But they worked. They set each morning in motion; they stitched each day to the one that had gone before. They were somehow crucial to crafting an experience of that library that has stayed with me over the decades since and that still shapes the way I work.

In time, I became Arts Editor of *Trinity News*, so when I wasn't in the Lecky I was in the publications office in House Six, and when I wasn't immersed in books I was immersed in music. That role was revelatory. New music poured in to me from the major record labels' offices in Dublin and from independent labels in London. My name started being added to the guest lists of the city's clubs and venues. And all I had to do was listen and write and ask others to do the same. It was like being handed the keys to the sweet shop.

This was still, more or less, a time before internet. (My first forays online required a trip from the Arts Block to the computer science lab, where I would interlope on terminals running Unix or something similarly opaque.) On today's internet there is a surfeit of writing about music; it's a debased currency. But back in the Dublin of the early nineties, there was an appetite for more words about music. When I took on the arts section of the paper it was two pages long – I fleshed out the arts team and pushed the page count to eight. I owe a debt of thanks to the editor at the time, who was very accommodating towards this expansionism, calculating I suppose that music and movies meant more to most than the second-rate circus that student politics was already then becoming.

It was a great time to be a music-loving student. Just as the wider economy was starting to enjoy better times after the 1980s, so Dublin's music scene was on an upswing. The combination of higher disposable incomes and better venues were altering the economics of including Dublin on a European tour. More and more bands passed through the city. And more DJs too, music's new heroes, who flew in to play pounding sets in riverside venues to sweaty and euphoric crowds, off their faces on Ecstasy and whatever else was doing the rounds.

I would occasionally travel to London with friends to see bands that weren't going to be playing Dublin. The only way to make it affordable was to go by bus and boat – a lot of travel for a two-hour concert. Looking back, there's something otherworldly about those pilgrimages; they required an excitement and a commitment that have been lost to me over the years. And a camaraderie too. One moment sticks in my mind; it must have been 1992 and it was probably a trip to see Nick Cave. We were on the bus, in the middle of who knows where, and it was pitch black outside. Someone passed around their headphones so that everyone could listen to a tape recording (a tape recording!) of the just-released debut single of a new band, Suede. It felt like being present at the birth of something. Suede became an important band for a few years – their second album, *Dog Man Star*, remains one of the finest ever recorded if you ask me – but they were at their most intoxicating at the moment of their emergence. You could feel it viscerally, from the very first bars, in the pulsating drummed intro to that first single. Sharing that moment so unexpectedly on a night-time coach to London sticks with me still – I have lost touch with those friends, but I owe them many of my best memories of my time at Trinity.

I studied English. My final-year dissertation was on the 'disembodied voice' in Beckett's later work. There was lots of Derrida in it. There was lots of Derrida in a lot of things back then. My supervisor was Terence Brown, a wonderful teacher with a wonderful mind. He didn't have much time for Derrida. And he thought the idea of focusing on something as obtuse as disembodiment was a bit beside the point when dealing with a medium – drama – that requires real bodies to be on real stages. This struck me as straightforwardly wrong in Beckett's case (and still does I suppose). But it also seemed to me the response of someone too old to keep up. What insufferable shits so many of us must have seemed so much of the time.

Once that final academic year was over, most of my friends moved on, but I still had another year to go. If it hadn't ended in abject anticlimax, my year as Ents officer would have been the most purely enjoyable of the five I spent at Trinity. The position felt like a pretty seamless way of building on my time as arts editor, perhaps even of edging towards a career doing something related to music. I could have done without the mortifications of the electoral process, but I recently found a battered copy of my campaign poster and although it's a bit of a graphic-design monstrosity, in the photo I look young and very happy. Those were good times.

I got to spend the next year working in the slightly shambolic beauty of the Ents office, planning events for the student population, and spending my evenings out at any number of concerts around the city. In essence, it seemed, I was being paid to love music. I had a free apartment on campus. I enjoyed the convenience of an unofficially acquired key to the pedestrian gates in the university walls. I was able to lean on invaluable support from the Ents crew and the rest of the Students' Union. I found unexpected fellowship and friendship in a community of past and present Ents officers from across both Trinity and UCD – I can think of few better ways to experience Dublin in your early twenties.

And yet. In the natural run of things, an Ents officer's year culminates in May with the Trinity Ball, an explosion of hedonism that in its heyday had etched itself into the musical annals of the city – back in the day, acts like Public Enemy and The Smiths had headlined. Those Edenic times were long gone by the mid nineties, but the ball remained the telos towards which every Ents officer's year was orientated. Mine was cancelled. The bands had been booked. The tickets had been sold. But the ball quietly died because the university authorities couldn't resolve an unrelated industrial dispute with the cleaning staff. It was due to be held on 10 May 1996; the board of the university cancelled it on 24 April. I still came into work the next morning, but I had nothing to look forward to from my remaining time at Trinity but the slow and embarrassing process of unpicking many months of careful planning. I occasionally wonder what might have come next had the ball gone ahead. As it turned out, all thoughts of working with music faded swiftly. Within months I had moved a few miles south to study with Richard Kearney, a choice to which I can trace most of the events that have shaped my life in the two decades since.

Aengus Collins (TCD 1991–95; English and Psychology) lives in London, where he is Country Forecast Director at the **Economist** Intelligence Unit. Whenever possible, he still travels to watch Nick Cave play live.

OUT AND ABOUT IN PARIS AND DUBLIN

gráinne maria lina hayes

MY SINGLE BED was toe to toe with another bed in which someone had just sat up. Black wavy hair and a wide smile.

'Oh! I'm glad it's you!' the girl said, although we'd never met before.

I smiled back, my cheeks tight with tear stains. It was my first morning in Trinity Hall and one would have thought I'd been sent off to university in Afghanistan. I had cried at the gate at Glasgow airport, blubbed some more on the plane and looked out at Dublin's grimy streets in silence in my aunt's car on the way to Dartry. Before Trinity, I had never been away from my family for more than a night's sleepover nearby. I wouldn't even go on a French exchange without my sister.

Fortunately, Trinity Hall in the early nineties proved to be a mellow introduction to college life. To secure a room in halls, one had to come from beyond the Pale so there was me – the Irish-Portuguese girl who grew up in Scotland – my room-mate and classmate Ruth Doyle from Wexford, Damian Agnew who was Irish but grew up in Hong Kong, Sybille Chrissoveloni from Greece via London, and a posse of new friends from the North and all over Ireland. We bonded over pints in the Buttery and walked back from the bus stop in twos and threes along Trinity Hall's chestnut-lined avenue, past an unkempt tennis court we'd play on in Trinity term. We'd spill into the sitting room of the Victorian main house and sing along to someone's guitar until we were hoarse. We must have sometimes moved our festivities to other parts of halls because I still have a letter from the ever-patient Warden, Professor Florides: *Further to the disturbances in Kitchen 61 Top Corridor last Friday/Saturday night, I regret to inform you that a fine of £10 has been imposed on you for your involvement in these disturbances.*

At the weekends, Ruth and I would deconstruct life, literature and men over breakfast at 5 am in the aforementioned Kitchen 61 at the end of our corridor, and then part ways: myself to sleep after a night out, Ruth to cycle to Islandbridge and row at dawn.

I read law and, for Michaelmas and Hilary terms anyway, took my course's eight lectures and two seminars a week as something of a maximum. These were generally accomplished (or not) by noon, so what to do with the rest of the day? I dived into a variety of College societies with varying degrees of success, defeating the Hist auditor in a Jaffa Cake Impromptu Debate on 'pleasure is the creator of existence'. I also scribbled occasional album reviews for *Trinity News* and, for the first time in my life, auditioned for various plays. In Players, the importance of the role seemed to be inversely proportional to the time spent in rehearsals. With roles such as 'Sign-holder' in Caimin Collins' fourth-year play, and 'Soldier Two' in a rebellious production of Oscar Wilde's *Salomé* (featuring a burly Scots King Herod, clad solely in an assortment of black bin bags), I was thoroughly occupied.

The afternoons thus filled, there were the evenings to contemplate. As adults-in-training, this meant not only gigs, pubs and balls but also early forays into the world of home entertaining. My 'events' inevitably started with a list. One, stuck into my second-year diary, features an urgent reminder to *NICK SOME GLASSES!!* across the top. The lucky guests were *Will, Damian, Gavin, Aaron, Aillil, John O'C, Dicko, Ruth, Aoifinn, Sybille.* Note the male-to-female ratio, which mirrored the drinks-to-food ratio. *Cocktails or punch?* to start, followed by *vodka, wine, mineral water, peach schnapps, coffee and Baileys.* This entire *soirée* would miraculously cost £40, apparently. Another night we hosted a (quasi-)legendary toga party, sheets *de rigueur*, to which I wore a fetching pale blue flannel number. We were later to be found boogie-ing, still in togas, at a Leeson Street nightclub down the road.

These were the final few years before mobile phones took all the guess-work (but also some of the magic) out of being out and about. The accepted means of contacting someone in rooms, for example, was scrunching up a note and wedging it behind the panel of doorbells. It wasn't a very reliable method for tracking someone down. Many of the messages went something like this one I stuck into one of my diaries: *Hi, like where are you? I called around in a splendid mood. PS might go to Thing Mote later.* As a result, evenings often ended up being a bit of an adventure and nothing like what had been planned. A walk across Front Square always brought a chance meeting or five: the 'Front Arch to the tree' route is one of Dublin's favourite shortcuts (the tree in ques-tion, at Nassau Street Gate, was cut down in 2009, although another has been planted in its place).

When I think of it now, Trinity's geography is metaphorical as well as physical. A semi-sheltered site in the heart of a city; open and closed at the same time. A place, which provided shielded chances for nascent interests to flourish. Step out of Front Arch and all the possibilities of the city lie before you. Walk inside later and, when the porter closes the gate door behind you, it's just you, the Campanile's moon shadow and the sound of laughter across a cobbled courtyard.

FROM THIS protected place, I began to imagine journeys further afield. I still sometimes envied my Dublin friends – Sorley, Carla, Ellen and others – who could just jump on a bus and go home at the end of each day, but my eye had begun to stray beyond Dublin. I set off inter-railing around Europe with Ruth after first year with my ankle in plaster because I was too impatient to wait for a few more weeks until my cast was off. Buoyed by this trip, my sister and I travelled to Egypt the following summer. I remember standing by the sea near Alexandria, another city with a library at its heart, shifting my feet from side to side on the burning sand, watching the women swimming in their ballooning chadors. By the end of second year, Erasmus beckoned. The question was not 'if' but 'where'. I noted in my diary: *Sounds like most of last year's students had a bit of a mare – especially the ones in Paris II. WON'T be going there.*

Naturally, I landed in Paris CDG a few months later. Université de Paris II Panthéon-Assas is highly prestigious, but like other arms of the Université de Paris, it's more like a giant faculty than a university like Trinity. In Assas, the only subjects are law, political science and economics, yet it is bigger than the entire Trinity student body. *Really weird – absolutely huge!!* I wrote in my diary after my first lecture in a cavernous auditorium, crammed in with a thousand other students. The idea was true French egalitarianism – to give as many as possible the chance of starting the course, although in fact only half would make it through to the following year.

Another surprise was that a good number of Assas students wore suit jackets and carried briefcases. Assas had a reactionary slant that sometimes warped into a more ugly side. I hear things have improved now, but it happened several times that an Assas student would come over to us to offer, quite openly, a casually delivered insult to my fellow Erasmus friends from University College London, who happened to also be Jewish or second generation British-Asian. These closed souls were the minority however. Within a few weeks I was once more composing long lists of dinner-party invitees, listing friends who were Tunisian-French, Algerian-French or just plain French, and others from Italy, Turkey, Canada and Holland. This time, judging from the lists I've stuck in my diary, the *soirées* were for twenty-odd people, with a dozen more arriving later for the 'afters', all squashed into a miniscule Paris apartment.

Doing Erasmus in one of the world's most expensive capitals takes a certain ingenuity, particularly in relation to finding accommodation. In my first week I went with my TCD classmate Emma Boylan to see a studio advertised for two. Emma played rugby and cricket for Trinity and wasn't about to be fobbed off: '*C'est où, le lit?*' she queried, looking around the tiny room. We watched, astonished, as the woman pushed a button – *et voilà*! A single bed levered out from the wall and took up the remaining floor space as we darted for the door.

Another night, a pal and I were invited by a new Erasmus friend for dinner. A pineapple dominated her tiny Formica table. 'I love pineapple,' I said, wondering what was for main course. She started cutting it up and served out careful slices. Yes, reader, the pineapple was *le dîner*.

If this sounds vaguely like hardship, it was, of course, the opposite. I eventually found a room in a flat just off Place Monge, which for all its closeness to Saint-Germain, had the relaxed, homely feel of a provincial square. Veiled women and the grey dome of the Paris mosque gave the area a Parisian cosmopolitan edge. Myself and another pal, Elizabeth, who reminded everyone of Olive Oyl from Popeye, painted my room in our undies as we had no 'painting clothes', drinking wine and smoking cigarettes, feeling wonderfully grown up – although of course much of the fun was because we weren't. Elizabeth au paired in the sixteenth arrondissement and I visited her once, counting the (I thought) endless stops from central Paris on the arching lime-green number nine Métro line and meeting her at a park called Ranelagh. I remember sitting on a bench under the plane trees, thinking of Dublin as she wrestled with a chubby three-year-old. I made my excuses and went back to *ma belle vie*.

My memories of that year in France are impressionistic. Peering down from the gods at Madame Butterfly at the Opéra de Paris. Saturated colours at the Barnes Collection exhibition at the Musée d'Orsay. Sipping wine on the steps outside the Sacré Coeur and watching the sunset over Paris with my fellow Erasmus classmate Bobby and his best pal Mim, an effervescent Iranian-British girl with ridiculously long eyelashes. Slowly sipping an excruciatingly expensive cup of tea to make it last at Café Marly outside the Louvre, and visits to myriad other galleries. Dancing to Maceo Parker at the Bataclan. Playing table football at Café de la Plage. Eight of us packed into a Renault revving up the Champs-Élysées, MC Solaar on the radio. Learning to dive in the pool of an ivy-covered house in the hills above 'St Trop'. Using broomsticks as mics while visiting Emma's friend Anna in Rouen. Being grabbed by a friend as a current ripped me away while a group of us skinny-dipped in the Loire. Zooming around on a motorbike without a helmet or jacket (in November!).

Even taking the Métro was an experience; the elegant wrought-iron arches of the entrances; each station with its own character and the heady whiff of humanity when the doors opened. *Got out at wrong metro so walked around for a while. Very cold but Paris looked beautiful in the dusk*, I wrote.

PARIS, APRIL 2016

I still have my diaries from TCD, although the letters and tickets now fall out as I turn the pages; the Sellotape has long ago lost its stickiness. Memory can be a *faux ami* – there in those pages is how it really was, then.

To my complete delight, I'm back living in Paris again, this time with a family in tow. The places I spent time in then and now have swapped around. Fate plays its little jokes. Tomorrow we will walk a few blocks to the Jardin du Ranelagh and press coins into the hand of the cap-wearing man at a nineteenth-century carousel. We will sit with friends on a bench under the plane trees, watching as our kids spin around with sticks in their hand, trying to spear the metal hoops placed almost out of reach. I've swapped the infamous Ed discount supermarket and solitary pineapples for canapés at gilded embassies.

Those are not the only changes, however – one might have hoped for some of those, more than twenty years on. There are other changes. On the park bench, between holiday plans and jokes about school, we parents murmur about attacks. At school, our kids crouch under their desks in practice lock-downs hiding from 'a robber'. I now hesitate to take the Métro at rush hour, although like everyone else I do it anyway. I haven't yet been back to the Bataclan, now synonymous with grief, but I will again, alongside hundreds of others. Today we ate in a restaurant a block away from there, and it was packed. We have to live.

Not only live but, as much as we can, remain open and fearless in our dealings with others. It seems to me that that's what my Trinity years – out and about in Paris and Dublin – were all about. Not so much the experiences themselves, memorable as these were, but the people I encountered along the way.

And I can't help thinking that being open-minded and unflinching towards the newcomer and the other remains essential. Even now, when, at the periphery of our busy and privileged adult lives, it can sometimes seem that shadows are lengthening across Paris and elsewhere, and instinct tells us to turn inwards. Especially now – and not just when it was easy to do so, when every second day brought a new friendship, when our greatest dangers were self-induced and life was a sparkling stream of experiential (if not always academic) firsts.

GRÁINNE MARIA LINA HAYES (NÉE HEHIR) (TCD 1991–95; Law) is Head of Political Affairs at the Irish Embassy in Paris. Before her diplomatic career, she was a Brussels-based EU correspondent for Dow Jones Newswires and the **Wall Street Journal Europe.** Her writing has been shortlisted for the Shiva Naipaul essay prize.

LIFE LESSONS

fionnuala breathach

WHEN CHOOSING where to go to college in 1991, my attraction to Trinity had nothing to do with the academic accolades of the medical alumni, or historic reputation, or university rankings. I simply wanted to be 'in town'. Living in Mount Merrion, next door to Belfield, reduced the appeal of UCD. I envisaged myself transitioning to college life surrounded by an eclectic blend of luminaries from other faculties, in a city centre haven steeped in history. Of course I swiftly realized that the Faculty of Health Sciences, situated at the south end of the campus, was the suburbia of TCD. Medical students were notable for their earnest stride along College Park en route to the hub of all things scientific. Yet there was always a relentless draw back toward the Arts Building, the soul of campus.

Early in my second year, when I had recently moved into rooms in Front Square, my younger sister died unexpectedly and suddenly. I was propelled into unimaginable grief and surrounded by friends who were kind and supportive but still new to me. This pivotal time in my life is inextricably linked with Trinity for that reason. I grew up overnight, with the sense that I was living among the shadows of generations of occupants of Front Square before me. This loss informed the outlook of my college years. It weakened and strengthened me. It made me a better doctor.

Our class was that healthy blend of enthusiasts and more passive participants, all with a shared incredulity that we would spend the next six years together – to our eighteen-year-old selves a third of a lifetime thus far – unified in pursuit of a degree that would secure our place in society as responsible tax-paying grown-ups. There was a respectable attendance at lectures scheduled for mornings or early in the week. Thereafter, we tended to drift toward the Buttery, or Lincoln, or Stag's Head. And of course the summer evenings were memorable for the Pav, appropriately chosen to host our ten-year reunion.

Those from Northern Ireland or from farming backgrounds (and indeed the exceptional soul who might be fortunate on both counts) were marginally less broke than the rest of us, but we were happy to park our smouldering resentment for their generous grants when they bought pints in the Lincoln on grant day. The abolition of fees came in 1996, so that while we enjoyed one fee-free year, the majority of the class was in significant debt by then. The strategically positioned College Green bank was gushing in its enthusiasm to shower us with loans on the day of graduation, which we willingly accepted in the celebratory spirit of that promise-filled milestone. And so was fuelled the debt-laden existence of our generation.

Activism in Trinity in the early 1990s was dominated by the Supreme Court's X Case ruling in 1992. The provision of contact information to women seeking to terminate pregnancy was illegal, and led to the prosecution of student groups who provided contact information in their leaflets. I would have considered myself a passive observer to this activism that ignited around the time of my sister's death. Indeed, my allegiance lay pretty firmly on the pro-life side of the fence. My views have softened since, and providing information and support to women who terminate pregnancy for foetal abnormality is an aspect of my job now that is enormously important to me and to my patients, who find themselves in extraordinary difficulty in the face of a complex pregnancy.

I still consider myself to be 'pro-life' in the sense that all practitioners engaged in the business of childbirth and reproduction are. My attraction to a career in obstetrics most likely came during the course of the Medical Overseas Voluntary Elective (MOVE) in the summer of 1995, where along with two of my classmates I spent eight weeks in a Finnish mission hospital in southern

Ethiopia. There I did my first delivery. Blankets were scarce at the clinic and the newborn was wrapped in newspaper. The privilege of guiding a baby into the first moments of its life took my breath away, and still does.

Although the principles of childbirth remain unchanged in the two decades since my graduation – indeed those principles have changed little across the millennia – significant advances have occurred in medical and societal aspects of this job since the 1990s. Our ability to manage the more complex elements of obstetrics and gynaecology continues to advance, and I look back at student experiences and recognize the rapid pace at which many aspects have changed. Even toward the latter years of my undergraduate training, HIV medicine was at an early stage in evolution. Highly effective three-drug therapy for HIV was incorporated into clinical practice in 1996, and HIV patients were among the sickest occupants of the wards at St James' Hospital, where I spent most of my clinical training time. The public fear that surrounded this disease permeated to health care workers. I recall one HIV-positive woman who was receiving effective antiretroviral treatment and was attending a Dublin maternity hospital, being told by the hospital staff that the bathroom labelled 'Out of Order' was the one designated for her use only.

Today I conduct many student teaching sessions, and wistfully wonder how my earnest twenty-first-century teaching style compares to that of my own educators. Professor Patricia Crowley conducted one memorable tutorial outdoors in the non-leafy grounds of the Coombe Hospital on a balmy June afternoon. We were all instructed to buy ice-creams, and we sat outside debating whether a pregnant woman's listeria infection could have been acquired through eating EasiSingles. The consensus was that it was unlikely that there was any actual cheese in the putative product, and that we were all more likely to succumb to the microbes of our ice-creams.

The OSCE format for final exams (Objective Structured Clinical Examination), resembling a speed-dating circuit, was always a traumatic affair and I remember declaring after the obstetrics version of this endurance test that I never wanted to see a pregnant woman again. Dr Paul Bowman, a portly man a few years shy of retirement, played the role of a pubescent teenager with menstrual difficulties. The consultation was rendered difficult by his high-pitched declaration that he was 'a martyr to me monthlies ...' Now my role in coordinating such exams is an altogether more regulated affair, with each simulated patient consultation requiring more credibility, oversight, standardization and a good deal less hilarity.

I returned to an unchanged Coombe seven years later, in 2003, to deliver my firstborn, under the care of the wonderful educator and clinician Dr Bernard Stuart. This event had been preceded the previous year by my wedding at the Trinity chapel on a glorious August day, when Front Square never looked more beautiful.

And so I consider Trinity to be associated with the happiest and the saddest days of my life. I am extraordinarily fortunate to be engaged in a job that I love, a circumstance I attribute in no small part to the wonderful and disparate group of classmates and mentors and colleagues that I met during my fleeting six years at Trinity.

Fionnuala Breathach (TCD 1991–97; Medicine) is Associate Professor of Obstetrics and Gynaecology at the Royal College of Surgeons in Ireland and the Rotunda Hospital Dublin. Having completed a Fellowship in Maternal Fetal Medicine at Columbia University, New York, her specialist area of expertise is in the management of high-risk pregnancy. She is married with four children.

JURIS ERRATUM: RUNNING FROM THE LAW

turtle bunbury

IT WAS quite comfortable to sleep on; that I do remember. *Wylie's Land Law*, I mean. A hefty tome of maybe 1400 pages of legal jargon pertaining to Irish property, equity, trusts and succession. It wasn't a work I became overly familiar with, mind you, but I can still just about feel the impressions of the cover upon my forehead. Sometimes I got through a couple of pages before it happened. Mostly it struck me on page one. I'd think, 'Maybe I'll just have a wee nap before I start, clear the auld cranium a little.' The book would be shut and carefully positioned. My head would lean forwards and I'd nod off, listening to the whirl of papers and biros and distant whispers emanating around the Berkeley Library.

It was certainly a mellower sleeping spot than the house where I lived on Heytesbury Lane, a short stumble from the east end of Baggot Street. Technically speaking, there were five of us in the house: four young men, one courageous young lady, all students. However, in the ensuing decades I have met many people who tell me, with much authority, how they spent so many nights in our house that they were practically entitled to squatters' rights. Ours was a party house, for sure. It wasn't supposed to be a party house, of course, and yet, in hindsight, perhaps all the chaos was somewhat preordained.

My Berkeley snoozes rarely lasted more than thirty minutes. When I awoke from my slumber, I would invariably put the nice book away and head outside for a smoke. And then, trance-like, I'd drift across to the soft green playing fields where familiar faces were sure to be soaking up the rays or the rains with some nutritious wheat juice at the Pav. Many a moon might wax and wane before I made it back into the library.

Model student I was not. From the age of eight through to eighteen, I was locked up in boarding schools, one in Dalkey, the other in Scotland. I remain convinced that the Oxford and Cambridge Examination Board botched up and gave me someone else's A Level results. They were too good. Having hitherto assumed I would be reading art history at Dunstable Polytechnic or some such, I found that I had unexpectedly qualified to read law at Trinity. My parents were so thrilled they banished me on a ten-month trip around the world and I duly headed off to paint gates in Virginia, master the art of poker in Hawaii and flog encyclopaedias door-to-door in the suburbs of Australia.

Globe-trotting was such enormous fun that by the time I started at Trinity in October 1991, I couldn't take it seriously. A college in the centre of Dublin, brimming with joyous youth, surrounded by amazing pubs? Immensely exciting. My knowledge of the capital prior to this was limited to a few days on the razz at the Dublin Horse Show, and a handful of 'cinema' trips with my older brother, which basically involved sneaky scoops in Bruxelles where a prematurely stubbly chin served in my favour. But now I was old enough to drink legally – and could there be a finer city in the world to enjoy such a pastime?!

I was formally registered on 4 October. Hazy memories of my first stroll across the now-so-familiar cobbles of Front Square: a hasty dash through a long string of enthused faces trying to convince my fellow Junior Freshmen and me that if we joined their camogie team, sci-fi club, theoretical society etc., we would get all our books at half price forever more. It all seemed more akin to the American high schools I had seen in movies than a solemn seat of learning. I was deeply relieved that initiation ceremonies were not part of the process. Someone presented me with a library card, someone else took me to see the Berkeley and Lecky libraries, after which I sought out some bad company and fled to a pub.

I've kept a diary since I was eight, and these days I play a game when pals come to stay. I ask them to pluck a 1990s diary off the shelf, any diary. Now choose a page, any page. And when they do, the chosen page unvaryingly finds me either in a pub or at a party, or on my way to one, or recovering from the last one. Frequently I am all of the above at once. Midway through my first law exams, for instance, I find myself consuming a bottle of Buckfast at the Pav and then, fast-forward a half-dozen hours, I'm doing knee-bendy dance manoeuvres down at Screwy-Lewy's on Leeson Street.

Trinity itself plays an embarrassingly small cameo role in those formative years. I blame the law. I just could not grasp it as a subject. It confused me. It made me sleepy. Here's a sample I copied directly into my diary from one of our books about constitutional law: 'The terms are not so unambiguous as to prohibit an interpretation of them aided by a consideration of the apparent intention of the legislature in enacting the bill.' It's lines like that that had me pinned to my chair in tremendous horror, reaching for my pouch of rolling tobacco.

There were maybe a hundred people in my class and I am still in touch with a number of them to this day. They were a good, kind-hearted, intelligent bunch. It seemed to me like they'd all known each other for ages but that cannot have been right. Indeed, many of them were as giddy as me, euphoric at the prospect of living away from home for the first ever time. I think my year roaming the globe had perhaps made me a little aloof, or maybe I just thought of myself as too cool for school, but I was slow to mix with the class. I probably didn't help my cause when I raised a hand during one of our first lectures and asked 'What's your *auktass*?' I can still feel a couple of hundred eyeballs swinging around to see what eejit would ask such a question. My Scottish education hadn't prepared me for terms such as Oireachtas.

Somehow I survived my Junior Freshman exams intact although, reading my diary, I cannot see how this was possible. Fortunately I did not deceive myself that all was well. I realized that if I didn't buckle down, all this studying law would be a colossal waste of time and money. So I signed up to study for Schol, the voluntary exams, on the basis that it might spur me into action. Victory would also secure me free education for the rest of my time at Trinity as well as complimentary rooms on campus, not to mention the strange rumours that I'd be entitled to graze a sheep in Front Square and march around the Buttery with a cutlass. Emboldened by my decision, I allied myself to a sagacious friend who was also sitting Schol and we both went to stay with his fabulously strict mother superior of a mother in Athlone. She did all that she could for us, turfing us out of our beds before the dawn, time-clocking the hours we spent at our desks and keeping us far from the temptations of Bacchus et al.

It might have worked but the questions did not go my way. Failing Schol was the knockout punch to my fleeting visions of becoming the new Perry Mason. I went on the batter and forgot to stop before the summertime exams came. And then I failed them too. Which meant I would have to do re-sits later in the summer. Fifteen law exams in one year. Everyone else in my class sat five. What on earth had I done to myself?

The situation was becoming increasingly untenable. A family friend urged me to meet with a circuit court judge of his acquaintance. Down I popped to the Four Courts where the genial Justice enquired about my legal ambitions. I told him of my miserable plight and admitted that I was contemplating abandoning the course. He leaned in close, glanced discreetly left and right, and said, 'I don't blame you, son. Get out while you can.'

So I did. Or at least I transferred.

A non-academic friend by name of Stu put the notion of a transfer into my head when I called into him for a refreshment one morning. 'I don't understand why you're not doing history anyway,' he said. I've always been obsessed by history, an inevitable consequence of growing up in a big old house surrounded by historic paintings and furniture. I lapped up history in my school years. I read history books for fun. I never let a historical epic leave a cinema unseen. The notion that I could actually study the subject at university level began to make my ears shake.

Fast forward to the winter of 1993, and you couldn't have found a cheerier student than the 22-year-old from Carlow who was now seated close to the front row, learning about Viking Dublin in the age of Sitric Silkbeard and how the Tudor viceroys all went demented trying to govern Ireland. I was overjoyed to be studying such topics. Now, it would be erroneous to say that I was henceforth a student of terrific diligence and resolve but I did have a considerably jauntier stride whenever I strolled or cycled into Trinity to attend a lecture.

I subsequently spent a year at Groningen University, where I mastered a different form of Schol – or Skol, if you will. The life of an Erasmus student studying history in Groningen was preposterously easy. My weekly agenda comprised of four hours of lectures, two of which were conducted by a lecturer with severe hypochondria who quite frequently cancelled them at the last minute. For the remaining 166 hours of each week, I was left to my own devices in the northern Dutch town. What's a guy to do? However, at least my chosen subject was history and, between the boldness, I read plenty of books about the long-term origins of the Vietnam War and why the South lost the US Civil War and why the Dutch are boring. The last topic was probably the oddest but they took it so seriously in Groningen that we spent an entire term studying it; a flat landscape and a 400-year-old democracy were cited as the two main reasons.

I made it all the way through college and left with a perfectly good history degree. I honestly can't now recall if it was a 2:1 or a 2:2. I remember that when it was conferred I had Jonathan Swift's beady eyes looking at me reproachfully; my main thesis – an unremarkable work – was an examination of Swift, who was about as convoluted and barmy a man as one could possibly find to write about.

I've never been called upon to show my degree to anyone but the historical itch was firmly upon me by the time I donned the gown for the graduation ceremony. Within a month, I was on a flight to Hong Kong where the next chapter of my life was about to begin. History would have to go on hold for a while because, much as I enjoyed my historical studies, Hong Kong just wasn't yet ready for all my newfound knowledge about Sitric Silkbeard. I assumed when I left Trinity in 1996 that I'd probably had my fill of history and that a new career would come my way before long. Half a decade would pass before I realized that my love for the subject was absolute and I yielded with a familiar elation when history came full circle to grip me once more.

Turtle Bunbury (TCD 1991–96; Law and History) is a bestselling author and award-winning historical consultant, whose roles include global public speaking and research for corporate bodies and television production companies. He is a frequent contributor to historical television and radio programmes along with print and online media, including **National Geographic Traveler**, **Vogue Living**, **The**

World of Interiors, Playboy, The Australian, The Irish Times and The Irish Daily Mail. His latest book is Around the World in 1847.

TRUE COLOURS

penny storey

I CAME to Dublin in 1991 from Belfast. Though I grew up in Northern Ireland in the 1970s and 1980s, I experienced 'the Troubles' indirectly through the media. What remained once the daily digest of bombs, military and civilian attacks, internment, political prisoners and protest had filtered through was a pervasive but subconscious awareness of threat, a state of mind that I carry as a specific memory.

On one regular, everyday journey with my parents, an armoured Land Rover transporting British soldiers pulled in front of our car. A helmeted head stuck out of the roof with a rifle trained on the road opening out behind. Leaning into the open back doors were two more soldiers, the rifles across their knees casually pointing in the direction of our car. I was only five or six but knew that here was danger.

When you live with something, you notice its absence more acutely than you ever register its presence. Arriving in Dublin that October of 1991, the most striking thing was the absence of threat. At first the quiet was unsettling – but what a revelation it was to understand that this is what normal should feel like.

If you're not from the city it's hard to plan the move. You don't get an offer until what feels like five minutes before you start and with not enough rooms in Trinity Hall in Dartry, it's a bit of a lucky dip. With no idea of what to do or how to do it, I boarded the Dublin train where I met the friend of a friend of a woman I used to work with – and we headed off to look for a flat together.

There was not a lot left to choose from. After something of a mild panic, we grimly agreed to take what was probably the last available collection of rooms in the city. They were in a basement, cost £27 a week, had an electric meter that must have been a nice little earner for the landlord, a rubber attachment on the bath taps for a 'shower', and no central heating. It flooded while we were home for Christmas, and was so cold in January that the three of us who lived there had to sleep in the same room. In the background, a soundtrack heavily dominated by brainwashingly repetitive hits from the sixties and seventies blasted out from Denis O'Brien's nascent radio empire and in the corner sat a massive brown boxed TV set, on which we watched John Major win the 1992 UK General Election. As there was no washing machine and no phone, the year was marked by regular pilgrimages to a launderette on the South Circular Road that only ran cold water through the machines no matter what the cycle, and to the bank of payphones at the intersection of Harrington Street and South Circular on a Sunday night, to queue with scores of other students for a five-minute call home. This was also the spot where many of the most enduring friendships of my life were forged.

The most valuable part of my first-year education was entirely extra-curricular, and mastering the art of hanging around was a full-time occupation. I had come to Trinity so that I could stay in Ireland, and I was staying in Ireland to row, specifically to train with a very talented UCD student. In rowing, like so many sports, hanging around is very structured. You're either waiting or recovering. While you wait – for a full crew to arrive, for equipment, slip access, race schedule, a break in the weather – you are talking over the best last race or worst last session and mentally preparing for what you're about to do. If you're recovering, you stretch, eat, drink, pitch the boat or talk over the best last race or worst last session. This was not the form of hanging around being practised by my newly minted, very urbane arts friends.

We had to either stay in the library or go out – to the Buttery, or the back bar in Kehoe's, which was still a single long red wooden bench – to get warm enough to sleep. It's hard to get up at 6 am when you've been dancing in the sitting room until two in the morning. It's a tough choice between evening circuits and spag bol with whoever might be dropping by. It's no fun coming back on Saturday afternoon, wet and cold, to a flat that is also wet and cold. The rowing didn't last.

Though I never perfected the art of the ramp (which may explain why I couldn't see that boy clearly enough at the time), with new friendships secure I went back to DULBC in second year. The coach was a student, a Senior Sophister, and the only person I had ever seen researching training schedules from books. From a rag-tag group of women with various skills, mixed motivations and varying physical attributes emerged a finely tuned crew in a pitch-perfect boat that sat under starter's orders at the final of the College Eights at the 1993 Henley Women's Regatta.

I did try to keep my hand in with the hanging around, and efforts expended there absented me from a few training sessions – on the water in Islandbridge the day after the 1993 Trinity Ball was not my finest hour. That Wednesday before we flew to London for the regatta was the last day with my non-rowing friends before we all scattered for the summer and then on to our Erasmus destinations, and my reluctance to leave them was partly responsible for me missing the flight to London (luckily I was put on a later one). But I had never been so well prepared for one race. As a unit, we knew exactly how many strokes it should take us to get down the course. The drilling was so deeply ingrained that even without instruction from the cox each of us knew precisely when to change gear.

We had rowed three heats to qualify, defeating Liverpool in a loosener – coming down the course in 5' 45" – then Reading in 5' 25", with a few errors that got us over the jitters. The semi-final to qualify out of our group would be the biggest challenge. If we could beat Tufts University from Boston, the final would be straightforward and the cup would be ours. This crew of Amazonian Americans was so well matched that they might well have been clones of each other. Our coach Dave had watched them warm up, practise and race their early heats, while we, like horses too easily spooked, were sent away from the course to do some structured hanging around. Tufts pushed us down that course in 5' 09" and over the last 500 meters we inched away with every stroke to finish two-thirds of a length ahead of them. It was textbook but it was tough. As it turned out the final was tighter than we expected, the winning time was 5′11″, the distance a canvas – the surge of a strong release from the Lady Eleanor Holles schoolgirls lifting their boat over the line just as ours was at the slowest point of the stroke. It was devastating and not a word was spoken as we lifted the boat off the water. The years at Trinity were a time and place when we all did things for the first time – and that was the first time I ever cried after losing a race. It was also the last time I ever rowed a full season.

When I came back for fourth year, after Erasmus in Lille, many of that crew had graduated and moved on. I never went much to the Pav, but was delighted that a picture of us hung on the wall of fame in there for a while. It was an official photo taken on the water so the one person you couldn't see was the coach on the bank, recording everything we did in order to calculate what we needed to do next, and who deserved the most credit.

If I could read the runes, I might have been able to foresee that more than twenty years later I would be living in Boston with the man that boy on the ramp became, rowing recreationally on the same stretch of the Mystic River where the Tufts crew had trained. And still hanging around, albeit virtually, every single day with that wonderful woman I met on the train, and the others who came to eat and dance and hang around with us as we moved across the city and into our adult lives.

Since graduating, **Penny Storey** (TCD 1991–95, English and Psychology; 1995–96, M.Phil. Textual and Visual Studies) has professionalized her art of hanging around universities. She worked at Trinity in the Student Records and Admissions Offices before joining the telecommunications research centre CTVR as a manager. She is currently living in Greater Boston with Neil Ardiff (TCD 1991–95, French and History of Art), where she is a co-director at the policy research center CIERP housed at the Fletcher School, Tufts University, and is studying for a Ph.D. in Higher Education at UMass Boston.

TRINITY WITHOUT THE PIMM'S

austin duffy

MY AMERICAN WIFE insists on Trinity every time we're in Dublin. It's not what you'd think. As my father says, America is just as old as anywhere else. Besides, once you get beyond a hundred years everything can be vaunted, and the States has plenty of venerable institutions. So it's not the age of the place *per se*, but the Book of Kells that draws her in. She does the tour every time. (An artist herself, by way of majoring in illustration, she views the anonymous monks as the *sine qua non* of graphic design, the origin myth of pretty much all that came afterwards in her field.) The last time, I admit to having left her on her own. The BoK doesn't do it for me I'm afraid. I went for a browse in Hodges Figgis on Dawson Street and met up with her afterwards for a pint in Grogan's. She turned up excited, laden down with a plastic bag full of old maps – nineteenth-century Dublin et cetera – that she was going to put to use in some sort of collage, I think. I'm sure I'll get it when I see it. (This year, while I return to our apartment in Washington DC – and my job as a medical oncologist at the National Cancer Institute – she is staying on in Dublin to take up an international residency at the MART in Rathmines.)

So on each occasion I have to make a decision about Trinity. And each time, it seems hard to credit that I actually went there, that the place existed as the living, breathing focal point of my life for six years, as opposed to merely what every tourist appreciates – no small thing either – that cold historicity, that cocoonment from Dublin as you cut through the Arts Block and across Front Square, where I lived once for the period of a year, my final one, from 1997–98. (My last act as a student was to close the Front Gate behind me to get a 5 am taxi to the airport, en route to six weeks of post-finals hedonism in Vietnam. Attempted hedonism, I should say – the experience was fabulous but not all that different from my college one, apart from the humidity.)

Can I stipulate that it was an immense privilege to go to Trinity, and agree that you don't have to look very far at all to see the enormous size and shape and statistical unlikelihood of that privilege. (Outside my apartment building in DC at the moment they're digging a big hole in the ground. No fun in the Baltic winters they get here, and – at the risk of racial profiling – I'm guessing the men in it don't have health insurance, much less have they been asked to write nostalgically about their third-level educational experiences.) And then there are the backs of others. My mother's secretary wage in an auctioneer's office that went direct every Friday from her boss's hand into my BoI account; she had sole possession of it for the fifteen minutes it took for her to walk down Clanbrassil Street (Dundalk) to the bank. It's a poignant thought now, but back then I went straight to the Lincoln Inn. And thus it was for many of us who did not come from money, cheered on from the sidelines as the first college-goers in a long file of people who had laboured in some other menial zone far beneath their gifts. TCD was not unique in this regard but perhaps, in the context of Irish society, it was the first manifest part of what the Americans now call social mobility.

I studied medicine. It staggers me to think back now on how little thought I put into making that decision. (I genuinely thought there were only one or two options.) It's even more staggering that it worked out so well, but I only realized that afterwards, long after Trinity I'm afraid, thousands of miles away in the oncology ward of Wellington Hospital, New Zealand, where it suddenly occurred to me that I could do this thing and even thrive at it. Prior to that, and especially during college, I was infuriatingly non-committal, muted about participation in anything that required me to back myself and therefore lose a bit of the self-effacement I took to wearing like a mask, and which of course was its own conceit. For a long time, remembering this reticence and dwelling upon it led to a degree of ambivalence about my college years. For certain I can't lay claim to the archetypal Trinity experience – though I suspect I am in the majority there – and which I would struggle to define anyway. The Strauss Ball perhaps, Pimm's parties in the Provost's Garden, the Hist, the Phil, the whatever. I didn't do any of those things and it is not with pride that I attest on behalf of me and my buddies that, whilst attending the most unique university in Ireland, we superimposed upon it the most generic, transplantable experience. We could have been in Limerick for God's sake, but it's not really a complaint. Did anybody really have that experience? The answer is yes, of course, a few heroes who were better able to run without hesitation into the centre of things at an earlier age and – I realize now – are only to be admired. (Recently I had the great pleasure of meeting one of them by chance, in The Stag's Head over Christmas, and who I instantly remembered from fresher year and his run at Student's Union rep. His schtick was to drape himself in the American flag, his slogan: 'I'll bring your daddy home'. Genius. I probably didn't even vote for him. I probably didn't vote at all.)

I hung around with six or seven lads, all still great friends. The centre of gravity was the kitchen of whatever flat one or other of us was living in. I laughed my head off ten times a day, minimum, for six years. But I was a minor player, always holding back on the periphery, a little cowed by the dominant personalities of the others, who were smarter, funnier, more knowledgeable about the world, even though none of us knew anything. In all of that time I probably laughed more than I spoke. And this, I think, is where the ambivalence comes from, or used to come from: that when I looked back I saw someone who was not an individual yet, whether out of immaturity or provincialism or a simple lack of experience. Maybe those are all the same thing. Either way it used to be a source of frustration for me that I didn't make as much of that whole time as I could have. When again would you get six years with so little of life's pressure bearing down? I could have learnt Russian for God's sake, or windsurfing, or karate. Or for that matter donned a tuxedo to drink Pimm's in the Provost's Garden. What is Pimm's anyway? Did they wear a tux to do it?

It didn't help that as medical students we were relegated to the Hamilton building and its modern sterility. There was a general lack of lounging around – not enough gaps in the timetable. If you made it in to campus you might as well go to lectures, which were an unreasonable 9 to 5. (More often than not I didn't bother. Two girls in our class – Teresa, Ruth, thank you! – took excellent notes. We spent hours in PrintBiz on Nassau Street photocopying them in the run-up to each exam.) It seems quaint now to think these end-of-year pressures were the closest thing to fear. Although there was also the anatomy building of course, tucked away, quietly fearsome, like the reptile house of a zoo. And Professor O'Brien, who was liable to pick you out with her red laser as it jumped around the amphitheatre to ask you about some obscure ligament or nerve root or artery. (The most terrifying part of dissecting your first dead body is the video they show beforehand. Two people fainted at the sight of some old guy wearing a white coat telling us about the do's and the don'ts, the ethics of how to behave and about the – totally unrecognizable by the way – person of the departed. After that it was as mundane as you can imagine, another thing to try and skip.)

I did have some of my own unique Trinity experiences. I saw Brad Mehldau in the Hyde lecture theatre, before anyone had heard of him. I collapsed after the pre-Med Ball cocktail reception in the Buttery, never making it to the Burlington. (Woke up the next morning with a bicycle tyre mark that ran down the back of my white shirt.) And after finals a group of us ganged up on our friend from Clonmel and undressed him – he'd worn the same lumberjack shirt every day for six years. With some sense of ritual we set it on fire in Front Square. Most of the memories are mundane, very pleasant to recall – my final year when I shared rooms with my pal The Gal, a psychiatrist now in Toronto, the hours we stood smoking at our first-floor window, looking out at what my father calls the passing parade, milling around beneath us, and like us, not overly concerned about all that much.

In fourth year – the beginning of clinical attachments in one or other of the affiliated hospitals – our class split into two and you had to chose between the Meath/Adelaide or the newer, more academic, sterile St James'. My mates chose the former, which was the traditional choice of all the characters, and smokers too, more or less. To St James' went the conscientious, the dutiful, the earnest. And me, to everyone's surprise. As strikings-out for new ground go, it was not exactly the stuff of ballads, but it felt massive at the time, a conscious attempt at some sort of self-assertion. This is not *post-facto* narrative shaping:

I explained it thus at the time, to my friends who thought I was nuts, but they were also too decent to say they knew what I was getting at.

After fourth year, Trinity itself began to fade. The hospitals reared up instead, frightening places. On consultant ward rounds, you'd hide at the back but the bastard would always remember you were there. All your ignorance highlighted, standing around some poor fucker's bed. They alone seemed to pity you. The best you could do was make your stupidity amusing for everyone else, the interns, SHOs and registrars on the team, whose actual job it was to know these things. (They mostly didn't.) It was only later you realized they were grateful to have you there as the lightning rod, representing an obvious target for the wrath emerging from on high. A consultant whose first name was Napoleon gave me shit for not listening to somebody's eyeball for a *bruit*. I didn't know it was a thing. (It's not really.)

I've gotten over the ambivalence, and any self-criticisms directed backward at that young man from Dundalk, whoever the hell he was, and on the way to becoming, funded by his mother's wage; foolish, naive, as uncultured as you can imagine, holding back on the edge as if waiting for something to happen. He was all of those things of course, but that seems perfectly OK to me now – that there was no rush for life to begin, nor should there have been. What was Trinity for me? Friends for life. A nice and famous place as the backdrop to early adulthood, where all sorts of things were put on hold. As I said, I laughed my head off ten times a day, minimum, for six years. Hard to top that really.

Austin Duffy (TCD 1992–98; Medicine) comes from Dundalk. After completing a medical internship in St James' Hospital, and a period of travelling and working overseas, he returned to Ireland to complete specialist registrar training in the field of medical oncology. In 2006 he moved to the United States, completing a fellowship at Memorial Sloan Kettering Cancer Center in New York, before moving to Washington DC, where he is currently a practising medical oncologist at the National Cancer Institute, specializing in the development of immune-based treatments for gastrointestinal cancers. Duffy is also a writer. In 2011, he was awarded RTÉ's Francis MacManus award for his short story 'Orca'. His debut novel **This Living and Immortal Thing** was published in 2016.

FEELING LUCKY

paschal donohoe

I HAVE SO MANY different memories from my time in Trinity but one feeling permeates all of them – the lyrics change but the tune stays the same – and that feeling was the sheer luck of recognizing, there and then, that I was having a wonderful experience; one which would immeasurably change and improve everything that would follow it. I knew at the time that it was not something to be taken for granted, and I felt it from my very first day on campus.

I studied politics and economics from 1992 to 1996 and my earliest memory is of Freshers' Week, and walking through Front Gate into the bustling market-place of societies. Like many a Junior Freshman, I joined lots of different clubs, but three in particular stand out: the Phil, Young Fine Gael and the Fencing Society.

Even though I never managed to attend a single meeting or joust with the Fencing Society, I remember always using it as an example of all that Trinity had to offer – there was something so enticing about waving a sword or stick at an opponent. Alas I never made it to a single duel and I've resisted the temptation since then! However, the other two societies played a big part in much of what happened to me during the rest of my time in College, not to mention in the years after.

The Graduates' Memorial Buliding – home to Trinity's debating societies – meant a lot to me. My first experience there was of participating in the Maiden

Speakers' Debate. I had debated a lot in secondary school but nothing prepared me for that first night in the GMB. Standing by a box that, to my anxious mind, appeared to exude hints of both the greatness and humiliation of previous speakers. The silent audience, and being unsure as to whether the silence was because they were bored or enthralled. That same audience erupting into a roar, the reason for which would be inexplicable at the time, but would play in slow motion in your mind for days afterwards. At the end of Junior Freshman year I was elected Secretary to the Phil and spent a wonderful summer in the top floor of the GMB writing to potential guests and organizing the schedule for the year. Each week was locked in combat with our great rival, the Hist, to get the biggest crowd and best speaker. I loved it.

I also had a great time as part of Young Fine Gael, and my stand-out memories include a series of lunchtime meetings between TDs and members. Conferences, at home and abroad, were a source of sheer fun as much as any political deliberation, but in the end, I found it a bit too much. I wasn't consumed by politics – that came later! – and at the end of my second year, I remember consciously deciding to withdraw from it. At that stage I began to think I might try to become a public representative later in life and I reasoned that it would take up enough time then, so best focus on other things in College. That's what I did, and for the last two years of college life I was not involved in YFG at all.

I suppose that was because I was enjoying so much else.

First of these was my friends. I arrived in College as a shy teenager and making friends within my huge class, not to mention within societies and across the college, was great and scary – all at the same time. Unfortunately, the cut and thrust of a busy life means that I have lost contact with many of them in the intervening years, and that is a genuine regret. But those with whom I have kept in contact matter to me as much now as they did then. Weddings, baptisms, fortieth birthday parties, and the sadder events that come with getting older, have all flowed from those formative friendships.

The second was my subjects – I loved them, and their study eventually led to a career in public and political life. Politics introduced me to everything from game theory to Athenian democracy and the study of checks and balances in American political institutions. Through Antoin Murphy I first learned about

a subject that continues to fascinate me – the economics of monetary integration. Little did I realize then that concepts of real economic convergence and
convertibility would have such seismic political and economic consequences.

Economics was equally stimulating, and was brought to life by the history
of monetary economics and the economics of transport. I remember the head-
spinning difficulty of quantitative economics and the fact that I barely passed
that subject made me realize that life as an economist was not for me. Oddly
enough, though, it was the study of economics that made me realize how
important politics was and is. The nature of political and public institutions is
fundamental to the performance and design of an economy.

A great pleasure has been the experience of meeting former tutors later
in life. Sean Barrett lectured me in the economics of competition in transport.
To my occasional discomfort, he has acted as transport spokesperson for the
University Senators in Seanad Éireann, and to this day I always leave a debate
or conversation with Sean knowing more than I did at the start.

Finally, my time in Trinity is defined by a vivid sense of place: climbing
the stairs in the GMB, feeling at home in a building, cherishing the fact that I
had a key for it. Walking through the Front Square early in the morning, on
the way to lectures; the Lecky Library, where I always sat in the same row of
desks, adjacent to the Berkeley Library and looking out on the green of Fellows'
Square. The temptation to spend time out there, as opposed to wrestling with
textbooks, was always great. I resisted it most of the time, but wish now I'd
spent a little bit less time in the library and more time in the sun. The seminar
rooms in the Arts Block, where I realized the difference between an essay and
an argument or thesis that you could stand over and defend. The long banks of
computers in the Arches, where Sunday afternoons where spent typing essays.
The café in the Arts Block, where coffee on an hourly basis was a prerequisite.
The Pav and the Buttery, where Thursday and Friday nights pulsed away in the
company of friends. The society posters, layered on top of each other by week's
end – but the walls bare again on Monday morning, all set for another week of
agitation or fun.

Of course there were difficult moments and challenges along the way. The
stress of exams. The pressures of student and social life. The occasional feelings of solitude, and the rest, that are natural when you are a tiny part of a

huge organization. But what a place and what a time. I loved it all and to this day, never walk by Front Gate without that same, long-ago feeling of luck and gratitude for the years I spent there.

Paschal Donohoe (TCD 1992–96; Politics and Economics) is the Fine Gael TD for Dublin Central and the Minister for Public Expenditure and Reform. Prior to this he was the Minister for Transport, Tourism and Sport and has also served as Minister for European Affairs at the Department of An Taoiseach and the Department of Foreign Affairs. Paschal was first elected as a TD in Dublin Central in February 2011, where he topped the poll. He was a member of Seanad Éireann from 2007 to 2011 and served as member of Dublin City Council from 2004 to 2007. Prior to Trinity College, Paschal attended St Declan's CBS, Cabra.

THE ACCIDENTAL ART HISTORIAN

brenda moore-mccann

I CAME to Trinity later than most, as a mature student. It was not my first time at university – I had previously studied medicine at University College Dublin in the 1960s. However I had always had an interest in the arts, and throughout my twenty-year medical career I had taken a number of extramural courses in literature. When I decided it was time to explore this interest more seriously, I opted for a diploma course I had heard about in Anglo-Irish literature at Trinity. By then, however, the course had been upgraded to a degree and as I was already juggling the running of a family-planning clinic and my own family, I decided that it would not be feasible to take on such a commitment. So I enquired if there were any other diploma courses available. And that was how I came to enroll in the Purser-Griffith Diploma in the History of European Painting in October 1990. As often happens in life, I became an art historian almost by accident.

I was very keen to do the diploma in Trinity as in my youth, Catholics were prohibited from entering the college without permission from the then Archbishop of Dublin, John Charles McQuaid – it felt like a second chance. The course consisted of two lectures and one seminar per week. With the support of my husband and the last son still at home, I was able to continue working while studying for the diploma.

Entering university as a mature student requires a number of significant adjustments. Arriving with experience in a different sphere of life, where I had been in charge of doctors and nurses, and treated patients, it was strange to take my place among a diverse group of people from a younger generation. It was as if one was divesting oneself of one persona and acquiring another that was, as yet, completely unknown. There were times when I felt it was important to bite my tongue to allow space for younger students to air their opinions. Another aspect of the age difference was my relative closeness in years to some of the lecturers, and the fact that the younger students were the same age as my own sons. However, the apparent gulf between generations did not last for too long as we gradually all became part of the same great adventure. As there were a number of other mature students besides me in the class, the initial temptation might have been to align oneself exclusively with them – however, I made a special effort to integrate as much as possible with the younger students (without ignoring the older ones either). Part of this was to try and sit in different places in the lecture theatre, as well as chatting over coffees or lunches. The field trips abroad were huge fun and greatly facilitated that closer integration. I remember in particular one trip to Rome, when one of the younger students burst into song in Borromini's church of Sant'Ivo alla Sapienza. In such exquisite surroundings with excellent acoustics, the effect was electric. Another memorable moment – though rather more intimidating – was when one of our lecturers, the much-loved and fiercely exacting Eddie McParland, asked me to explain the mythological scene on the ceiling of Palazzo Pamphili on the Piazza Navona (he knew that classical civilization was my second subject). Luckily I knew that it depicted the life of Aeneas by Pietro da Cortona, and somehow I managed to get through it!

So why leave the field of medicine? 'Didn't you like it?' 'How could you leave medicine when taxpayers have paid so much towards your education?' 'Why did you choose art – it's so different!' And (plaintively/anxiously), 'What are you going to *do*?' These were just some of the questions I was confronted with once my decision became known. I found some of them revealing of the ways in which society in general evaluated both disciplines. At the root of much of the incredulity lay a particular understanding of the relative merits of both fields. Medicine, it appeared, was clearly superior to art. Apart from the social prestige of the profession, it was also a more useful, important and intellectual profession than art. The latter, while nice to have on one's walls or to look at in museums at home or abroad, was merely an indulgence, a luxury. It did not really matter. Depending on my assessment of the sincerity of the questioner, I gave short or long answers. The short one was that as I had worked in medicine for over twenty years in various capacities, I felt that I had repaid the taxpayer through practice, teaching and publishing. And I had loved medicine and would dearly liked to have done more work, if specific retraining facilities had been available at the time. I had always worked part-time once my family arrived because, for me, it was important to be there for my children, but also because of the family dynamics. By this I mean that my husband, whom I had met at medical school in UCD, took on the task of pioneering the creation of a National Stem Cell Transplant (Bone Marrow) Unit during the 1980s. The onerous nature of such an endeavour required that one parent had to anchor the family. Yet I had always nurtured the idea of getting back to work full-time as soon as the time was right. That time did eventually come, but with it also came the realization that it would have to be something other than medicine. This was because of immense changes in diagnostic procedures and therapeutics, coupled with the lack of retraining opportunities. Pondering all these realities took five years, but then, it was time to move on.

While still practising medicine, I began the diploma course. Within a couple of weeks it was clear to me that this was something I had always wanted to do – that is, to understand more about art and the ideas surrounding it. As one of my sons remarked: 'At least now you will know your art from your elbow, Mum!' Art had always been part of my early youth through trips to Greece, Italy and elsewhere with my parents, and the enthusiasm of one of my aunts for Evie Hone. As a medical student, I was enthralled by a guide at the Uffizi in Florence who made the paintings come alive. Now was my chance to do the same! At the end of the course I got the Purser-Griffith scholarship. I had to go on. So I resigned from medicine and pursued the degree course, and subsequently a Ph.D.

While going through the degree, one of my lecturers, Catherine Marshall, mentioned an Irish doctor to me who was better known as an artist, writer and critic living in the United States. The work of this artist, Brian O'Doherty (aka Patrick Ireland), became the subject of my BA thesis and then my Ph.D. Subsequently it became the first book on his work. Discovering this artist was a serendipitous pleasure but also a challenge. Dealing with a living artist may not always be easy but in my case I think it was aided by the fact that we were both chimeras with a shared medical training and involvement in the world of art. But more than that, O'Doherty's work, to my surprise, brought me to all of the areas I had long wished to pursue outside of medicine: literature, poetry, music, theatre, art theory and ideas, politics and Italy. It was an incredible journey intellectually that stretched and at times puzzled me, but almost always was a delight. My new persona had arrived!

As mentioned earlier, I had studied classical civilization alongside art history. It was such a pleasure to find affinities with writers from a couple of thousand years ago. At one stage in the course I remarked to Professor John Dillon that it seemed as if we had learnt nothing in the intervening centuries. He replied that a few thousand years was only an eyeblink in the vast aeons of time. On one occasion I had to meet him in his office to discuss an essay I had written. When he opened the door, I walked over to a vacant chair. I then realized that it was his and apologized profusely. Being the gentleman he is, I had to stay there until the end of the interview.

At the end of the three years I had to decide which of the two subjects would be the major for my final fourth year. This was difficult but in the end I decided that my interest in contemporary art history might provide more opportunities later. As it turned out, this was the right decision, and through it I have been lucky enough to meet some extraordinary and creative people, visit wonderful museums and galleries worldwide and still feel that I too can make a contribution to our culture. Directly from my experience in Trinity, I have been able to lead an enriched life, which has also made an impression on the family, all of whom engage in creative pursuits at a professional level.

In 2008 the School of Medicine in Trinity, led by Professor Shaun McCann, my husband, inaugurated a series of medical humanities modules for first-year medical students to which I was invited to contribute. At first I was reluctant (understandably, I had concerns about nepotism), but then I was persuaded that I was probably one of the only people in Ireland with degrees in both medicine and art. This gave me the opportunity to bring my dualistic experience together. Rather than teach a course on art history, I decided to invent a course, which would demonstrate areas of overlap between the two fields. At a basic level, both employ the same tools to perceive a world. The course is interactive, and utilizes art as a tool to show the processes of how we look and see; the nature of the fragilities involved in the perceptive process and the illusions we accept in trying to make sense of the world. No prior knowledge of art is required. Oscillating continually between medicine and art, the artwork in effect, becomes a proxy for the patient. Art and medical imagery are shown side by side, and the hope is that by juxtaposing two largely different ways of thinking, a richer, more critical appreciation of life and the approach to medicine may occur.

For me, at least, to discover an alternative way of thinking to that which more and more relies almost exclusively on the reductive nature of the scientific method, was a liberation. I found, even though they may have lived hundreds of years ago, that there were artists who expressed what I had always intuitively felt about certain issues. These artists and writers became in a sense my friends. I admired those who often had to make their statements in paint, ink or another medium in a hostile sociocultural environment. Thus the happy 'accident' whereby I became an art historian has not only enriched my own personal life but has convinced me of the vital necessity for greater understanding between the sciences and the humanities. They have more in common than is generally thought.

Brenda Moore-McCann (TCD 1992–96, History of Art and Classical Civilisation; Ph.D. 2002, History of Art) is a medical doctor, art critic and writer on the visual arts. She works as a freelance lecturer teaching art history and also devised and teaches a medical humanities module to medical students at Trinity College Dublin. She has published widely, including the first monograph on the artist/critic/writer Brian O'Doherty (aka Patrick Ireland). She is an Assistant Professor (Adjunct), Trinity College Dublin; a member of the International Art Critics Association; a Member of the Programme Board of the Royal Hibernian Academy and an Honorary Patron of the Contemporary Irish Art Society. She is currently writing a book on the Rosc exhibitions, which will be published in 2017.

ENTER, WITH FLOUR

hugh o'conor

JEAN-PAUL IS SITTING in a bathtub. In case there was any doubt about it, the word BATH is painted in black on the side. I am standing behind a large wooden flat, wearing a long, emerald dress, holding clumps of flour in my fists, waiting for an orchestral piece from the Monkees' soundtrack *Head* to finish. As soon as it does, Teri Garr can be heard speaking the words: 'Quick! Suck it before the venom reaches my heart!' (She's playing an actress on a very fake-looking western movie sound stage, an arrow sticking out of her chest.) On cue, I take a running jump, hurl myself through the newspaper-covered wall of the living-room set, and land onstage Players' theatre in front of a lunchtime audience of about twenty (at least four are stoned).

It is 1 pm on Monday, 24 October 1994, and I am nineteen years old. I throw the flour in the air to simulate dust and collapse, face-first, on the ground. The play begins.

FRESHERS' WEEK had gone by in a blur. I joined Players as I was doing drama and theatre studies, and my classes would be in the same building – the wood-wattled Samuel Beckett Centre, which had only been open a year or so by then; Michael West's essay in the 1980s edition of *Trinity Tales*, 'Autumn Testament', tells wonderfully of the Lombard Street days. My single honours class numbered about twelve, so we went in search of fellow mischief-makers. We didn't have to go far.

The Freshers' Co-op, a musical revue and staple first show of the season, was duly auditioned for, upstairs in Players' theatre itself. Dougal Thomson's *Asterix: Man, Myth or Mackerel?* was being co-directed by the already legendary powerhouse team of Pauline Turley and Lucy Ryan, second- and third-year students on the Players committee. We waited fearfully in the lobby, looking at homemade posters of past productions Blu-Tacked to the walls, and wondering why we were doing this to ourselves.

Ushered into the theatre, I stood before the pair, notebooks ready, eyes assessing. They were aware I had acted before, and asked smart, interesting questions. I don't remember what piece I auditioned with, but I remember thinking it hadn't gone well, and left downhearted as always.

Parts were posted next day on the bulletin board in the main corridor. Shoulders were patted. Martin McKeown was Asterix. They had taken pity on me. I would be Obelix, who was sad and silly and didn't have to do very much, which meant more fun hanging out backstage and less terror while standing on it.

I went full method for the Belgian giant – pillow under the t-shirt, and grapes for nipples, which invariably burst during the shows. Lines were forgotten. Cues were missed. Parents were offended. We're planning a reunion tour in 2019.

IT WAS my father who had insisted I go to college. I worked sometimes as an actor by then, in summers between school, but he didn't want to hear about that. He was a musician and a music teacher, and as he always warned prospective students, music is a hard, often heartbreaking life, and if you can do anything else for a living, for God's sake do it. Something to fall back on; a degree in something, at least. I wanted to make films, I thought, since I had been doing that throughout my teens, and writing stuff, so drama studies seemed a good compromise. My father, it's safe to say, was not overly delighted.

If you got enough points, it came down to an interview at the Beckett Centre. I attended with two other nervous applicants. When faced with the panel alone, I overcompensated for fear with an unearned arrogance. I revealed that ultimately I wanted to make films, which I could immediately tell wasn't what they wanted to hear. They asked what I was reading; Franz Kafka's *The Trial*, I replied, triumphantly – which was, tragically, true, and no doubt incredibly annoying. The face of Brian Singleton, now head of drama, betrayed no emotion.

Afterwards, I said goodbye to the other two, and walked out of Front Square, convinced I would never return. But a few days later, the news filtered back. Bizarrely, miraculously, I was in.

DRAMA AND THEATRE STUDIES classes consisted of studying the history of theatre-making around the world, pretending to read lots of plays in the library and watching lots of bad VHS copies of plays taped off the TV in class. In second year we'd start writing a bit, and maybe even begin making our own work. In third year you'd study specific chosen subjects in detail. By fourth year you'd complete your thesis, and potentially put on a play in the Beckett Centre. It all sounded pretty full on.

The reality was, first and second year mainly consisted of – Players.

What was exciting about Players was that anyone could put on anything they wanted, as long as it was agreed to by the committee. Two shows ran for a week, Monday to Saturday, lunchtime or evening. So after class we'd rush to Players and start planning shows of our own, or help others with theirs, then go to see a show, retire to the Buttery to talk about it, get hammered, end up at a party with lots of other students, try to get off with them (and sometimes actually even succeed) then come in late and hungover to class the next morning, scrawling HELP ME GOD HELP ME into a notebook and feigning interest as a lecturer discussed the use of masks in seventeenth-century Kabuki theatre, all the while waiting to rush back to Players and repeat the same thing over and over again.

My first big audition was for a production of Eric Bogosian's *Sex, Drugs, Rock & Roll*, which was being directed by a third-year student, Jason O'Mara, an actor and director who other students spoke of in hushed, reverential tones.

The audition was held in a large white room off the Buttery. Jason was sitting behind a desk with an assistant, looking 100 per cent the chiselled leading man he now is. I did my audition piece – a monologue from the play about a homeless man who collects bottles and cans in Manhattan – and finished with an attempt at a dramatic flourish. Jason didn't say anything. Neither did I. Finally, he spoke.

'Good. Try it again. And this time, don't show it, just feel it. Trust me; we'll get it if you do.'

I took this in. I tried it again. It felt better.

Jason worked us insanely hard. He was part of the older Players gang who had come up through the ranks, and were now its stars and leaders. They were funny and welcoming and brilliantly talented and sexy as fuck. *Sex, Drugs, Rock & Roll* went down well and was chosen for the Student Drama Awards in Galway. We trooped over on the train and stayed up late in Kinlay House hostel and laughed and cried and got off with each other and performed the play in a warehouse on campus and won an award and it felt amazing.

What impressed us most was their drive, their ambition, their compassion: people like Jason and Pauline and Lucy and Brídín Murphy-Mitchell and Justine Mitchell and Ciara O'Callaghan and Evelyn O'Rourke were making brilliant shows, and taking time to care about each other, too. Michael Cregan and Michael Parke lived in rooms by the Beckett Centre, and as well as being the perfect example of a loving couple, welcomed us in and made us feel at home; they inspired us to become better people.

We tried to follow in their wake. Shows were put on to impress each other, but also just for the hell of it. We saw and performed Stoppard and Churchill and Pinter and Fo and Ionesco and Carr and Shakespeare and Marlowe and they may have been terrible, but that wasn't the point. Steve Wilson and Martin McKeown put on a stage production of *Reservoir Dogs* and got a mention and quote of approval from Quentin Tarantino in *Empire*. Karl Golden wrote and performed two monologue plays that absolutely destroyed us. Simon Doyle directed a production of *Ubu Roi* called *Snooks* that influenced me hugely. Will O'Connell formed his own company, I Smell Burning, and did a production of *House of Blue Leaves* at the City Arts Centre that I still remember vividly, with Will mournfully, unwaveringly playing the piano to an assembled cast that included Sonya Kelly and Charlotte Harrison, while the rest of us sat in the audience, in bits.

IT WAS all this inspiration that led me to end up backstage, wearing a dress, with flour in my hands, about to launch myself through a newspaper-covered wall and into the twenty-minute comedy piece, *Tex & Ned*, that we performed one week in second year. I had written a few stories with these crazed neighbour characters in a copybook. I cobbled them into a script, and together with some friends we managed to convince the Players committee to let us put it on.

During the show we ate raw eggs, delivered long speeches about the futility of war, and beat the shit out of each other on numerous occasions. The only other character's job was to throw a brick through the window – willing friends rotated the position – then appear at the end, waving, as we danced offstage to the strains of 'Beatle Bones 'n' Smokin' Stones' by Captain Beefheart. It was insane, Beckett-lite nuttiness and we all should have known better.

At the end of the show's run, Brian Singleton sat me down and warned me that if I kept on the way I was going and didn't knuckle down to work I might not make it to the end of the line. He doesn't remember doing this, but I do, and I took his advice seriously.

Hugh O'Conor (left) *as Tex and Jean Paul Van Cauwelaert as Ned,*
Trinity Players 1994.

It was time. Although we all continued to go and see stuff at Players, I only did a few more shows in third year. And in fourth year, I focused, inevitably, on 'real' work. By that stage, the Jasons and Paulines and Lucys had gone, emerging blinking into the real world, and we were on our way out too.

But that day, as I waited in the wings to make my entrance, there was nowhere I would have rather been: 'Quick! Suck it before the venom reaches my heart!'

And off I went, crashing through the wall, into the imaginary world we all briefly, magically shared.

Hugh O'Conor (TCD 1993–97; Drama and Theatre Studies) is an actor, director and photographer. Not always in that order.

AN INNOCENT ABROAD

alex massie

HALF A LIFETIME AGO. What a thought that is. The years pass and the temptation to wash one's youth with nostalgia is as ever-present as it proves irresistible. We were younger then, after all, and all things seemed possible.

Dublin in the 1990s was another place. They did things differently then. I arrived in the autumn of 1993 following a disagreement with Cambridge University. I knew precisely nothing about Ireland, having neither Irish relatives nor any previous experience of the country, but Dublin saved me from spending my undergraduate years in Durham and that, by God, still counts as one of my life's greatest blessings.

So there I was, an innocent abroad. I bought copies of *The Ginger Man* and *The Beastly Beatitudes of Balthazar B* and reckoned them travel guide and self-help manual respectively. This may have been unwise. But back then, in that particular time and place, everything was an adventure.

Dublin was changing and it was, I now understand, a rare privilege to be present for the years when modern Ireland was, in so many ways, born. The 1990s were a hinge moment in Irish history; closing the door on one era and opening another to the next. When I arrived I was struck by the fact it seemed as though any young Irishman or Irishwoman's most precious possession was a visa entitling them to live and work in the United States. Five years later all that had changed; a future could be built in Ireland too.

They were, then, years of light and transformation. Years in which the nation's emerging sense of possibility was perfectly in tune with our own hopes and dreams. The scale and pace of that change remains breathtaking. Ten years before I arrived in Dublin the producers of *Educating Rita* – much of it filmed in Trinity – reckoned that 1980s Dublin looked more like 1960s Liverpool than Liverpool itself. The city seemed soaked in faded grandeur; there was an attractively shabby melancholy about the place. Much of Temple Bar was still untouched – trees sprouted from crumbling rooftops – and large areas of inner Dublin were, effectively, little more than derelict land.

It was, it is hard to remember, still an age in which Bewley's was considered the height of coffee. I remember a friend – Ciaran Power – returning from a summer in San Francisco with a suitcase full of Starbucks beans. This, we all agreed, was the very acme of sophistication. We were the last pre-mobile-phone generation of students; the last for whom notes left on Front Arch noticeboards were vital, and the last for whom computers were things you found in a lab. A different world entirely.

So Trinity was a great romance. It was Tim Campbell, with whom I had shared five years incarcerated in a Perthshire educational penitentiary, who first persuaded me to think about crossing the Irish Sea. In our first term we shared what could only be reckoned a hovel on North Great George's Street. Tim discovered rowing early on; I was swallowed by the GMB. I joined the Phil and the Hist on the first day of Freshers' Week and that was that.

Eugene Downes was auditor of the Hist that year and Jim O'Brien president of the Phil. There followed a tug-of-war for my affections that was won, in the end, by the Phil. The Hist was a little too solid, a touch too dependable, consistent and respectable for my tastes. The Phil, by contrast, had – or so it seemed to me – a raffish quality. The Phil's worst years might be very much worse than the Hist's poorer sessions but the Hist could never, or so I became convinced, touch the heights the Phil might reach in its better years. (As a general rule – though there were always dishonourable exceptions – the Hist nurtured more politicians than the Phil.) So that was Wednesday and Thursday nights sorted for the next four years. Motions reflected the times: there were the annual debates on abortion and Northern Ireland, for instance. That they were 'annual' said everything. No one's mind was ever changed on either subject but they were grand evenings of fierce and passionate disputation. Post-debate parties could be interesting too. You have not lived until you have seen a Liberal Democrat MP play 'The Sash' on a tin whistle in a Dublin pub.

Competitive debating was very different then. It had not yet been professionalized. Reading *The Economist* was the limit of our preparation. We held to the idea of the amateur; preparation and research was a kind of cheating. Anyone could win with knowledge; winning without knowledge was, we decided, the real test. This ensured victories were rare.

Matthew Magee, another Scottish exile, became my preferred debating partner. We were a cup team, not a league team. That is, on our better days we could give almost anyone a decent run for their money; on our worst we could lose to anyone. Consistency was not our forte. The world championships held in Stellenbosch, South Africa, were a case in point: we began very badly and things then got much, much worse. We finished fourth-last and were, officially, the worst English-speaking team in the world.

Four months later, we became the first Phil team – and only the third TCD pairing – to win the John Smith Memorial Mace, then as now the unofficial British and Irish championship. No one before or since has completed a double like that. Joe Guerin, by then president of the Phil, greeted our improbable triumph in fine style, telling *Trinity News* he felt 'like Khrushchev when Gagarin first ventured into space'. This was cutting it a trifle high but the point was well made.

I hate to think how many days – weeks, months, years in fact – were spent lounging and arguing the toss on the blue sofas of the Hist's Conversation Room. Many more, certainly, than in the library or lecture theatres. Those were strange lands for me, doubtless filled with monsters and therefore best avoided. Notionally I was embarked on a degree in European studies and then, following a change of direction, history. The department never seemed very interested in my attendance, however, and I was happy to reciprocate. University was for living, not studying. (I flunked third year history, which required passing no exams, by accepting an invitation to attend the Cannes Film Festival with my then girlfriend, Domenica Scorsese, when I should have been in the library writing long-overdue essays.)

Dublin was my real subject, however. These were the years in which, one by one and far too often, grand old Dublin boozers were ripped apart and refashioned to offer a facsimile of the authentic experience offered by the Irish pub at Frankfurt Airport. The fake became real because it was, I assume, presumed that tourists preferred the familiarity of bogus authenticity over the real thing. But the best of them – The Long Hall, The Palace, Neary's, Grogan's, and so on – retained a kind of immunity against this progress. For a while I lived with another girlfriend, Amanda Keogh, and Sheena Concannon in a tiny flat on Dame Street and revelled in the fact that all life's essentials – a 24-hour Spar, Iskander's kebab house, a bookmaker's and The Stag's Head – were within fifty feet of my front door. Bliss it was to be alive.

By then I'd expanded extra-curricular activities to move from the GMB to House Six and the publications committee. After years in the doldrums, *TCD Miscellany* was rescued by Ben Walsh and he bequeathed it to my care. Production values were close to non-existent but I still have, somewhere, copies of the magazines we produced and, though painfully earnest, they're hardly as bad as they might have been.

There was a strong Caledonian influence in Pubs. Matthew Magee co-edited *Trinity News* (with Amy Mahon), Graham McKendry was sports editor and Robin Gray served as news editor. Our proudest – the term is relative – achievement was a successful campaign to persuade the SU shop to stock Scotland's other national drink (and noted hangover cure), Irn-Bru. A shadowy organization known as PICT – the Preserve Irn-Bru Campaign Taskforce – lobbied the SU to this effect and earned vastly more coverage in the student press than their actions really warranted. But we ran PICT and, conveniently, we ran the press too. Enlisting the British Embassy to assist our efforts in boosting Scottish exports produced an invitation to attend the Embassy's 1997 general election party. We were first to arrive and last to leave and we were not invited back.

This wasn't our only racket. Nick Royle somehow persuaded the CSC to recognize and fund the Dublin University Soccer Appreciation Society, an organization which existed chiefly to subsidize Guinness and Carlsberg in Doyle's bar as we watched football on the TV. Occasionally other events were held. After one, Mark Lawrenson, the former Liverpool and Ireland defender, scandalized the committee by ordering a white wine spritzer. I've looked at him askance ever since.

Players became another obsession. Simon Carswell was president then. I flirted with the idea of drama school before coming to my senses. Still, by virtue of having taken the lead role in Heiner Müller's *Hamletmachine* (directed by Phil Levie) I can technically – if also weaselishly – claim to have played the Dane. The best production in which I featured was a performance of *Under Milk Wood* directed by Niall O'Driscoll. It was all a hoot.

Ah, what adventures! Trips to Leopardstown with the agreeable chancers from the Racing Society; a shambolic expedition to Kerry to make some kind of terrible zombie movie with the Video Society; Friday nights at Dalymount Park supporting Bohemians; occasional days of cricket in College Park. All this and much more besides.

Above all, perhaps, there was talk. Endless chattering and discussion in the GMB, House Six and Players; countless arguments and larks in The Stag's Head and elsewhere that cemented friendships forever. Dublin was, as least for me, an intoxicating blend of the exotic and the reassuringly familiar; like Britain but subtly different in a hundred various ways. I dare say I'd do a lot of things differently if I had my time again but I cannot regret the things we did. Those were the days, my friends, and we'll always have Dublin.

Qualified for nothing else, **Alex Massie** (TCD 1993–97; History) left Dublin and became a journalist. He joined the staff of **Scotland on Sunday** in 1998 before quitting and going freelance in 2003. He currently lives in Edinburgh and is a columnist for **The Times** and Scotland Editor of **The Spectator**. He is still not writing a novel.

HOW I LEARNED TO STOP STUDYING AND LOVE THE LECKY

anna carey

FIRST OF ALL, an apology. If you were attempting to study downstairs in the Lecky Library at any time between October 1993 and June 1997 but were unable to do so because a short, skinny, dark-haired girl (probably wearing Levi needle-cords, suede Converse One Stars and a t-shirt originally intended to be worn by a small child in the 1970s) was having a long conversation in a stage whisper louder than most people's actual voices, that girl was probably me. When I think of the Lecky, I don't think about writing essays and reading books about Brecht – though the fact that I'm now entitled to put BA (Hons) after my name shows that I must have done all of these things there. I think of my social life.

In my defence, I wasn't the only one. The Lecky was a strange place in the mid 1990s. This was partly because an acute shortage of desks meant that quite a lot of the students had to sit on the floor, and also because the Lecky was seen by many (though not all) arts students as both library and unofficial social club. People were always stopping to have conversations and leaving notes on friends' folder pads when they weren't sneaking glimpses at the current object of their lust or just graffitiing the desks (like the passionate Rod Stewart fan who carefully carved the words ROD THE MOD, FOREVER YOUNG across several in the German section).

In fact, the Lecky, and indeed the Arts Block as a whole, was a hotbed of hormones. Most of my friends had a library crush at some stage, a stranger who would be referred to by a nickname until his or her real name could be discovered. In a pre-internet age (arts students only got email accounts automatically in Michaelmas term 1995, when I was in third year, and we had no access at all to the brand-new World Wide Web), students would share gossip and ask for 'any info' on various boys they fancied by scrawling on the backs of the lavatory doors (and all over the frames). I'm not sure that reading scurrilous gossip on the back of a loo door was exactly what I had hoped university would be, but it was always entertaining.

I decided I wanted to go to Trinity as soon as I was old enough to think seriously about going to university, which was around the same time that my sister Lisa started her Trinity English and history degree in 1989. The fact that she went there – and sneaked me into one of her lectures to see David Norris talk about *A Room with A View* when I was about fourteen – made going to Trinity seem almost a matter of course, like going to the same school.

It wasn't the only reason, of course. I knew I wanted to do an arts degree, probably drama or English, and Trinity made sense for a number of reasons: it was in the city centre (as a suburban northsider, there was no way I wanted to drag myself from Drumcondra all the way over to Belfield and its surrounding dreary southside suburbs every day). The classes were relatively small. And it was old and it was beautiful.

If I'd had any doubts about where I wanted to go, they were dispelled in summer 1992, when I tagged along in the car as my mother dropped Lisa off to that year's Trinity Ball. In honour of the college's 400th birthday, purple spotlights were turned on Front Arch, while buckets of glitter were flung down from the roof. I gazed on enviously as Lisa and her mates walked through the magical, sparkling gates. Why would I go anywhere else?

I wanted to study drama and history of art, but after I made an embarrassing failure of my drama audition in spring 1993, I changed my CAO application to German, which I was studying at school and which, thanks to Edgar Reitz's recently aired TV epic *Die Zweite Heimat*, I had started to find romantic and strangely beautiful. And so, in October 1993, I began my German and history of art degree. One of my best friends from school was also studying

German, which made those first few months less daunting – though like most Freshers, I still had plenty of days when I wasn't sure what to do with myself.

But I always felt at home on campus, and by second year I was having the time of my life. After endless conversations with my friends throughout my schooldays about how boring everything was and how much we yearned for something, anything, to happen, suddenly we were in a place where every-thing *was* happening. Each Thursday and Friday night the queue to get into the Buttery snaked out across the cobbles of Parliament Square; when the warm weather kicked in, everyone decamped to outside the Pav.

For two of my undergraduate years, 1995 and 1996, there was no Trinity Ball. In 1996 the Ball was cancelled because of a security guard strike and even though the strike was called off at the last minute, it was too late for a proper ball. Instead, hastily photocopied signs appeared all over College urging everyone to descend on the Pav for a BYOB ball. In the end, so many turned up that they had to close all the gates by about nine o'clock; I was lucky enough to be inside by then, enjoying the chaos, but some friends ended up climbing over the railings.

I remember those years as a time of excitement, freedom and lots of new friends, many of whom are still my friends today. It was the people who made college for me. The intense friendships (which sometimes became more than friendships), bunking off lectures in favour of endless conversations in corners of the Arts Block, sitting on the boxy seats known inexplicably as the chocolate boxes. When, recently, I read *Tender* by Belinda McKeon, who was a couple of years behind me in College, I marvelled at how well she had captured one of the university arts student's greatest privileges: the ability to devote entire days to one's friends on a regular basis.

Once I was downstairs in the Lecky working on an essay when a passing friend, on whom I had had a library crush the previous year before transfer-ring my attentions to a less worthy boy, asked me if I wanted to get a coffee. I distinctly remember thinking, 'In the future, what will seem more important – this essay or hanging out with someone I like?' That afternoon, I chose my social life. Twenty years later, I don't remember what the essay was about, but I'm married to the boy who asked me to go for the coffee.

I would not recommend this approach to the younger generation, however, not least because I actually did care about my subjects and my ability to regularly put off studying in favour of spending three hours drinking hot chocolate in the JCR meant that I often ended up panicking about various exams and essays. I was generally able to pull these things off at the last minute, but it always stressed me out and I sometimes fell on my face; I had a full-blown panic attack in two exams, one in first year and one in fourth year, and had to go off and finish the exams in a room by myself.

My relationships with each my two departments were very different. Despite my initial terror at the German department's total immersion approach (from the very first day, all classes and lectures were conducted entirely in German), I felt quite at home in that slightly eccentric and sometimes flaky section of the Arts Block's fifth floor. I had almost complete freedom in choosing essay subjects, wrote my fourth-year dissertation on Brecht and Weill's *Threepenny Opera*, read lots of Kafka and studied Expressionist cinema, nineteenth-century feminism, the novels of anti-Nazi exiles and many, many different versions of the Faust legend (after I missed one Faust Projekt class, a friend told me it had been about Lessing's *Faust*. When I expressed my surprise to hear that he'd written one, she said, 'Anna, they all wrote a *Faust*').

Just a few feet away on the fifth floor was the history of art department, which adopted a more traditional (and, to me, dull) approach. It also lived up to all the social stereotypes associated with the subject: as the North Dublin state-school-educated daughter of public servants, I was very much in a minority. In second and third year, class trips to Italy were organized, which cost several hundred pounds. Financial assistance was available for those who qualified for it – which I didn't – but the few of us who simply couldn't afford to go were made to feel that we weren't sufficiently interested in our course.

I've never wanted to romanticize Trinity, to be one of those people who found excuses not to leave, who defines herself by her time in college. But I was very happy there, and whenever I take a shortcut through the campus now I feel a great amount of affection for the place. And if I had ever taken Trinity's charm for granted, I certainly didn't after I started my master's degree in journalism at DCU in October 1997.

DCU's remarkably ugly, dreary university campus was within walking distance of my parents' house. Every day for a long, miserable year I would trudge past the bus stop where, just a few months earlier, I boarded a bus that took me into a place full of fun and drama and loud conversations. And then I would walk down Collins Avenue to DCU, where the library was always as quiet as the grave. And where I never saw any glitter.

Anna Carey (TCD 1993–97; German and History of Art) is a journalist, author and scriptwriter from Dublin. She is a regular contributor to **The Irish Times** and RTÉ. She is the author of four books for young adults and her first book, **The Real Rebecca**, won the Senior Children's Book of the Year at the 2011 Irish Book Awards.

ROOMS

barry mccrea

I HAD BRONCHITIS in the Freshers' Week of 1993. More crippling than the illness, though, was the terror of missing out on some marvellous group that might constitute itself in the first days of college and then close its doors on new members forever. The thought of lying coughing in the little bed in my teenage bedroom in Glenageary while this went on in town without me was intolerable, so with ignored advice ringing in my ears, I prepared to haul myself the six miles to Front Gate. There was a further problem. Having a lung infection made it impossible to smoke, but smoking represented all I was going to Trinity to find: prohibited pleasures, fascinating and maybe dangerous people, some vision of life that I hazily thought of as 'European'. Not smoking in this crucial first week was a risk I could not run, so I limped first to Mrs Burke's chemist in Glasthule where I bought a box of clove-based herbal cigarettes, then got on the number 7 bus to An Lár.

I had come to study French and Spanish and at the Mod Lang Society reception I struck up a conversation with a glamorous-looking girl with short black hair who was a Senior Freshman in Spanish and who told me all about the department and the lecturers. I was on the hunt for interesting people but I must have cut quite an unusual figure myself as I stood there, my face a deathly yellow pallor, rattling and wheezing and wreathed in a thick, clove-scented mist.

'My voice isn't always like this,' I explained to my new friend in a gravelly, bronchial growl. 'I know I sound like Phyllis from *Coronation Street*.'

She offered a more dignified example: 'Or Marlene Dietrich.'

I **WAS** one of those Dubliners people complain about. I arrived in Trinity with a group of friends already, a few always-slagging-each-other boys from my secondary school and some better-read, more mature girls from the convent school across the road. In the early nineties, the European Union with the newly unified Germany at its centre was the horizon of newness and promise to which we looked, and many of us had come to Trinity to do modern languages. But town, too, was for me the first new frontier. The Dublin I had inhabited before was entirely contained within a suburban triangle from Ranelagh to Sandyford to Bray, and on arrival in Trinity that social space seemed suddenly cramped and far away.

There were more rooms in the house of Ireland than I had known. I was shocked and delighted to discover that the Anglo-Irish ascendancy really existed, people whose surname was the name of the town they were from; I made friends with a 'poetess' from Kerry who referred to everything she thought interesting as 'cosmic'; there was a Russian, rumoured to be a genius, who had come or fled from Ekaterinburg to study Italian. For the first months of college my Dublin friends and I lost each other as we discovered the true smallness of the world as we had known it, and spent our time in thrilling new friend-ships with people from Castlecomer and Dungannon and Manorhamilton, and learned about the life and literature of Vienna, Paris and Castille.

As I memorized new idioms and archaic grammatical forms in my language classes, I was slowly inventing a kind of private language of my own. I did four translations a week, into and out of French and Spanish respectively, but I was also performing another act of translation every day. Since I was from Dublin, I continued to live, or rather sleep, at home. I would sit reading or translating in the Lecky until half nine, and then, dizzy with new words and ideas, rush over to the Buttery, and then, dizzy with drink, I would get the last number 7 back out of town to Glenageary. I commuted every day between the vast world of pubs and poetry around Trinity and the little family circle, between the 'continent' of town, and, as it were, Coronation Street.

Like the rest of my friends, I was fascinated by my lecturers and the art-soaked lives I thought they must be leading. Trinity was a foreign country in which we had all chosen voluntary exile; I found it hard to imagine that they, with all they knew and all they could make us feel, also went home at the end of the day to houses in Dublin.

I hovered on the edges of the GMB – filled with intimidating boys who when they talked about 'the Labour Party' meant the British one, and who argued in the style of the House of Commons even when they were in the Buttery – and tried a few 'cosmic' coffees in the Bohemian headache of the Junior Common Room. But I joined and participated in no societies, not Mod Lang, not *Trinity News*, not the Literary Society, not the Cumann Gaelach. They were all thresholds I could not bring myself to cross, because, even as externally I navigated these wide open social spaces, running with the rest from O'Neill's to the Stag's, internally I was tightly locked inside a private, tiny room – the psychological space referred to as the closet, whose bolts bar entry to all sorts of places.

In secondary school, homophobia had been an unremarkable feature of the everyday world, part of its backdrop, like chalk-dusters or the rugby pitches. Those slurs, which had echoed in the classrooms and yard of school, fell silent in the cobbled squares of Trinity, but I could not find anything more than this quiet truce. My eyes darted all over campus seeking signs of possible romance, in the sweaty heterosexual intriguing of the GMB, among the morning smokers on the ramp or the Erasmus students with bright Invicta bags locking their bikes at the 1937 Reading Room. I hung around Books Upstairs and the Gay & Lesbian section of Waterstones, and saw other furtive glancers, but nothing ever moved beyond silence.

In my classes on the fourth and fifth floors of the Arts Block, however, I was startled to discover the passions I was looking for in the pages of the books we discussed: in French Romanticism, in Lorca's dreaming gypsies, in the cursed French poets rolling into bed together after a long night on the green fairy.

Trinity kept opening new and unexpected doors. I had heard people talking about 'rooms' in College, and finally discovered with a shock that there were little flats hidden in the granite buildings on campus. I had heard a rumour about an out gay man, a fourth-year from the North who lived in campus. I found out where, knocked on his door, blurted out my secret, and was invited in for a chaste tea in his rooms. Soon after, elated with the feeling of unburdening myself of my secret, I came out again, this time to my 'Marlene Dietrich' friend who accompanied me to a meeting of the Gay Soc in another set of converted rooms near the JCR. She left me there after a time, like a mother leaving a child to his first day at school, and I was taken on my first outing to The George. It was a pub with a small bar space and dance floor upstairs; a tiny room into which I crammed a host of huge, frightening feelings.

MONEY WAS always on our minds and the standard calculation of a fiver a day to cover coffees, food and pints had to be earned over the summer. There were still poor employment opportunities in Ireland, and in any case, those of us in modern languages had residency requirements to fulfil. People went to Germany either because they were studying German or because work was so plentiful, or to France, where there was a generous minimum wage, the mythical SMIC. I headed to unemployment-ravaged Spain because it was the language that needed most work and because my head was filled with Mediterranean visions of sensuous adventure. When the British Airways stewardess heard that I was off to Spain not on holiday but to look for work, she filled three plastic sacks with packets of peanuts and mini-bottles of red wine and handed them to me as I stepped off the plane.

Spain was a glorious, boiling disaster: I was robbed, fired, cheated, and fired again and after six weeks of wandering the beachfronts of Catalonia and the back alleys of Bilbao I ended up back in Glenageary washing dishes in a retirement home. But my halting Spanish was filled with new idioms and vocabulary, new words for old and new ideas; I had discovered there were more rooms inside me than the closet.

My old circle of school friends found each other again on campus. Girls came back from Germany with shaven heads and unshaven armpits, boys came back from Spain and France hugging each other and wearing coloured wristbands. We had returned with cartons of duty-free Lucky Strikes and Diana cigarettes, along with new takes on nudity, menstruation, sexual freedom, egalitarian economics, togetherness.

It was as though we had carried bits of Europe back to Dublin, the way soldiers from the trenches were said to have brought back the seeds of French flowers on their muddy boots to bloom in the ditches of England. But in fact, Europe had been there all along before we left: under the corridors of the fifth floor of the Arts Block were the sands of the Costa Brava and the grass of the naturist parks of Hamburg. As our knowledge of the languages and literatures we were studying grew, word by word, poem by poem, so did the pool of acquaintances, friends, potential lovers. None of us had ever seen a website or sent an email. No one had a mobile phone. The place to find 'sensitive' information about people was in graffiti in the toilets in the Berkeley Library. As you walked through campus you would see notes fluttering on the doors, like Buddhist prayer trees, as people told each other where they would or would not be, when they would return to their rooms, whom they could or could not see. Once a friend could not find a piece of paper and wrote her note for me on a big brown sycamore leaf.

A scholarship in second year entitled me to my own rooms on campus, a physical manifestation of the new spaces, which had been opened up inside me. Someone else told everyone they were gay, and then another, and another, closet doors flying open like the drawers in *Mary Poppins*. It seemed to be happening all over An Lár. The George added new adjoining spaces. Two new gay bars – the Front Lounge and Out on the Liffey – started up. Weekly gay nights were established in other venues: the narrow rooms of the old pubs and clubs threw themselves open to accommodate our rapidly expanding selves and dreams.

It felt as though the city, too, was on the verge of its own kind of coming out. It was in part the early stirrings, of course, of what was to become the disappointing Celtic Tiger. But in the classrooms of the fifth floor and in the dark corners of the Buttery, I felt as though we were making an imaginative leap from Phyllis to Marlene, from the bedroom of adolescence to the backrooms of Berlin, out of the cramped closet and into open, airy spaces which, one by one, were being unlocked.

Barry McCrea (right) *with Léan Ní Chuilleanáin and Caitríona Ní Dhúill.*

Barry McCrea (TCD 1993–97; French and Spanish) is a novelist and Chair of Comparative Literature at the University of Notre Dame, where he teaches in its campuses in the US and Rome.

FINDING MY WAY

aoife mclysaght

GOING TO COLLEGE: a classic rite of passage. A new place, a whole new bunch of people, an opportunity to reinvent yourself as one of the 'cool' crowd. I pretty much scuppered this chance on my very first day when, unable to find the Chemistry Large Lecture Theatre, I asked a passer-by for directions. It wasn't just random – I chose someone who really looked like they ought to know their way around. And this particular passer-by very kindly didn't just point me in the direction of the lecture theatre, but told me that, happily, he was walking the same way, and would walk along with me. Whereas two of my classmates – and best friends of over twenty years' standing – first met each other in similar circumstances, when one asked the other for directions (like a cool person would), I had chosen to ask a professor. And not just any old prof: I was escorted to my first lecture by Professor Simms of the maths department. As someone who has spent quite a bit of time and effort trying to dispel the image of professors as older white men with crazy hair and tweed jackets with leather elbow patches, it rather pains me to say that Professor Simms really is the picture of a professor – and he had just walked me to my first lecture. How embarrassing! How uncool.

During my years in College I found my intellectual home, and that was in the genetics department. I started to gravitate towards genetics as early as

Junior Freshman year. I remember distinctly those lectures with Professor David McConnell. There were over 200 of us in a packed MacNeill lecture theatre (I found my way to this one on my own), as he told us about the early days of genetics; the golden era when so much of the information that we can now take for granted was discovered: that genes are made of DNA, that the sequence of the DNA is read as a code by proteins in the cell, and that that sequence determines a huge amount about us (and every living thing on this planet) and sets the parameters and limits on other characteristics and traits. The thing that really grabbed me during lectures was how McConnell led us through the experiments and the results, and challenged us to place ourselves in the minds of those pioneers of genetics and to interpret their experiments. This was fun! (I am so not cool.)

During our Senior Freshman year we would have to make a decision about which subject we would choose for our moderatorship. I was definitely leaning towards genetics, but I wanted to be certain. I decided to get myself a job working in the field for the summer before Senior Fresh year and I was lucky in that the Irish National Centre for Medical Genetics had just opened in Crumlin Hospital. I had then, and still have, a fondness for that hospital; the staff there had looked after Niamh, one of my younger sisters, a lot over the years, and it was there in March of that year, 1995, that she breathed her last, difficult breath. I decided to volunteer in the genetics unit. I worked for free, and in return the hospital gave me a contribution to my bus fare and a wonderful opportunity to learn.

I spent that summer working on a diagnostic test for Fragile X Syndrome, the most common form of heritable intellectual disability. I was trained in by the wonderful Dr Shirley McQuaid, herself a graduate of the Trinity genetics department, and the boss, Dr David Barton. During my placement, it so happened that Professor McConnell from Trinity came to visit the new unit. When I heard about this, I panicked a little – had I misrepresented how much I was acquainted with the prof? I knew him, surely, but I was a face in a few hundred – he didn't necessarily know me … The day came and, as he was being shown around, I heard David Barton say to McConnell, 'We have one of your Trinity students here this summer.' When they came around the corner and saw me, McConnell reacted with, 'I don't know her at all – she's not one of ours!' Oh the mortification. I quickly clarified that I had only just finished my first year as a science student, and that he didn't know me personally. I felt like such a fraud!

Genetics was all about figuring things out, about solving puzzles, about thinking. It was so much more rewarding, so much more stimulating than those other subjects that seemed to be all about memorizing (I'm looking at you, biochemistry). During Trinity term of my Senior Freshman year, we had an exam in this area called 'Problems in Genetics', where we had to deduce genetic maps, figure out inheritance patterns, and interpret experimental results in genetics. I enjoyed this exam the way people enjoy crossword puzzles and riddles.

One Saturday as I was quietly working at my weekend job in my dad's nursery, my sister Emer came running to find me, telling me that someone called Professor McConnell was on the phone. Apparently I had done quite well with those problems, and he thought I should work in the department that summer.

My first paid job in genetics was a six-week summer placement in the Trinity Genetics Department working for Dr Andrew Lloyd in the Irish National Centre for Bioinformatics. 'Bio-what?' you might ask. I did too – I had never so much as heard of this mysterious new topic before. Nonetheless, Andrew rather optimistically asked me to help write a course in it, and I equally optimistically agreed to do so. Bioinformatics, sometimes called 'computational biology', is a meld of genetics, computer programming and statistics. I started doing bioinformatics that summer with Andrew, and I haven't stopped since.

There's a very special thing about Trinity genetics I've observed over many years, which is that students are really welcomed in as members of the department. Almost immediately, my eleven classmates and I were told that we weren't to bother with 'professor' and 'doctor' and that everyone in the department just goes on first names. We weren't treated as lesser than the lecturers – we were just people at an earlier stage in our career. This ethos was extremely important for the process of our intellectual maturation. We were encouraged to think and to (gasp!) have our own ideas. Just stop for a moment and think about how well the Leaving Cert prepared us for that ...

Being only twelve in the class, we became a close-knit bunch. There were rumours (still unconfirmed) that in previous years genetics students had become so competitive that some of them would hide library books so that the others couldn't access them. Maybe these were fabricated cautionary tales, but in any case, we decided that we were not going to be like that. In those days, scientific papers were still printed on paper and stored on shelves. It seems hard to believe now, when everything is easily and readily download-able in electronic format, but back then we had to go to the library to find the reading material for every lecture and then make photocopies. This was time-consuming and a real pain. The weekly journals were bound together into large volumes, and we'd usually need only one paper from a given volume. We could feel our biceps growing as we carried stacks of these to the photocopier room. (Cue Monty Python's Four Yorkshiremen sketch: 'In my day …') We set up a system whereby one member of the class would assume responsibility for this task each week and make enough copies for everyone. We spent a fortune in photocopier cards and became firm friends.

When we got sick and tired of lunches at the Hamilton Café (a common ailment) we usually went en masse to Clockwork Orange, a greasy spoon at the top of Westland Row, right beside Sweny's Chemist of lemon soap fame, immortalized in *Ulysses*. This is where I discovered the joys of a 'chicken melt' – a mayonnaisey chicken sandwich, cut into triangles arranged pointing upwards on the plate, with cheddar cheese melted over the top. Served with chips, it is a dietician's nightmare. We gobbled them up.

We did have our own version of hiding the library books though, albeit a less devious one. Rather than creating a false advantage by disadvantaging class-mates, we instead made sure that no single one of us could ruin the night out of the others by staying in to study, and making the rest feel guilty for not doing likewise. Somehow, we had an unspoken pact that we should always socialize together, and that this was definitely OK, because if none of us was studying, then we had nothing to feel guilty about. Our usual haunt was Kennedy's pub on Westland Row, which we declared to detest, but still kept returning to anyway. It was something of a genetics tradition: one of the guys in the class ahead of ours used to save up his pennies so that he could pay for his pint in the most irritating way possible, just for the pleasure of annoying the surly barman.

When we weren't in Kennedy's, it was usually a house party, and usually my house. (Not being independently wealthy, I lived with my parents – so I really ought to say it was their house.) The first of these happened on the spur of the moment when, after a small departmental party, someone remembered that the new series of *ER* was starting that evening. We landed into the living room in my family home and took command of the TV. At some point, my parents gave up and just decided to go to bed but we continued late into the night, occasionally bursting into raucous song. Blur's 'Song 2' was a favourite due to the easy lyrics, which involved shouting 'Woo-hoo' over and over again.

The years passed. We graduated and spread out, but kept strong connections. Two of my classmates went so far as to get married to each other (which is overdoing it, really). Myself and another classmate ended up living in the same neighbourhood and we see each other every week. Many of us try to meet up for a meal every now and then.

While some of our original twelve found a niche in different areas, over twenty years later eight of us are still active in science. I'm a faculty member back in that same department that nurtured me as a student, where I hope to repay that kindness to the next generation. Every now and again I hear stories from the students, rumours they have heard about crazy parties that happened years ago. I recognize some of the details, and know that it was us – but I just smile and say nothing.

Aoife McLysaght (centre) *with, from left, Kate Joyce, Emma Jane Joyce, Rebecca Goulding and Lisa Bouchier-Hayes.*

Aoife McLysaght (TCD 1994–98, Genetics; 1998–2001, Ph.D. Genetics) entered Trinity at eighteen and, apart from a stint in the University of California, Irvine as a postdoctoral researcher, basically hasn't left since. Since 2003, she has been a faculty member of the genetics department where she lectures and leads a research group. In 2009 they discovered the first ever examples of completely newly evolved human genes and current work focuses on using evolution to identify disease genes. Aoife spends a lot of time sharing her enthusiasm for genetics, evolution, and science in general by giving talks and arranging events in such places as Science Gallery and the Electric Picnic, as well as contributing to radio, TV and newspapers.

SINKING SUN

mark pollock

SITTING HIGH above Front Square, I was looking out of the open window of House Twenty-Five in the Rubrics, the last of the May sun casting the Campanile's great shadow across the grass. Wyclef Jean's 'Gone 'til November' was playing on my CD player and I was feeling the intense sense of belonging I had forged over the last four years at Trinity start to dissolve.

On 10 April 1998 I had had an emergency operation in Manchester to try to repair the detached retina in my left eye. I had already completely lost the sight in my right eye as a five-year-old, but now the cloudy green soup that filled what I had always called my 'good eye' was obscuring everything. I couldn't see through the mix of gas inserted by the doctors and the debris kicked up by their interference. But, if I bowed my head for a minute or two at a time, the gas bubble floated upwards, pushing my ragged retina onto the back of my eye.

And, as it hovered in place, I stole moments of the greens and browns of Library Square with its perfect grass and its two massive Oregon maple trees. I saw glimpses of the greys of the Campanile, the cobbles and buildings of Front Square beyond it, as far as Front Gate. All in soft focus with the thick sauce of the sinking sun pouring over it.

THE FIRST TIME I walked through Front Gate, I was wearing a green sports jacket, green trousers a shade darker, brown brogues, a mint green shirt, all topped off with a multicoloured tie. This shocking ensemble had been my work-experience uniform in school and now, in 1994, it was part of my attempt to impress an interview panel. If I impressed them, I would get into Trinity; if I didn't, I wouldn't.

I had nowhere near the points to get in. And, when I say nowhere near, I mean four A Levels off the mark. When I got my results in August 1994 I assumed that Trinity was out of the question, but my dad, who knew very little about university entrance rules, decided he would argue my case. He got nowhere on the phone, but after he posted and faxed multiple copies of a letter he had devotedly composed and written out with his very best fountain pen to various Trinity offices, it eventually landed on the right desk. Despite all reasonable expectations, he got a response and I got an interview.

Dad had drafted in my school rowing coach, Bill Jacques, to support my application. Bill had been a classics scholar at Trinity in the 1960s and after a stint in Africa he taught Latin in my school, Royal Belfast Academical Institution. Bill knew I wasn't going to become a classics scholar like him, but after seven years of coaching, he believed in me as a person. Most importantly, during his time in Trinity he had been a member of Dublin University Boat Club and I suspect he thought I would fit in there. So he and my school principal, Michael Ridley (who could not have been impressed with my academic record either), sent letters to Trinity arguing the case as to why the university should give me a chance.

And so it came to be that in early September 1994, dressed in an outfit that looked like I'd lifted it off a mannequin in House of Ireland on Dame Street, I passed through Front Gate and into the covered arch. I passed the sports club notice boards with team sheets pinned on them, the hexagonal wooden blocks underfoot wobbling as I headed for the Dublin University Boat Club board. A recruitment letter explaining the history of the club had a photo of the Senior VIII racing at Henley Royal Regatta the year before. This is what all the effort was for – since I was fifteen years of age, I had wanted to be in that crew. The problem was that I had to get into College first.

I crossed the cobblestones, the red bricks of the Rubrics in the distance, veered right through the gap between the 1937 Reading Room and the Old

Library, and towards the ramp leading up to the Arts Block where the smokers congregated. I made my way towards the Business Studies, Economics and Social Sciences Faculty offices for an interview with the department head and a lady from special needs.

The interview went as well as an interview can go for an eighteen-year-old trying to explain his surprisingly poor results and desperate to be accepted regardless. Sitting there wearing fifty shades of green, all I remember is that I wanted in so badly that I proposed taking up French as a second language if it would help (of course, this ignored the fact that I had only scraped a pass in GCSE French). After the interview, I leaned on the Arts Block wall overlooking the coffee dock, not yet aware that they had decided to offer me a place in BESS, nor of how much time I would ultimately spend sitting on that wall with mates and girlfriends and girlfriends-to-be.

WE WHO ARRIVE as the sun rises above the Islandbridge boathouse are rewarded. We stand on the bank beside unbroken water, above the channel of mist clinging to the river's dip. We push off the slipway and the sun chases us and the mist up the river towards the church at the Boohouse bend, breaking the silence only with the swoosh of our boat and blades cutting the water.

This memory is a collage of many years of mornings as a Dublin University Boat Club oarsman. I only remember the mist and the calm days now, even though in the winter of my first year in Trinity we spent months, regardless of conditions, rowing two equally matched VIIIs side by side. I was in a new club; no track record. Each day, each stroke, I was on trial. Our coaches, two Trinity alumni – Nick Dunlop and Raymond Blake – were looking on, trying to pick their VIII for the upcoming season.

As a schoolboy oarsman I had watched the distinctive black-and-white striped t-shirts of DUBC's First VIII cross the line first so many times. Now I had a chance to earn my own 'stripey', as those t-shirts have been known since the club's formation in the mid 1800s.

If I was to make it onto the Senior VIII, I would have to radically improve both my strength and technique. We were tested every six weeks. A single rowing machine sat in the middle of the long room of the boathouse, the winter's breeze blowing in the double doors of the balcony. The river rushed over the weir and our coach, Nick, sat with his clipboard ready to take notes. We, the DUBC hopefuls, waited in the wide hallway watching as one of our potential teammates went head to head with the machine for a pain-filled, 2000-metre flat-out test.

Like the daily crew rowing sessions, single-sculling time trials, the runs, the circuits and weights, this was part of the selection process for the DUBC Senior VIII. We stood in that hall with crew photos from the previous hundred years watching over us – sepia-coloured rowers standing static, with large moustaches, coxes and other crew members reclining in front of them with their cups, their Henley medals, their stories – and we felt part of something bigger, part of a club, its history offering us a chance.

'**CAPTAINS, SECRETARIES** and guests, welcome to this year's Halloween Massacre!'

I spoke from the stool I was standing on at one end of the boathouse bar, dressed in my black boat club blazer with its white piping on the seams. It was my job as captain to welcome our guests to this invitation-only reception – guys in black tie and girls in cocktail dresses, all either officers in their sports clubs or competing for the university, and many for Ireland. I proposed a toast to their sporting success and pint glasses of double gin and Woody's fruit-flavoured alcoholic mixers were raised in the air and promptly drained. Back at College, another 300 or 400 people who had bought tickets for the main part of the night were gathering in the Pav, and would soon be joining us.

Outside, the first of the double-decker buses we had hired to transport the crowd to Islandbridge arrived, a stream of students pouring down the approach to the boathouse. Inside, the veneer of respectability was on the slide. As the second, third and fourth buses dropped off more and more people, the DUBC House and Grounds team swung into action.

We were selling the gin and Woody's concoction for half nothing and had named this cocktail a 'pint of chat'. And there was lots of chat, a lot of laughing, and most importantly, the chance to meet and talk to that girl you'd seen while sitting on the wall in the Arts Block the week before. Many relationships started – and sometimes ended – on those nights at Islandbridge, including a few of my own. Everyone was so full of energy; life was so fit to burst with potential.

It is difficult to separate those nights at the boathouse because there were simply so many of them, always sponsored by one or more of the drinks companies. Each year there were two carbon-copy events, one month apart. The Boat Club ran the Halloween Massacre in October, and in November the Knights of the Campanile held our Captain's Reception. During my time as secretary of the Knights, this clutter in the events calendar was of great concern to one former president. At one of the formal meetings, complete with Irish whiskey, jackets and Knights' ties, I remember minuting his concern that the Boat Club might be getting too much free product from the drinks reps. I also remember reminding him (of course through the chair, as per the comedically formal protocol at these meetings) that the Boat Club had in fact donated a free keg to the Knights the last time the Knights ran out. What I didn't minute was that the complainant had brokered that deal with me on the night – he was clearly too pissed to remember.

The morning after that 1996 Halloween Massacre I was woken by tapping on the window of my ground-floor room, 23.01, Boat Club Rooms in the Rubrics. It was the chief steward, or perhaps someone from his office, tipping me off to get down to the boathouse to clear up the debris from the party before the College authorities arrived, ready to hand down punishment for the mess.

I jumped on my bike and got there before them, spending the morning clearing glass from the floor and the effects of the 'pints of chat' from my head. The other lads were counting the cash and banking another massive profit. With the club members working for free, no overheads and a serious amount of free product from the drinks companies, we made over £4000 at every party.

Unfortunately, in the 2000s parties like the Halloween Massacre and The Knights Captain's Reception at the boathouse ended altogether, which is a shame because so much of university life is about learning from experiences outside the lecture hall – the marketing, sales, financial and organizational education that came from being given the space to make mistakes, to learn from them and do better next time.

THE 1998 ACADEMIC YEAR ended and that sight from the window of House Twenty-Five of the Rubrics – the last of the May evening sun casting the Campanile's shadow across the grass, the glimpses of the greens and browns of Library Square and its two Oregon maple trees – became some of the last things I would ever see.

I didn't sit my finals but at graduation in November, my name was read out in the Exam Hall alongside everyone else in my class. The only difference was that I was led onto the stage to receive my degree alone. With my class and family in front of me, I was given my *aegrotat* degree, an unclassified honours degree awarded to people in special circumstances.

Special circumstances seem to have been the theme of my Trinity story from its start to its end. The sense of privilege that I feel having been allowed in at all has never left me. I doubt I will ever really know who created the opportunity for me in the first place. Whoever you are, I am so grateful; thank you.

In the postscript to my undergraduate days, that theme follows on. Over the subsequent twenty years, Trinity has been a constant in my life – it was where I lived with my guide dog, Larry, for three years in the 2000s when I first went blind. I launched my career as an adventure athlete and motivational speaker there. I made my first documentary and co-wrote and published a book with Ross Whitaker, a friend I'd made while we were both at Trinity, and I trained at Islandbridge and won silver and bronze medals rowing for Northern Ireland at the Commonwealth Games with friend and fellow Trinity graduate Brendan Smyth. It is where a girl called Simone George taught me how to dance salsa in the GMB kitchen and it is where I proposed to her five years later, standing between those Oregon maple trees in Library Square.

In 2010, four weeks before we were due to be married, I fell from a second-storey window during Henley Royal Regatta and broke my back. Now Trinity is helping me to explore the frontiers of spinal-cord injury recovery. Their scientists are combining an innovative electrical stimulator over my spinal cord with a drug supercharging my nervous system as I walk hundreds of thousands of steps in my robotic exoskeleton covering miles and miles of Trinity ground towards whatever the future holds.

Mark Pollock (TCD 1994–98; BESS) is an explorer, innovator and collaboration catalyst. Mark has competed in ultra-endurance races across deserts, mountains and the polar ice caps, including being the first blind person to race to the

South Pole. He won silver and bronze medals for rowing at the Commonwealth Games and set up a motivational speaking business. In 2010 Mark was left paralyzed after a fall. Through the Mark Pollock Trust he is on a mission to find and connect people around the world to fast-track a cure for paralysis. Selected by the World Economic Forum as a Young Global Leader, Mark is on the board of the Christopher and Dana Reeve Foundation (USA) and is a Wings for Life Ambassador (UK). He is the subject of the acclaimed documentary **Unbreakable: The Mark Pollock Story** and has spoken at Davos, Wired and TEDx Hollywood. He has been awarded the Trinity College Alumni Award and honorary doctorates by The Royal College of Surgeons in Ireland and Queen's University Belfast. He holds a diploma in Global Leadership and Public Policy for the Twenty-First Century from Harvard University, as well as degrees from Trinity College Dublin and the Smurfit Business School.

Mark Pollock (centre) *on the water at Henley, 1997.*

ACT ONE

simon carswell

MY NUMBER was 94498989. It was a four-year sentence. I arrived an innocent, wide-eyed teenager from Limerick, still wearing clothes my mother bought me and sporting a dodgy hairstyle, a product of some ill-judged self-pruning. (What male barber could be trusted with Titian ringlets on a lad heading into Trinity, dahling?) I left a twenty-something graduate, rehabilitated, still with the dodgy hairstyle – oh, and with a wonderful, future wife.

My time at Trinity was anything but a sentence, of course. The friends I made in the lecture halls of the Arts Block, in the black-box Players Theatre, on the cobbles of Front Square and in the bars of Pearse and Lombard streets remain my closest to this day.

I recall three things from my first day of Freshers' Week in Trinity: pedestrians on Grafton Street can be very slow to jump out of the way of an energetic eighteen-year-old on a racer; there were many students in Trinity with English accents (and most not even from England); and there were so many societies and clubs worth joining that it appeared there was little time for the important stuff. The important stuff, I quickly learned, happened outside the lecture halls.

My friend Shane O'Neill, a fellow blow-in from Limerick and my wingman on that first day in October 1994, set himself the task of joining the most obscure clubs he could find. Within a few hours was a proud member of the TCD Aikido

Club. 'Tell da boys I joined d'Aikido Club!' he said repeatedly in a thick Limerick accent. He threw some moves he thought resembled the Japanese martial art, demonstrating his acting chops, and stomped off to the Samuel Beckett Theatre for four years of drama studies, luvvieness and general mayhem.

The Arts Block and the history department was my destination, but the real action turned out to be in Shane's corner of campus. The card that mattered most at the end of Freshers' Week, it turned out in hindsight, was not my Trinity College student ID, but my membership card for Dublin University Players, the college drama society.

I auditioned for the Freshers' Co-op, the rite of passage for all new thesps. Boasting of my pre-Trinity days earning a few quid playing piano in bars and restaurants, I landed the task of writing an opening blues number for *Cinderella*. For the life of me I can't remember how the tune went. My abiding memory of those performances was hoping that the male singer I accompanied could struggle through some rather curious sweats and shakes.

The show had to go on, and it did. Mostly. Except for the Thursday night. About a dozen of us, each playing a different James Bond, and thirsty, decided it would be far better to use our free Guinness pint vouchers before our scene rather than wait until after the curtain call. When time ran away on us, a shout went out and our rental (the collective noun for a group wearing bad tuxedos) of Freshers downed our pints, grabbed our fake guns and sprinted to the theatre for our entrance, shaken and stirred. For the next four years, the shows continued to go on. That piano and I became close.

In Players, there were two and sometimes three shows a week, about forty shows a year. It was our laboratory and we, the players, were mad scientists conducting wild experiments. There was little risk of anything blowing up our faces, just slight bruising to our egos. Some experiments ended badly, others spectacularly, though all fired even greater creativity. The remarkable writing by Ken Slattery in *The Lads* or the jaw-dropping acting by Sonya Kelly, Jason O'Mara and Mark Huberman, among others, stick in my memory. A big-cast, stirring production of Dylan Thomas's *Under Milk Wood* next door at the Beckett was another high watermark of those years on the boards.

One personal highlight was *Lovers (Winners and Losers)* by Brian Friel, which I directed in my first year with my friends Shane and Kathy Fox (now husband and wife) acting alongside Will O'Connell and Leah Hamilton. I recall being transfixed by their performances and Friel's language as I stood in the darkness of the wings, trying to feel for the right notes on the piano.

Another high point was the musical *Jerusalem!*, written and composed by the talented Neal Rowland (now a screenwriter), Stephen Swift (a regular on stage at the Gate Theatre), my friend David Horan (an established Dublin theatre director) and myself. This 'Epical, Biblical, Comical, Musical!' stretched our creative muscles with songs such as 'Things Won't Be Quite The Same Now That You've Been Crucified'. (I still play it.) The muscles hurt more from the laughter of being around such funny people for long periods.

We later brought the show to a drama festival hosted by an engineering college in an eastern suburb of Paris. (Yes, it puzzled us too.) The show was performed under a screen with French subtitles. The engineers loved us. My memory of the week is skulking around the streets of Paris drinking strong coffee and smoking our own rolled-up cigarettes. I didn't drink coffee or smoke but felt I had to; it was Paris after all and we were artists.

David and I became 'Nicotine Buddies', the title of one of the songs of our short-lived band that we thought would see us through our difficult 'second musical' phase. There was talk of writing something about the 1916 Rising, Ireland's answer to *Les Misérables*. I particularly liked the idea – floated by a fellow Player – of building a giant Styrofoam GPO for each night of the show that could be destroyed during the performance. We dreamt big in those days. We even joked, too, about the idea of writing a follow-up musical called *Paris!* and bringing it to Jerusalem. All those Guinness-fuelled fantasies came to nought.

One of the most rewarding parts of *Jerusalem!* was collaborating with such a large group of people, many of whom I didn't know well beforehand. When I first landed in Players, I was surprised at how small a collective the drama society was, controlled by the omnipotent ten-person Players committee. I had hoped during my four years that we could swell the society's membership ranks and make it more inclusive. We did. During my year as treasurer, the theatre's annual budget topped more than £20,000, most of which came from box-office receipts, evidence of the vast dramatic output by so many during those years.

Some money was made on savings from negotiating cheap booze purchases and creative sponsorship deals with the newest college drinks rep, who hadn't found us out yet. A Fosters Ice promotion was judged such a success that, on delivery, it left us with one of the worst hangovers of my college years. Our friends and occasional collaborators, the debaters of the Hist and the Phil, sunk to new lows, alcoholically speaking, with their drinks deals, settling for the latest saccharine alcopop that did no one any good – though hats off to the quantity they could negotiate (and drink).

As for the spending side of the balance sheet, Players' coffers were severely depleted by sending almost the entire society membership to Queen's University in Belfast for the annual Irish Student Drama Association – or ISDA – festival in 1997. My memory of handing out fivers to guarantee the return of train tickets (for accounting purposes, you see) ensured a roaring business at the Queen's Student Union bar on the first night of the festival. When the anti-Trinity taunts came, we were ready. 'Sorry, I don't speak Mexican,' was the comedian's response to us rowdy, south-of-the-border hecklers.

My out-of-Players, extra-curricular hours involved piano-playing in a restaurant in Monkstown: easy money requiring as few hours as possible away from the devilment of Trinity. During the summers, it was singsongs in a Connemara hotel bar and – for one summer only! – in The Dubliners Irish pub in St Paul, Minnesota. My near-average singing was complemented by general buffoonery and poor attempts at cheeky-chappie Irish humour during these summers. It reached the heights of:

Guest: 'Can you play "From A Distance"?'

Me: 'Yes, how far?'

The ability to belt out a song scored me access to great Trinity parties and encouraged the good people who ran Blazes Restaurant (RIP) in Temple Bar and George's Bar on South Frederick Street to serve us until our singing sounded so amazing that we couldn't stop.

After three years of being something of a wandering troubadour academically, I hit a high note with the history of the Irish in the First World War under the guidance of Professor David Fitzpatrick, who helped me salvage a respectable degree. His seminars were always lively, whether it involved singing Orange or nationalist marching tunes in his course on fraternities in

Irish history, or cooking dishes with wartime rations. It brought us back there.

My final-year attention span was a battleground: a fight between the soldiers and chaplains of the First World War on one side and the 1998 ISDA Festival in Trinity on the other. Along with festival director Ryan Meade, fellow deputy director Rachel Burden and a committee that included Vanessa Berman (the aforementioned now wonderful wife) we staged a memorable festival with lots of drama, on stage and off. One of the students assigned to be a liaison officer to one of our professional judges took her liaising a little too literally. We scored an astonishing sponsorship deal with Guinness that allowed us to fill the DA Club (once again, RIP) with cut-price pints and many punters. One of the post-show festival nights featured an early outing from aspiring stand-up comic Des Bishop, then a student and actor with UCC who was practically heckled off stage. 'All that sperm and you were the fastest' was the put-down that drew the most laughs.

In the end, DU Players scored a best production win for our own staging of *Twelve Angry Men* and the festival even produced a profit. Yes, a profit. From a student enterprise. It surprised us too. As a result, the festival committee enjoyed a weekend away in that Connemara hotel, including a rather drunken murder-mystery game and naked night-swimming.

In my final year, I had the good fortune of making my home in a second-floor bedroom of House Seven overlooking College Green, thanks (I think) to my ties to Players. At times, when I should have been studying, I found myself standing, staring out the old sash windows at the people below as I wondered how many others had stood there and stared over the centuries.

I counted myself so very lucky then, and I still do. Why else would I remember that eight-digit student number with a broad smile almost twenty years later?

Simon Carswell (TCD 1994–98; History) lives in the United States, is married to Vanessa and has two daughters, Amy Rose and Kate. He is Washington Correspondent with **The Irish Times** and the author of two books, **Something Rotten: Irish Banking Scandals** and **Anglo Republic: Inside The Bank That Broke Ireland**. While at Trinity he was a proud member of Dublin University

Players, and served as chairman in his final year. He has not appeared in, composed music for, directed or produced any professional theatrical productions. Yet.

REVOLUTIONARIES IN SLIPS

miranda kennedy

I ENROLLED in Trinity the year that divorce became legal in Ireland. This fact was so astounding to my twenty-something, left-wing American self that I talked about it endlessly – especially to the parents who were the reason I'd ended up on this tiny conservative island. My dad, an American married to a British woman, was offered a chair and a professorship in Trinity in 1995. I was already in college elsewhere, but never mind, they said breezily. You don't really like it in upstate New York anyway. And Ireland has Joyce and Beckett … and the sea.

They were right. I probably thought about it for a day before I walked swiftly over to the administration building in Vassar College to announce that I was leaving. Vassar was small and very beautiful and very liberal. I was miserable there. It was full of supremely sophisticated, privileged Manhattanites who made me feel like a midwestern country bumpkin, which was certainly not how I liked to think of myself.

I didn't especially want to do as my parents wanted me to, but the idea was compelling: of reading *Ulysses* in Dublin, of claiming it as my own dirty little seaside town. It was enough to justify the extra year Trinity told me I needed to do there if I was to achieve a Trinity degree. True, I did sometimes refer to my two years at Vassar as two years of 'basket-weaving and sonnet-writing' but it was an exaggeration. Still, it seemed this was how the Trinity administration saw it – as not quite up to snuff. The upside was that I got to spend three years in Dublin rather than only two. Three years is enough to make a place feel like home, to make you committed to it. From the moment I arrived, an Irish-American reverse migrant to Ireland's green shores, I was committed.

Still, I fought the home-ness and right-ness of Dublin. I was twenty, after all, picking up and leaving my cool New York life to follow my parents to a tiny irrelevant spit of land. So part of me was relieved to find out that Ireland of 1995 was in social turmoil. It gave me some leverage and distance at Sunday dinners with my parents and younger sisters at their newly purchased Georgian house in Glenageary. Divorce only became legal this very year. Can you imagine what that has meant for generations of Irish women? I delivered so many righteous American zingers at our dinner table, it's a wonder they survived it, really.

If I found it hard to fit in right away, it was also partly because Ireland is, in many ways, such a strange bird. How could people be so irreverent about everything – from God to their marriages – and yet defend a set of laws and social expectations that seemed a century out of date? How was it that no one I knew went to church, but everyone pretended Ireland was properly Catholic? No matter how much Joyce I read, I couldn't quite get it. And Beckett just made me confused and despairing about everything, so he wasn't much help.

STARTING A literary magazine at College was less of an effort to understand Ireland, as it was to try and change Ireland. I had an idea that I would revolutionize this country, with the help of my band of like-minded friends. The magazine was called *Harlot*, for God's sake; it was fairly clear we were trying to spit in the eye of something. If you'd asked me what I was spitting in the eye of, specifically, you probably wouldn't have wanted to stick around for the answer, because it wasn't exactly concise. It would have included rants and teary-eyed bits of Irish poetry, and it would have been delivered over pints in The Stag's Head or The Lord Edward. If I try to make it more concise now, I think was the ideas of a Church-run state and The Patriarchy that got me most animated.

I was an outsider picking fights with a country I didn't know, but for the first time in my life I really cared. Moving to Dublin helped me discover the idealistic spark in myself – something was lit in me during my years at Trinity.

Leaving the cosy nest of my upstate New York liberal arts education for a big university in a city forced me to decide what mattered to me. That's what *Harlot* was about. It was deciding to care, and acting on it. I'd always figured I would be a journalist, in the back of my mind, but I hadn't done a whole lot to make that happen. Now I was determined to make this magazine succeed. First, though, we had to make more than three fellow angry feminists read it, an ambitious-enough goal, given our publication's name.

In fairness, we didn't choose the name 'Harlot'. The magazine had already existed, as a rather more elegant and subtly ironic publication, years before. For years it lay quietly dormant, until we came along and hijacked it with all the subtlety of a rhino waving an Uzi. We were 'rejuvenating' the publication, 'making sparks fly'.

The band of renegades I found to start it up included a couple of half-Irish, half-American girls; a law student from Northern Ireland; and two rebellious Dubliners who studied English with me. Together, we provided the vision that was *Harlot* magazine of late nineties Dublin. We wanted to rival *Piranha*, the gossipy newsletter run by Dublin lads with D4 accents, and which we thought was especially cruel to women.

I'm not sure how we thought we'd steal readers away from *Piranha*, unless they were buying *Harlot* to take the piss. We probably needed a better marketing strategy – every single issue that we put out had a hot pink cover. The magazine was what we liked to call 'pro-sex feminist', which makes me cringe deeply, in my soul, and which basically meant 'we still want to shag guys even as we rant against the system that's rigged against women'. One of our issues was dedicated to the theme of 'erotica'. I admit I had only a vague notion of what erotica actually was until we looked it up in the dictionary, which will tell you the justice we did to the topic.

By day, we'd tramp through Dublin's soft rain into coffee shops and lunch places, searching for a woman in charge, or at least an offbeat-looking café owner who might hear us out. It was hard to get past the name. By night, we'd throw fundraisers in the basement of some city-centre club.

For these events, the required attire for us *Harlot* ladies, or Harlotines, as we called ourselves (to rhyme with harlequin, get it?!) was, basically, a slip. Yes, that's right – we all donned short, filmy undergarments. In the dead of winter we were allowed to wear tights – otherwise, no tights, no shirt or sweater on top. 'Take off your coat, ladies, no self-respecting harlot covers up!' we'd say to one another, and rush out to buy another frilly slip. We bought them at Jenny Vander, the pricey vintage shop in George's Street Arcade, and must have single-handedly justified its entire stock of vintage negligées; who else was buying them? After all, vintage does mean used!

My personal favourite was peach-coloured, a lovely polyester number edged with grubby bits of lace; I remember trimming off the dangling bits ahead of one of our fundraisers. I still have it – it is beyond ridiculous to think of myself prancing through the Dublin drizzle in that thing.

But the uniform was great for morale. We definitely stuck together, we *Harlot* girls. On any given evening, we could be found deliberating editorial questions such as whether to include the work of men in our pro-sex feminist publication (the answer, unsurprisingly, was yes). Ahead of publication, we'd spend night after night crouched over a single computer in the borrowed office of a friend who happened to be a graphic designer. He showed us how to use his software, and after a few rough starts, he let us at it on our own. It would take us many, many nights to finish, and many packets of Spar own-brand crisps and packaged buns, but eventually we figured out how to lay out the whole magazine ourselves. I remember proudly cycling it to the printer in a huge manila envelope.

Unfortunately, the feminist theory that guided us broke down a bit when I got into a spat with one of my *Harlot* sisters over, of all things, a fellow we both fancied. It nearly ruined our friendship, and forced the magazine to take a publishing hiatus. I'd like to be able to say that when we brought it back, we brought new maturity and humility to its pages. In fact, I think one of our final issues featured a photo essay we'd shot of ourselves re-enacting the fairytale of 'The Princess and the Pea'. It was our own feminist retelling, featuring me, the princess, in pink hot pants, displaying a bruised rear end. That was not erotica so much as high comedy.

But we had something to say, or at least, we had fairy tales to retell, and we found a way to do it. Inside the vaunted cobblestoned squares of Trinity, and the confines of this Catholic island nation, I was set free to become myself.

Miranda Kennedy (TCD 1995–98; English) was inspired by her days as editor of **Harlot** to pursue a career in journalism. She moved to New York and worked as a reporter and editor for four years before moving to India to report on South Asia for the US public radio network NPR. In 2011 she published a book about her time in India called **Sideways on a Scooter: Life and Love in India**, and is working on a second book about religion in America. She is an editor at NPR and lives with her husband and daughter in Washington DC.

Miranda Kennedy (far right) *with fellow 'Harlotines'.*

PILLS, THRILLS AND BELLYACHES

declan lawn

ALL I COULD THINK OF as I lay on the floor of my little room was that I didn't want to die in House Seven. Or anywhere, for that matter. I was twenty-one years old and hadn't had nearly enough fun yet.

But there I was, in a foetal position on the floor of my room in Front Square, and the pain I was feeling was so intense that I couldn't move, or even cry out. A few hours earlier I had been cramming for my second-year exams, and had been suffering from a dull ache in my stomach. I had put it down to pre-exam nerves – but now here I was, at four in the morning, grasping my abdomen with both arms, paralyzed with pain, and imagining my obituary in *Trinity News*.

These days, in a similar scenario, I'd simply WhatsApp a hundred people for help, but in 1997 I was going to have to find salvation the old-fashioned way: by crawling to it whilst weeping like a toddler. Just getting to the door was torture – but then struggling to stand semi-upright whilst I opened the latch felt like skiing up a mountain. Out in the corridor I collapsed again, and it took me about twenty minutes to make it the four metres or so to my neighbour's room. I knocked weakly on the bottom of her door, and prayed with all my heart that she was in; we had the only two rooms on the floor, and there was simply no way I could handle the stairs.

After a few moments she opened the door, swearing loudly at the sight of the wretched creature at her feet.

'Ambulance …' I gasped, just as I passed out. Roughly ten minutes later I vaguely remember being stretchered out of House Seven, and soon after that I joined the dubious company of Trinity students who have been driven through Front Arch by the emergency services. My inflamed appendix, at the point of bursting, was removed a couple of hours later. There would be no summer exams for me that year. My second year in Trinity had come to a sudden and dramatic end.

Such moments in our lives often seem very different in retrospect. They take on a new significance when imbued with the full context of their consequences; it so happened that my bout of acute appendicitis was a case in point, because it set me off on a new path in Trinity, and later, in life.

Until that point, I had dabbled in *Trinity News*, and the publications office generally. My intermittent level of involvement was not commensurate to my interest, because truly I felt that writing and journalism were where my heart lay. What a wondrous thing, I felt, to be curious about the world, to investigate particular aspects of it, and to have it published for others to read! The idea seemed perfect to me, and indeed it still does.

But for my first couple of years in Trinity, I orbited the publications office like a diffident schoolboy who really wants to join the football match but instead leans against the goalpost with his hands in his pockets. I would write pieces here and there, and shyly deliver them on floppy disk to the cluttered office in House Six, where raffish and supremely confident publications types would sit around discussing the world and contributing to the permanent cloud of smoke that lingered like a nefarious Beijing smog. I never stayed for long; they all just seemed too confident and impressive.

But my exam re-sits meant that I would return to Trinity early the next year – in fact, around the middle of August. I had plenty of time to study, and plenty of time to think, and during the thinking time I decided that if I was serious about this journalism thing, I needed to jump into *Trinity News* with a bit more alacrity. I had to at least try.

And so late in August I climbed the stairs to an almost-deserted *Trinity News* office, where only the new editor, Oisín Tansey, had arrived to set about producing the Freshers' issue. I explained that I'd help as much as I could, and so it was that just by turning up when no one else did, I was appointed features editor. By the time the usual suspects returned to College a few weeks later, I had grown accustomed to sitting with my feet up on the desk, blowing smoke at the ceiling and formulating opinions about things of which I knew very little, and so they accepted me without comment as one of their own. I was in.

Over the next two years, publications became a big part of my life in Trinity. We took it seriously, and I learned a great deal about writing, and deadlines, and above all teamwork. I grew to love the heady stress of a production week, with the copy coming in, the paper being designed, the thankless and gargantuan task of persuading some reluctant local business to take a quarter-page ad. The night before we went to press meant no sleep and frenetic activity, fuelled by terrible coffee and Marlboro Lights and breakfast rolls from Spar on College Green at 3 am. Red Bull had just come onto the market, and there were often packets of ProPlus (the caffeine pills) lying around. I gobbled them all. If I ingested such a mixture today, I would undoubtedly have a heart attack on the spot.

When the paper was gone, at eight or nine in the morning, we'd go to The Dockers pub on the Quays, an early house where we would celebrate another victory in the war against time and finances and all manner of enemies. I've celebrated meeting many deadlines since then: for magazines and TV documentaries and news pieces, but looking back, I can honestly say none has felt quite so sweet.

We learned, as we went along, about all of those elements that make good journalism happen. We were ingénues, of course, and naive most of the time, but looking back even now, there were some stars among us; Colm Ó Mongain, now a presenter with RTÉ, Newstalk's Ger Gilroy, novelist Belinda McKeon, journalist and TV presenter Ella McSweeney, and many more who went on to do great things in journalism and broadcasting. There were others who went into PR and communications, and who also made to the top of those fields. These days some of us meet for Christmas drinks, and when I look around the table at them I often quietly think that it was quite a generation of *Trinity News*, in that many of them did exactly, in the end, what they said they were going to do.

For me too, it was what set me on the path towards professional journalism, and in fact, I can trace the trajectory with great clarity. My writing on *Trinity News* got me a column with *In Dublin* magazine, and I worked there after I left Trinity, where I became editor. That led to *Magill* magazine, and from there I got a job with BBC Northern Ireland as a reporter on *Spotlight*, and then I started reporting for BBC *Panorama*. The latter two jobs, which I still do, have taken me around the world and back again, and given me insights and experiences that I would otherwise pay to acquire. I wasn't right about a lot of things when I was twenty-one, but it turns out I was right about journalism.

Last summer I took my children for a walk around Front Square, and whilst doing so I experienced an overwhelming sensation that, although I may not be exactly advanced in years, a significant part of my life's journey has already happened. My nine-year-old daughter wanted to know about *Trinity News*, and what I did there. 'Well,' I said, looking up at the grand old buildings, 'it might sound weird … but it all began with a strange pain in my stomach.'

Declan Lawn (TCD 1995–99; English) edited **In Dublin** magazine after leaving Trinity, and then went on to edit **Magill** magazine in 2001. In 2002 he moved to Belfast to become a reporter for BBC **Spotlight**, the investigative current affairs programme. He started reporting for **Panorama** in 2004, and since then he has made dozens of documentaries for the BBC as an investigative reporter and more recently as a producer/director. His wife Breige was in his class at Trinity and they live in Belfast with their four children.

TRYING ON FUTURES

lynn scarff

IT IS OCTOBER 1995 and I am wearing my dad's flared, pinstripe wedding trousers along with other items befitting a grungy nineties teenager. My Junior Freshman year at Trinity College Dublin, where I will study natural sciences, is about to begin. I had just turned seventeen that summer, which meant I had a red line along the bottom of my student card, indicating that I was underage, for the whole of my first year. Interestingly, this didn't bother me as much as the fact that I was unable to vote in the upcoming divorce referendum. I remember being appalled by the notion that I was in college and yet not allowed to vote – what's up with that? The referendum was carried in the end but by an incredibly slim margin of just over 0.5 per cent.

Making my way to Front Square to check out what was on offer for Freshers' Week, I had mixed feelings of excitement and trepidation. My dream of becoming the next Jacques Cousteau had taken a U-turn at the last moment, when rather than go and study marine biology in Bangor in Wales, I changed my mind and put natural sciences in Trinity as my first choice on the CAO form.

The seduction had actually happened months earlier when I attended a weekend maths workshop for Leaving Cert students, at which my own maths teacher Mr Dunne was presiding. Sitting in New Square in the sunshine, chatting with my friends, I thought, this is the place for me. Who needs Wales?

When I recall it now I'm struck by how many of one's teenage years are spent defining our future selves. Trying on different books, music, places and even people to see if they fit, and adding them to the arsenal of what makes us unique. I was definitely still trying on a lot of ideas and potential futures back then and I felt an immediate response to Trinity. And so I changed my mind – broke up with marine biology and decided to study natural sciences. Incidentally my second choice was French and psychology – so yes, a lot of trying on …

I loved science but was equally happy in the arts. And here's the crunch – Trinity gave me the opportunity to explore both disciplines, to formally study science while informally studying the arts. In Freshers' Week I signed up to the Hist, the Phil, fencing, the Zoology Society, the Science Fiction Society, Trinity Arts Workshop and Players. Perhaps in a different university system I would have been more of a major/minor student, taking courses in different disciplines, but that wasn't on offer in the Irish university system at that time. So by day I was a science student and by night I learned about the arts – this may seem like an odd combination but I am now the director of Science Gallery at Trinity College Dublin, a space where art and science collide through events, exhibitions and education programmes. Would I have taken this route with a different university experience? I doubt it.

And I wasn't alone, a strange, lonely anomaly drifting from the science buildings at the northeast of campus up to the Arts Block and Front Square. There were many of my kin, but perhaps fewer drifting in the opposite direction – the science societies were mainly composed of science students. And in many ways that is what I seek to reverse within Science Gallery, by creating a space where genuine collaborations between disciplines can occur, ensuring that one isn't in service to the other.

But here's the thing: I didn't take part in the Maiden Speakers' debate; I didn't seek out a committee position; it wasn't about excelling in one arena. Instead, I attended events, debates, plays and workshops and met people, and had what I felt at the time were life-altering conversations about the nature of everything, and formed deeply solid friendships with people who fundamentally shaped me. It was in these interactions with my peers across the arts and sciences – intelligent and thoughtful individuals (for the most part; there were some godawful eejits but you never stayed in their orbit for very long) – that I learned perhaps the most. From critical thinking to good listening skills, it was in many ways my fellow students who contributed the most to my college education.

THERE WERE some memorable moments. In my sophister years I was involved in the Trinity Arts Workshop and specifically in a puppetry group. One of the final-year drama students was creating a show in the style of *Moulin Rouge* and I was taken on as the prostitute's left leg. To explain: the puppet was controlled by five individuals all dressed in black, with one person controlling an arm, leg or head. Moving involved seriously intricate movements that we had to perform in unison. At one point, we had to move our lady lasciviously across the stage singing 'My Funny Valentine' and ensuring that, while she had no body, the audience would imagine that she did based on the fluidity of our movements! That took a while to nail. I wasn't a physics student but I do remember drawing diagrams on the whiteboard of the key pivot points and trying to recreate that movement and coordination between five of us. I must have done something right because a week later the same director had me in the Grand Canal doing a water puppet show with a giant clown and an ill-fitting wetsuit.

AND SO in my years at Trinity I went from dissecting dogfish to building furniture for a play inspired by Magritte; from measuring over 3000 zebra mussels to making many ceramic pots; from learning in detail the animal classification system to learning how to use a darkroom. I walked up and down that path between the rugby pitch and cricket crease, from one end of campus to the other, and I loved every single second of it. Now with hindsight, those experiences and the societies that enabled them were forerunners of a new kind of cultural experience that many museums, galleries and science centres seek to recreate – they were creative platforms enabling participation and as welcoming of the amateur as the expert. They said 'You can do this,' and I did. And this combination of formal and informal learning experiences melded and meshed and gave me the confidence to cross disciplines and not be pigeon-holed into one.

AS I WRITE THIS, it is almost a year since the same-sex marriage referendum was passed by 62 per cent. This time I was old enough to vote. It's a different Ireland to when I began my undergraduate degree in 1995, but there are still too many people in our society who don't have access to the college experiences that shaped me and gave me confidence to pursue my passions. Perhaps the greatest legacy of those four years is that I have an almost zealot-like belief in the power of informal learning experiences and how they can transform lives – right now I'm just focusing on how to make those experiences open to the many and not the few.

Lynn Scarff (centre, front) *and friends outside the Pav.*

Lynn Scarff (TCD 1995–99; Natural Sciences) is the Director of Science Gallery Dublin. She has over twelve years' experience in developing and leading public engagement projects in science, arts and education. Her professional background was in the environmental and not-for-profit sectors and she has developed a series of programmes, exhibitions, events, books, TV and radio for these areas. She is passionate about science and arts and the potential of spaces like Science Gallery to be facilitators of transformation in people's lives.

AMBITION

katie holly

IT MIGHT SEEM STRANGE that it was my total and utter lack of ambition during college that determined who I am and what I do today. Nevertheless it's true.

I couldn't wait to start at Trinity. School for the previous six years had been boarding at a small all-girls' convent in my home county of Wicklow – a tiny pond. A constant routine of morning prayers, breakfast, classes, questionable lunch, more classes, hockey, folk group, school bank or magazine, prefecture, really questionable dinner, study, then bed. Study, though, frequently meant listening to Dave Fanning, then one of few ways to discover new music, and bed often meant convening with my friends Anna and Hogie in one of our dorms to talk half the night about music, or America, or what we would do when we got out of school. We would inevitably get caught, only to start the next day even earlier with detention, followed by morning prayers, and on it went. Anna and I were often compared academically, particularly in our Leaving Cert year, but the truth is that what I worked hard for, she could do effortlessly. She was smart, funny, generous and patient.

Spates of righteous teenage angst led me to think I might want to be a journalist and that, coupled with a love of reading – and an absolute surety I didn't want to go into pharmacy after my father – led me to elect to read

English and history at Trinity. I can't deny that the four-year degree, not to mention the campus right in the centre of Dublin, were also very persuasive. That my best friend Anna was also going there to study history was a comfort – while exciting, those first weeks in a new, vast, co-ed university were also completely nerve-wracking. At least we'd be together.

However, just before we were due to start, Anna developed bad headaches. Wisdom teeth: they had to come out, all four at once. Her face swelled up like Orville the Duck, and so she laid low until her face had returned to a less alarming shade and shape. I would have to face those first few days of lectures alone.

My sister, in whose footsteps I followed, advised me to be careful who you make friends with in Freshers' Week – you can spend the next four years shirking them. It was advice I took to heart, and I spent my early days like some kind of naturalist observing the peculiar specimen that is the student *homo sapiens*, sitting back, watching people in my lectures, in the Buttery, on the ramp. It didn't take long to spot my ideal group – the guy with glasses wearing a brown suit, the one in purple trousers who apparently was living in a tent on the cricket pitch, and a rake of their interesting-looking friends.

Lectures during that first term were a shock – I had been feeling fairly confident about my abilities, smug even, particularly after collecting the book vouchers myself and Anna both won as Entrance Exhibitions (but were desperate no potential new friends should learn about). But hearing people talk in lectures, I was rattled: what on earth was critical theory; was I a 'bad reader'? And had everyone read *The Canterbury Tales* except me? (I still haven't.) It didn't help that the group I ended up befriending were mostly English, so had done A Levels – I felt outranked and underqualified.

Friendships came: there was Helen, who did English and history like me, a bright spark with a beautiful voice. And Patrick, who was a fan of something called drum 'n' bass, taught me how to make the perfect rollie, and had hand-writing so wide that three words filled a page (we took notes by hand back then). We were probably one of the first years to be given our own personalized email addresses: a bunch of mixed-up letters and numbers. We laughed about what we would ever use them for. Anna befriended a lovely, brilliant English guy nicknamed Lenny, who was well versed on any topic, it seemed, and we quickly got to know his group: brown suit, purple trousers, the Robs, a slightly scary girl called Sinéad, and the others who used to live, or regularly convene, at the flat that became known as the Quagmire.

I don't remember consciously deciding not to join any of Trinity's many clubs or societies – in imagining my time there I thought that was exactly what I would do. But I think my feelings of being outclassed and in awe at my new surroundings prevented me. Besides, there were new and intoxicating friendships to attend to, and the freedom, after years of having every hour scheduled, to do just as I liked – like spend whole afternoons, or nights, watching movies or reruns of *Absolutely Fabulous*.

Dublin at the time was changing so fast – divorce was finally, albeit narrowly, legalized; the country was starting to boom, unemployment was falling – we never felt the anxiety of the previous generation about finding work. That first winter, in December 1995, Bill Clinton brought College Green to a standstill with his visit. Embarrassingly I was one of about four students to not skip class to watch him make his speech to a cheering crowd of thousands. The obedient convent girl lingered still – I had only around eight hours' lectures a week, but those I never missed.

The rest of my time was spent with friends. We'd converge in ever-increasing numbers in whatever café or bar we chose – the Alpha for a great fry, The Duke, Rí-Rá for dancing. There was excitement when a new bagel place opened in Temple Bar and we practically became squatters – bagels were rare and exotic back then. I felt like a sponge – reading more widely ever before, absorbing all kinds of new ideas, experiences, music. Hearing Nina Simone for the first time, played for me by my friend Malachy (brown shoes), I was sure it was a man singing. Malachy was an enthusiast and always had a new pursuit: learning the *bodhrán*, acting, dressing all in tweed.

Anna and Hogie had a flat on Leeson Street, which became a hub for all our friends. It was there that I met Séamus. It's rare to meet someone and feel as if you're already friends but that's what happened. We would stay up for hours doing totally silly things like prank calls (apologies to all the Michael Collinses in the phone book), and totally serious things, like watching *Free Willy*.

And so many other movies – emptying the coin jar to buy bottles of £2.99 Santa Rita and rent DVDs from Reel World on Leeson Street. *Before Sunrise*, *Reality Bites*, *Empire Records*. *Trainspotting* soundtrack on repeat. Anna – amazingly

– had a car, so we could go further afield on our adventures: ill-fated camping trips to Brittas, or Connemara, or wherever promised adventure.

Helen and Patrick were together, and in 1998 there arrived our first college baby, Áine. Anna and I were with Helen in Holles Street while she was in labour – I didn't really know anyone close with kids before so it was all new, and amazing to witness. At the time I felt like such a grown-up – now I smile at what babies we were.

We finally made it to America on a J1 in the summer of third year: myself, Anna, Sinéad and Aifric, a school friend who came to Trinity a year later. We found a bare one-bedroom flat in The Mission in San Francisco, slept all summer on blow-up mattresses and had the time of our lives. I worked four days to the others' five, and that extra day I'd buy a ticket to a morning movie and stay in the cinema all day: *Fight Club*, *American Beauty*, *The Sixth Sense*.

After finals we planned a return trip, this time with my friend Ger (Gilroy) tagging along. He'd heard our stories from the year before, and also had a bit of a crush on Anna. We agreed to help him and the friends he had in tow find accommodation. We were sceptical – they were the total opposite of our college selves: Head of the Pol Soc, active in publications, all driven and self-assured. But it was as if some alchemy happened in that casting – the bond grew so strong it led one of us, my current housemate Michael McDermott, to write a piece for the *Sunday Independent* naively entitled 'Friendship is Better than Sex'. I say naive because not too long afterwards, our San Francisco nine produced two couplings. Myself, Ger and Michael dragged that summer out as long as we could, and on returning to Ireland, still with no clear work goals in mind, I decided to go travelling. I visited Séamus and Anna who were working in Buenos Aires – we went to Iguazú Falls and got soaked under the cascade. Malachy was travelling around South America and I stayed on to meet him – he arrived in the middle of the night, full gaucho, with a poncho and a maté cup.

With spring rapidly turning to summer, I called no-longer scary Sinéad and asked what her plans were for the following year. She told me she had applied to do film production at DIT. I missed the deadline for her course, but got accepted to do a master's in film studies at UCD – basically a year of watching films from every era, place and genre, along with a small amount of production and screenwriting. That's where everything I had been absorbing coalesced: producing film was the perfect marriage of everything I loved – story, music, visuals, connection, big ideas and business (which I got from my dad) – and once that clicked, everything started to fall into place.

Looking back, I'm so glad that I didn't rush to assert myself in college; to excel in one society or another, and effectively begin my career. My secondary school self would have done that, were it not for the land I had when I arrived. It meant that college, for me, was about figuring out who I was and what was meaningful for me, and so much of that was friendships and experience.

People's lives go in such different directions, time speeds up, more demands are placed on us. But to me, all that time shared during those years is like a ball of threads bound up together – the threads may spread out and separate, and lead to different places, but they keep us connected.

Anna started drifting away from us in the years after college. It was gradual at first, and we really tried to keep her close, but that contact eventually dwindled to texts on my birthday, and at Christmas. And then nothing. Life takes people to funny places sometimes. The last time I saw her was at her mother's funeral. She seemed so alone. I still remember her mobile number. I wonder if it's the same.

It's a thread I miss.

For Anna.

Katie Holly (TCD 1995–99; English and History) is Managing Director of Dublin-based Blinder Films. Her credits include **One Hundred Mornings** (2009), **Sensation** (2010), **Citadel** (2012), **The Queen of Ireland** (2015), RTÉ's **The Savage Eye** and **The Pervert's Guide to Ideology** featuring Slavoj Zizek – which was like going back to college all over again. Her latest film, **Love & Friendship**, Whit Stillman's adaptation of Jane Austen's **Lady Susan**, premiered at the Sundance Film Festival 2016 and received widespread critical acclaim. Her next project is a feature documentary about Grace Jones, to be directed by Sophie Fiennes.

'IS THIS CLASSICS?'

chris binchy

IN THE AUTUMN of 1997 I was working as a chef in a restaurant on Andrews Street in Dublin, about to start a master's in creative writing in Trinity. One afternoon a few weeks before I was due to begin, I was told there was somebody asking for me downstairs. I found Brendan Kennelly waiting. He was a familiar figure around town – raincoat, carrier bag, head up, half-smile, taking in everything. He said that he had seen that I would be starting in Trinity soon and wanted to come in and say hello, that he was looking forward to working together.

It was an act of great kindness. Six years had passed since I'd been in college and I was feeling inadequate and doubtful. In the basement of my previous university there were two spaces on which the academic activity of the world above did not impinge. One was Dramsoc, from which generations of people had gone on to be nominated for BAFTAs, Tonys, Golden Globes, Oscars. The other was the Trap, a roomful of pool tables and arcade games that smelt of feet and rollies. Nobody who hung around in the Trap had ever, to my knowledge, been nominated for anything. I was a Trap kind of guy, which meant that when I left college in the early nineties, I settled into working in restaurants and hotels, occasionally writing short stories. When Trinity advertised a master's in creative writing, I applied.

The course, we had been told, would be taught in a house on Westland Row, the birthplace of Oscar Wilde, which had been recently refurbished to become a new centre for Irish writing. So recent was the refurbishment that it was ongoing, which meant that it wouldn't be ready until late Michaelmas term. Maybe early Hilary. What did this mean? It meant that until Christmas, our classes would be held in the Arts Block at night.

It was a familiar sort of place. It had no windows and smelled of feet and rollies. There were fifteen of us, split into two groups. I was with Brendan for the first term. The default setting of writery people is maybe something close to watchful. Sometimes hesitant or mistrustful. There might be an assumption that while you are not competitive yourself, everybody else is, so you better be ready to fight your corner. Put eight such people who don't know each other in a room and it might get claustrophobic. In retrospect all of this was in my head. On the first day, eight of us sat in a room waiting for Brendan to arrive. A lost student opened the door. 'Is this Classics?' he asked. 'Not yet,' said Sean O'Reilly.

Brendan arrived and we talked about where we had come from, where we were hoping to go. There were Irish and English and American and Italian people, a variety of backgrounds and experience, an age range of forty years. We were set tasks. For the following week we would produce a piece inspired by the senses. Any of the senses. You know – something short, to be distributed and read before we met again. I felt panicked all week but did nothing, then pulled an all-nighter to deliver 500 words about myself and my sister fishing in a lake, which finished with me kicking her. It was all from memory and had nothing to do with the senses. When we came to class, Brendan asked in his gentle way whether I would like to read it to the group. I said I would not, misunderstanding his meaning. 'Maybe you should,' he told me. I started reading. 'Louder,' he said. 'And slower. Maybe stand up.' I stood up and continued. 'Slower,' he said, 'and louder. Maybe lift your head.' I lifted my head and went on. 'Maybe you should stand on the chair,' he said. I am six foot four and in my time have turned a lot of furniture into firewood. There were risks involved but I did it. To a roomful of strangers I read my story about me being a bollocks to my ten-year-old sister while standing on a chair. Then I sat down. The class said encouraging things in baffled voices. Brendan was generous. 'And there is of course,' he said in the end, 'the symbolism of the fish.' 'Yes,' I said. 'There is that.'

In O'Neill's afterwards people remonstrated with me. 'What should I have done?' I asked. 'What choice did I have?' 'You could have said no,' they all answered, which was news to me.

Because the classes were held at night and because we weren't where we were supposed to be, there was a belief that normal rules did not apply. In the early weeks there was a lot of drinking. I think I remember people arriving to class with wine bottles clinking. Bread and cheese. People correcting each other's grammar with their mouths full. There was crying and some shouting but not, as I remember, much falling out. The things that people uncharitably might imagine a writers' workshop to be – people drunkenly emoting, getting het up over adverbs and punctuation – they happened.

But that's not to say it was easy. Having work that you have written – work that is personal and that may be, in some unquantifiable way, autobiographical – analysed, parsed and corrected is excruciating. Even when people try to balance honesty with consideration, it's a raw experience. You need to trust and respect the people you're working with, or at least find a way to listen to what they're saying without flinching, and thank them at the end. As I recall, we liked and trusted each other long before Christmas. The classes started at six and kept going for hours, discussions continuing as alarms went off in the background until eventually security guards would come and kick us out.

We were peripheral to the main action of College. I never went into the Buttery or the Pav, never ate in any of the cafés or restaurants. I never used a gym if there was one. I never rowed or went to the Trinity Ball or did any of the things that I thought I might do. But the general attitude that I got from the College was of benevolence. In UCD in the eighties there was a fear that, while lecturers and tutors were well disposed, the system might suddenly expel you if it ever managed to track you down. In Trinity, it felt that there was an abundance of things there for the taking if you found the right person and knew how to ask for them.

The first email address I ever had was given to me by Trinity. It did not feel like anything significant. Instantaneous post, I thought. Twenty-three hours faster than the regular sort. But I was not somebody who got a lot of post at the time and I knew nobody else with an email account in 1997 apart from my classmates, with whom I was spending most of my free time.

After Christmas, the Oscar Wilde Centre opened and we moved in. My group started working with Gerry Dawe, whose focussed style of criticism was different and complementary to Brendan's. Anne Enright came in as writer-in-residence and was brilliant and interesting. We had our own house with a code to get in the door. We had the use of shared computers and very overworked printers. The place smelled permanently of hot paper. At a time when nobody had mobile phones it was useful to have a place where you could meet people. And then go to Kennedy's.

I spent six months in Kennedy's drinking coffee that was made from ashtrays, served by Dublin's glummest barmen. We would gather and complain about the amount of work that had to be done, the degree of freedom that we had been given, the boundaries and the lack of boundaries. Sometimes the coffee would turn into pints and everything would get emotional and more funny. We sat there for weeks on end, going in to Oscar for workshops and occasional broadcasts from writers and publishers who came to tell us, in counterpoint to the encouragement we were getting, what was waiting for us in the outside world. Slush piles and remaindered copies and unearned advances. It did not sound easy.

You get from Christmas to May very quickly. Workshops finished up. Lectures tailed off. There were occasional tutorials but the end was coming. We were encouraged to publish a book of our work. Money was provided and we sorted out designers, printing, publicity, distribution. We launched it in Waterstones and did readings in Sligo and Galway. We gathered in Kennedy's to talk about how adrift we felt, how our co-dependence was being interfered with just when it was getting comfy. On one of the last occasions, I was ordering from a barman who had served me one hundred times without comment. This time he spoke. 'What is it you people do?' he asked. 'We are writers,' I said, just to see what it sounded like. 'Ah,' he said. 'We thought you were social workers.'

We put our portfolios together, got them submitted and then one day when we went into our building using our code, there were other people in the house. Strange people who looked watchful and hesitant and who didn't know who we were. That was the end of it. We had to move on.

Chris Binchy (TCD 1997–98; Creative Writing) is the author of four novels. His most recent book, **Five Days Apart**, is published by Harper Perennial.

ANY INFO?

belinda mckeon

I CAME to Trinity in the autumn of 1996: seventeen, boy-crazy, with long red hair and a crush on Hamlet, which was possibly the reason I'd opted to study English. My other subject was philosophy, about which I knew nothing, but I'd inherited a robustly maudlin nature from my funeral-loving father (this did not clash with the boy-craziness at all – see 'crush on Hamlet'), and philosophy, with its brochure page moaning *What's the point of anything?*, seemed like a good way to spend the next few years.

It's not hard to imagine what I would have worn that first day, walking through Front Arch with my school friends from home; I had a small wardrobe, devotedly put together from Saturday trips up to the second-hand shops in Dublin. I was probably wearing my Levi's flares with the comically trodden hems; the blue polyester shirt of some regional German soccer team; my battered green Converse Pro Stars, and my imitation Baracuta jacket, navy cord. Most of the clothes I owned had previously belonged to extremely skinny men in the 1970s. This was the tail end of the Britpop era; or rather, if you were seventeen and had just arrived in Dublin from rural County Longford, you thought it still was the Britpop era, and that it was still fine to talk about Blur and Oasis, but you were about to be set straight by a lot of witheringly cool people who smoked on the ramp and had English accents either actual or invented. Everyone said 'alright?' as a greeting, and everyone seemed to know who Jack Derrida was.

Yes, Jack Derrida. That's how I wrote his name down in my lecture notes those first weeks. Michelle Fuko, too, and John Boodria, and Roland Bart. It's hard to express the bewilderment I felt, sitting in those lecture halls, or trying to read the texts in the two anthologies we'd been assigned for critical and cultural theory; a 'text'? What the hell was a text? In school, we'd been told to read, say, from page fifty to page fifty-five in the Patrick Murray notes, and to learn it off by heart so that we could reproduce it in the exam; now the teachers were academics, delivering papers to us from behind their podiums as though we were also academics, not recent survivors of the Leaving Cert, and the reading list consisted of excerpts (what the hell was an excerpt?!) from Orientalism, and Discipline and Punish and Gender Trouble. Gender what? Nothing made sense. How could you just put words together like that? The words I could actually make out, I wrote them down phonetically in my four-section notebooks, and then I went to the library afterwards and wrote them out again more neatly, and I still didn't understand. I read the texts, but they were all footnotes, and *ibid.*, and *cf.* – what did any of this mean? I was very, very far from understanding.

The only comfort was that my first essay was not due until December, and exams were not until May, so I could remain undetected in my blankness and my panic until then. In tutorials, it was always the same people who spoke: an English girl called Natasha who wore long skirts and smelled of incense, a guy from Blackrock whose head was shaped like a square, and my friend M, who was from Mullingar, wore double denim and had hair like a Pantene ad. M was slightly older than the rest of us, having left another degree course to opt for English instead, so he was confident enough to expound on post-structuralism (that is, bullshit about it) in a tutorial. I think I had a crush on him, though I'm honestly not certain, which is odd, because I had a crush on almost every man I met. But he was the first male friend I'd ever had – my Longford convent school education really did a number on me – and just the fact of being talked to (or perhaps talked at) by a boy was intoxicating and overwhelming for me; there was no question of simply taking it for what it was. I analysed it endlessly in my diary. We spent quite a lot of time sitting over chips and gravy in the

Buttery, sniping at each other for some reason; what was that about? I can't work it out now. He bought me my first pint (of cider, Hudson Blue – the ads were everywhere, apples slicing through snow) in the Long Stone, on the last day of Michaelmas Term, when I had wanted to go to a society talk called 'What Is Postmodernism?', because I had an essay due and I still hadn't the first notion what it was. It's embarrassing to admit how green I was, how slow to do everything, from drinking to talking to boys to learning how to think for myself on the page, but I walked through Front Gate that Monday in October with caution and anxiety bristling on every surface of my body, and it was Trinity's job to shake at least some of that caution off. Of this business, most of my first year would consist. It was a tall order: I am still grateful that T, the beautiful English boy on whom I very definitely, from the first moment he walked into our philosophy class, had a colossal, dry-mouthed, scarlet-faced crush, was too stoned all through our first year to pay any heed to my lovesick staring and stammering. But I still should have tried to at least snog him. If there's an alumni fund I can contribute to in aid of the deprogramming of miserably cautious culchie teenagers, I'm happy to do so; I think it's a very worthy cause.

My closest friend was Anna, who commuted from Maynooth, through whom I met Susan, who took the DART in from Dalkey, through whom I would eventually meet K, who would become the 'friend of my life' I would later write about, poor sod, in a novel. All three of them were a joy, and just what I needed at that time: energetic, eccentric, irreverent, hilarious and surging with enthusiasm for Dublin, for the things it offered, the galleries, the cinemas, the places to dance or drink or sprawl out on lawns. We left fervent notes on one another's desks; we went shopping for second-hand books or second-hand ball gowns; we talked about our crushes in unflagging, forensic detail. These were pre-internet days – well, there was A Computer With The Internet On It in the Arts Block lab, but in 1996, I'm not sure what you could actually dial slowly into view on its screen – and people got information on the people they fancied via an early form of social media – the toilet doors. A person's name would be scrawled on the door in biro, followed by ANY INFO? and underneath, helpful souls would share the facts and qualities of which they were aware.

I began to feel truly at home in Trinity by the end of my first year there, when spring was beginning to unfurl its long, bright evenings over campus. I remember so clearly the joy of being 'stuck' in the library, which was not a stuck-ness at all, but a kind of camping out in the company of so many new friends: the frequent desk visits, the spotting sessions (*cf.* boy crazy), the tea breaks, the pub afterwards, or, as March gave way to April, the crowded lawns of the Pav. I went to the English Ball, and to the much-talked-of Trinity Ball itself, wearing a dress from the Harlequin and accessories from Jenny Vander; I still have the little Indian beaded purse I bought for £10, though it's long since battered beyond use. We went dancing at a club in Eamon Doran's in Temple Bar; the club was called Full Of Beans (or 'The Philippines' as I described it to my flatmates, drunkenly, just arrived back from my first night there) and we 'knew' the DJ, Jared, a dodgy English bloke with a moustache; we ate lunch, fries with pots and pots of tea, in the Alpha café on the corner of Clarendon and Wicklow streets.

At the annual College book sale, in the Exam Hall, I bought boxes of paperbacks, including an anthology of Irish poetry, which had been inten-sively annotated in blue pen by its previous owner, a man who used the book as a diary of a day before Christmas when he was on temporary release from Portlaoise Jail and was taking his two young sons shopping and sightseeing in Dublin. He recorded aspects of their day – 'a Christmas box for Shane', 'lit candles for Mammy', 'we shook hands and he said it was a deal' – and marked up the poems he loved. I kept that book for years, brought it to New York with me when I moved in 2005. Then one day I realized that Google would now surely allow me to look up the man, who had signed his name at the front of the book, and return his property to him or to his sons. Immediately I learned who he had been: Éamonn Mac Thomáis, the Republican author and historian, who did time in Portlaoise as a political prisoner in the 1970s. I found his son, Shane, who was by then also a historian and author, and sent the book to him. He wrote me the most beautiful letter in response, telling me what it had meant to get this time capsule of his father, then dead a couple of years, and sent me his own heavily annotated copy of the collected Hopkins. I never responded to that letter; I wish I had, to thank him. Shane Mac Thomáis died tragically not long ago, in Glasnevin Cemetery, where he was a much-loved tour guide. (The documentary *One Million Dubliners* became an inadvertent homage to him.)

My life began to change in a fundamental way that spring of 1997; I still lived with my school friends – in an apartment complex opposite St James' Hospital, where they were studying medical subjects and going to bed at a reasonable hour – but we were rapidly growing apart. I was an arts student, with only a few hours' classes a week and with friends who liked to talk about novels and paintings and even philosophy, and with a lot of free time to spend staring at gravy in the Buttery or drinking Hudson Blue outside the Pav. I was even starting to talk about novels and paintings and philosophy myself, thanks to some courses with reading lists I didn't have to approach phonetically: Writing Ireland, Literature and Sexualities, Free Will and Determinism. I was writing for the student union newspaper, *Aontas*, not realizing this was a very uncool thing to do; the following year, I would move to *Trinity News* and the pizza-encrusted offices of publications would become a second home. I was taking a weekly fiction workshop with the College writer-in-residence, Deirdre Madden.

That workshop was on Monday evenings in Deirdre's rooms off Front Square. The notices about it went up at the end of Michaelmas Term, and in a couple of hours one Sunday evening, by the miniature Christmas tree I'd bought on Thomas Street for the apartment, I wrote a short story about a girl who was obsessed with a dead neighbour boy. It began – I remember my friend M being particularly pleased about this, as he read my three pages in the Arts Block coffee dock – 'My friends just assumed that I was a lesbian.' It ended with the protagonist burning in a garden fire the memorial photographs of the dead boy, which she'd clipped from the local paper, an image at which M shook his head in what I decided to be admiration but was probably something else. Somehow, Deirdre Madden admitted me to the class, which sat for all of Hilary Term. I was the youngest by quite a distance; almost all the others were fourth years. Among them were a number who are now also novelists: Paul Murray, Léan Ní Chuilleanáin, Barry McCrea and Susan Lanigan. That this is a higher publication rate than the MFA programme I would take in New York ten years later surely says something about the quality of Deirdre's instruction. What I remember about those evenings in that softly lit room – we sat in a loose circle, on couches and armchairs and whatever other seating was available, and I think there was a gas heater – is the feeling of being taken seriously for the first time. Not in a coddling, sympathetic way, but rather in its opposite; I had been writing, and getting praise for my little stories, since the age of eight, so for me, praise was in fact the problem rather than the thing I needed. Deirdre set a standard so high, and so serious, that praise came to seem like something gauche, a lazy shortcut; instead, we were expected as writers to make clear and deliberate decisions about what we did with our sentences and our paragraphs. I wasn't treated any differently on account of still, essentially, being a child; I had to get on with it and produce my pages just like everyone else, and listen to them being keenly criticized, and I had, too, to get over my nervousness and make observations and suggestions about the pages of others. I had always written, but in a way that needed constant attention – grades, contest entries, school magazine publication; after that class, I began to write more quietly, more for myself, to try to get better at what I was doing and to learn from what I was reading; and I began to read in a different way, too. By the time I came back for my second year of classes, I was a different kind of reader. I spent months researching my winter essay, on female Irish poets of the early twentieth century, for my tutor, Lucy Collins. One is not born, but becomes, an Irish Woman Writer, the prompt read, riffing on de Beauvoir. Or 'Deboovwor' as I would have called her a few months previously. Oh well. What harm?

I go back all the time; I will never be free of the place, or perhaps it of me. The other day, wandering through the springtime campus of Rutgers, where I teach now, I got a sudden urge to head over to the Pav. Trinity shaped my mind and my heart and my sense of what the world was and could be at a crucial time in my life. It gave me my fiercest friendships and it gave me my first loves. Some of them were on the shelves of the Lecky. Some of them were at the desks, pretending to study. On trips back to Dublin now, I often use my library card just to ghost through those spaces, looking at the spaces stretching out under the high, sloping windows (the glass ceiling over which we never thought to chuckle ironically, or maybe some of the better-informed among us did); at the concrete balconies over which we used to toss notes to one another: MEET YOU ON THE RAMP IN FIVE MINUTES!! When I'm in Dublin now, I sometimes send a text saying exactly that to an old friend or two. And you know what? Within five minutes, they're very often there.

Belinda McKeon (right) *with Anna Martin and Susan O'Connor.*

Belinda McKeon (TCD 1996–2000; English and Philosophy) is a playwright, critic and novelist. Her debut novel **Solace** won the 2011 Faber Prize and was voted Irish Book of the Year, as well as being shortlisted for the James Tait Black Memorial Prize. Her second, **Tender**, was published to critical acclaim in 2015. Her fiction and non-fiction have appeared in **Granta**, **The Paris Review**, **The New York Times**, **The Guardian** and elsewhere. As a playwright, she has had work produced in Dublin and New York, and is currently under commission to the Abbey Theatre. She lives in Brooklyn and is an Assistant Teaching Professor of Creative Writing at Rutgers University.

A WARM COBBLESTONE

heather jones

ALL LECTURERS are poachers turned gamekeepers: students who enjoyed university so much they have made a career of it. This was certainly my experience. In Freshers' Week 1996, one sunny October day, I walked through Front Arch for the first time, to a tumble of voices, light and colour; pamphlets were thrust towards me; shadowy light inside Front Gate fell away to a riot of tables, shouting and milling crowds. I was there to study for the two-subject moderatorship in history and English but it took me some time to find the library: I joined about twenty societies before I had reached the Campanile that first day.

This *flaithulach* start to college was funded by a summer of hard work waitressing in Bewley's and sustained by a further bookshop job for four years. The economic weather was headed fair: the Celtic Tiger had just begun. Dublin was soon awash with part-time work for students; many of us juggled jobs and studies throughout the degree. Fees had just been abolished. I began university at less risk of debt than any previous generation.

Straight out from the discipline of the Leaving Cert, I was thrilled at the variety, the choice, the intellectual chaos, and the Catholicism – after the sheltered niche of denominational schooling, Trinity, somewhat ironically given its history, was the first time I had to constantly explain my cultural exoticism, coming from a minority southern Irish Protestant background. The Dublin of

1996 was very far from multicultural and there was frequently some ground to cover: one fellow student memorably asked me did we celebrate Christmas; everyone confused Protestantism with atheism. There was also the problem of class stereotypes. I had never heard the term 'horse Protestant' before: I owned not so much as a pony, to my new friends' dismay. An ordinary Dubliner, I was quite the disappointment to anyone hoping for stories of port and Georgian lawns. Fortunately Trinity was short of neither for all of us to enjoy and the identity shock soon dissipated in the realization that everyone was having one.

I sated my growing thirst for learning in the Berkeley, the Lecky, the 1937 Reading Room and barely missed a lecture; I was hooked. The excitement of honing an argument on a few skim-read pages, after perilously little sleep, was something wonderful, only possible to attempt when still a teenager. It rarely had repercussions, although I did once faint when giving blood in the Exam Hall, comically awaking to the forbidding, alarming gaze of Queen Elizabeth I. We were extremely young; most schools did not do transition year in 1996. Quite a few students had an alert on their College ID card stating they were still under eighteen in their first university days, debarring alcohol access. We all thought ourselves precocious, wanted to be writers, wore velvet jackets or sheepskin coats. The boys cut their hair like Noel Gallagher. For girls, it was the era of bad fake tan and 'the Rachel' hairstyle, in imitation of Jennifer Aniston in *Friends*. We posed on the grass in College Park along the cricket pitch in summer under the trees, with cheap cans of cider, feeling all of life open, fresh, exciting and ahead of us.

It doesn't seem that long ago and yet it was another world. Internet use was not yet widespread; I did not have a mobile phone until my finals. During my undergraduate years, no one used their College email – a newfangled thing we weren't sure would catch on – and only language students had full internet access in College. Meeting friends involved much old-fashioned lingering. We would gather at the Nassau Street ramp that led to the Arts Block, until every friend had shown up, or sit in the Buttery for hours discussing philosophy, theology and politics. The conversations were lively: among my peers were the future novelist Belinda McKeon and *Irish Times* theatre critic Peter Crawley.

Dark and brooding, the Buttery resembled a church crypt, badly lit in those pre-renovation days, with the faint scent of cigarette smoke from the night before; it had dingy glamour. Pre-smoking ban, I would return home throughout my first university year from the round of endless, exhilarating parties and socializing, reeking of toxic, acrid smoke, my long hair carrying its fumes around like a badge of honour: even though, like so many of my year from Dublin, I was still living with my parents, didn't smoke and barely drank, I was now a student. The prestige of the jump in status from suburban teenager felt delicious. When a friend gave me the cult red poster of Che Guevara, I felt I had arrived, even if I had no idea at eighteen who exactly Che was; unsurprisingly he had not featured strongly in the quiet world of Dublin Protestantism in which I grew up. Politically we were a cautious generation; the Arts Block foyer, with its split levels, steps and uncomfortable orange block seats, intended to dissuade student demonstrations and sit-ins, were unnecessary for us. The Celtic Tiger's purrs undercut radicalism. If there was one rebellion it was social: the rejection of some, though interestingly rarely all, aspects of Catholicism.

For the majority of my peers, coming from single-sex schools, Trinity was the first time they had been in class with the opposite gender. There was much first-year timidity, fear of looking stupid, exasperated lecturers trying to get shy students to speak in tutorials; enormous amounts of flirting and giggling too. In my case, coming from a mixed school, the ideas, not the presence of boys in class, were rather the novelty. Some English department courses stand out as feeling like a prise had been radically taken to my mind: post-colonialism was a liberating revelation; feminist literature an escape. Terence Brown, Eve Patton and Eiléan Ní Chuilleanáin inspired utter awe; Stephen Matterson, my tutor, wise counsel. In the history department, John Horne, Alan Kramer and David Fitzpatrick reframed my understanding of history forever and I started, without realizing, my future career path.

The end result was that on Trinity Monday in 1998, I was lucky enough to become a Foundation Scholar; the excitement such that I thought I might never sleep again. Five of us danced into the dark small hours of that morning outside the Rubrics. Schol brought accommodation, prestige, and, particularly importantly, hot food. Often, as a scholar, I led the traditional grace on Commons in Latin, diligently cribbed from an old cassette tape of a classics professor, and once, on Halloween, memorably incanted from the Dining Hall pulpit while dressed as Dracula, somewhat to the Fellows' astonishment.

Schol meant Trinity became my vivid term-time home. In the late 1990s few College rooms had been renovated; there were circular plugs of the kind used in the 1950s still functioning, along with vintage light switches, war-green carpets and old gas heaters. My aunt and uncle who had met at Trinity in that decade were able to enjoy the nostalgia when they visited me; my College generation learned to wear heavy jumpers in rooms in winter to fight the cold. The College experienced quite a few serious fires during my time, including the loss of the GMB attic with its archives; the electrical wiring in the older buildings was somewhat prolix. On one occasion, the College porters, who at that time for some unfathomable reason wore hats shaped like a French gendarme's *képi*, called to break up a party in ground floor rooms in New Square. Gamely a number of us decided that it was too early to call a halt and clambered down through a basement into an underground passage that ran under all the buildings on that side of the Square, resurfacing in another flat where the party surreptitiously recommenced. During the subterranean relocation, pints in hand, we could inspect the reams of electrical wiring that had gathered over decades beneath the buildings. Their complexity mirrored the Northern Ireland peace process. Their combustibility in those years was probably relatively similar. The Omagh bombing happened while I was in College; the Good Friday Agreement too, and, although the North was not that frequently discussed, there was always an underlying awareness for our generation that the future was changing, would be better. A talk at the Hist by Colin Parry, who had lost his son Tim in the Warrington bombing, was profoundly moving; shaking hands with this hugely compassionate, grieving man, was one of the most important experiences I had in university.

My association with Trinity began young and has lasted: there is a photograph of me aged about eight months following my mother's graduation, with her mortarboard lopsided on my infant head. Ultimately, I managed to wrangle eleven years of adult life there, staying to do a doctorate, in the inviting precincts of Trinity's squares and gardens. I may have finally taken the boat to London but Trinity's imprint has formed me. Joyce's 'dull stone set in a cumbrous ring' sneaks a warm cobblestone into the pocket of your soul; it never leaves you.

Heather Jones, aged eight months, wearing her mother's mortarboard.

Heather Jones (TCD 1996–2000, History and English; 2001–06 Ph.D. History) is an Associate Professor in International History at the London School of Economics and Political Science (LSE). She has a MSc from St John's College Cambridge, has held a Max Weber Fellowship at the European University Institute, Florence, and is a director of the International Research Centre of the Historial de la Grande Guerre, Péronne. Her book **Violence Against Prisoners of War in the First World War: Britain, France and Germany, 1914–1920** was published in 2011. She is currently researching the British monarchy at war 1914–1918.